A POETICS

A POETICS

Charles Bernstein

Harvard University Press

Cambridge, Massachusetts

London, England

1992

Library of Congress Cataloging-in-Publication Data

Bernstein, Charles, 1950–
  A poetics / Charles Bernstein.
    p.   cm.
  Includes bibliographical references.
  ISBN 0-674-67854-0 (cloth)
  ISBN 0-674-67857-5 (paper)
  1. Bernstein, Charles, 1950–   —Aesthetics.
  2. Poetics.
  3. Poetry. I. Title.
PS3552.E7327P64 1992
811'.54—dc20   91-19134
                                     CIP

Contents

a p o e t i c s

State of the Art

There is of course no state of American poetry, but states, moods, agitations, dissipations, renunciations, depressions, acquiescences, elations, angers, ecstasies; no music to our verse but vastly incompatible musics; no single sentiment but clashes of sentience: the magnificent cacophony of different bodies making different sounds, as different as the hum of Hester Street from the gush of Grand Coulee, the buzz of Central Park on August afternoons from the shrieks of oil-coated birds in Prince William Sound.

The state of American poetry can be characterized by the sharp ideological disagreements that lacerate our communal field of action, making it volatile, dynamic, engaging.

What I hear, then, in the poetries of this New American fin de siècle is an implicit refusal of unity that is the result of our prodigious and magnanimous outpouring of words. In saying this, I register my own particular passion—everywhere reflected in this book—for poetry that insists on running its own course, finding its own measures, charting worlds otherwise hidden or denied or, perhaps best of all, never before existing.

Poetry is aversion of conformity in the pursuit of new forms, or can be. By form I mean ways of putting things together, or stripping them apart, I mean ways of accounting for what weighs upon any one of us, or that poetry tosses up into an imaginary air like so many swans flying out of a magician's depthless black hat so that suddenly, like when the sky all at once turns white or purple or day-glo blue, we breathe more deeply. By form I mean how any one of us interprets what's swirling so often incomprehensibly about us, or the stutter with which he stutter, the warbling tone in which she sing off and on key. If form averts conformity, then it swings wide of this culture's insatiable desire for, yet hatred of, assimilation—a manic-depressive cycle of go along, go away that is a crucial catalyst in the stiflingly effective process of cultural self-regulation and self-censorship.

1

When poetry averts conformity it enters into the contemporary: speaking to the pressures and conflicts of the moment with the means just then at hand. By which I mean I care most about poetry that disrupts business as usual, including literary business: I care most for poetry as dissent, including formal dissent; poetry that makes sounds possible to be heard that are not otherwise articulated.

It is particularly amusing that those who protest loudest about the fraudulence or aridness or sameness of contemporary poetry that insists on being contemporary, dissident, different, and who profess, in contrast, the primacy of the individual voice, fanned by a gentile inspiration, produce work largely indistinguishable from dozens of their peers and, moreover, tend to recognize the value only of poetry that fits into the narrow horizon of their particular style and subject matter. As if poetry were a craft that there is a right way or wrong way to do: in which case, I prefer the wrong way—anything better than the well-wrought epiphany of predictable measure— for at least the cracks and flaws and awkwardnesses show signs of life.

Ideology, as in a particular and restricted point of view, way of hearing, tendency of preferences and distastes, everywhere informs poetry and imparts to it, at its most resonant, a density of materialized social being expressed through the music of a work as well as its multifoliate references. To pretend to be nonpartisan, above the fray, sorting the "best" from the "weak" without "ideological grudges"— as a highly partisan poet recently put it, as if to mark his own partisanship in the course of denying it—is an all too common form of mystification and bad faith aimed at bolstering the authority of one's pronouncements. As with George Bush's attempt to discredit "special interests", that is, all us "udders", in the end we find the center is a little wizard with an elaborate sound and light show, good table manners, and preferred media access.

What interests me is a poetry and a poetics that do not edit out so much as edit in: that include multiple conflicting perspectives and types of languages and styles in the same poetic work or, as here, in the same collection of essays. A poetry—a poetic—that expresses the states of the art as it moves beyond the twentieth century, beyond the modern and postmodern.

Which is not to say, exactly—moving beyond the distinction between prose and poems. Though if there's a temptation to read the long essay-in-verse, which follows these opening notes, as prose, I hope there will be an equally strong temptation to read the succeeding prose as if it were poetry.

Poetry should be at least as interesting as, and a whole lot more unexpected than, television. But reality keeps creating trouble for poetry, for it constantly changes the terms of what's possible versus wildly improbable or surreal, and poetry that runs the risk of being too cautious will find itself well outstripped by events (even).

I'm thinking for the moment of a McDonald's ad from Moscow broadcast only months after the crumbling of the Berlin Wall, during a time of turbulence bordering on economic chaos in the Soviet Union. This was not a farcical pastiche of conceptual art fronting as social commentary, but rather what we were led to believe were "real" Russians enjoying the communion of international packaging—just like Dave and Betty and the kids do in Syosset.

Our images of each other, and of other cultures, seem to go from ignorance to sinisterly deluded fabrication, almost without any middle ground. Poetry can, even if it often doesn't, throw a wedge into this engineered process of social derealization: find a middle ground of care in particulars, in the truth of details and their constellations— provide a site for the construction of social and imaginative facts and configurations avoided or overlooked elsewhere. But to achieve this end, poets would have to be as alert to the presents of their cultures as the designers of TV ads; which means a willingness to engage in guerrilla warfare with the official images of the world that are being shoved down our throats like so many tablespoons of Pepto Bismol, short respite from the gas and the diarrhea that are the surest signs that harsh and uncontainable reality hasn't vanished but has only been removed from public discussion.

That means we can't rely only on the tools and forms of the past, even the recent past, but must invent new tools and forms that begin to meet the challenges of the ever-changing present.

Innovation is a response to changing conditions. Which is not to say that the work "progresses", as in a technological model, or say "today we make a better car than we had did years ago". It's never a question of better. The details, the particulars, and how they are ordered keep changing and poetry is a way of articulating that.

Over and over again, in a panoply of poetry panels, our discussions again and again pummel the problem of balkanization or fragmentation: how to evaluate the fact that in the last twenty years a number of self-subsistent poetry communities have emerged that have different readers and different writers and different publishers and different reading series, even, increasingly, separate hierarchies and new canons with their own awards, prizes, heroines.

One response to this new proliferation of audiences is to lament the lack of a common readership. I'm not talking about those who want to resurrect a single canon of western literary values; the ethnocentrism and ideological blindness of this position is considered in several of the essays that follow.

What I take more seriously are pluralist ideas supporting an idealized multiculturalism: the image of poets from different communities reading each other's works and working to keep aware of developments in every part of the poetic spectrum. The idea of diversity, as it is advertised in almost all the latest college publicity, is the most superficial indication of this tendency; more significant is the introduction of multicultural curricula in the high schools and colleges.

My problem is not the introduction of radical alternatives to parochial and racist reading habits engendered by the educational system and the media, but that these alternatives are often ameliorative rather than politically or aesthetically exploratory. I see too great a continuum from "diversity" back to New Critical and liberal-democratic concepts of a common readership that often—certainly not always—have the effect of transforming unresolved ideological divisions and antagonisms into packaged tours of the local color of gender, race, sexuality, ethnicity, region, nation, class, even historical period: where each group or community or period is expected to come up with—or have appointed for them—representative figures we all can know about.

This process, more often than not, presupposes a common standard of aesthetic judgment or implicitly aims to erect a new common standard. In this context, diversity can be a way of restoring a highly

idealized conception of a unified American culture that effectively quiets dissent. For the twin ideas of diversity and the common reader evade the challenge posed by heterodox art, the poetries at the peripheries, to the very idea of a common standard of aesthetic judgment or the value of a common readership.

We have to get over, as in getting over a disease, the idea that we can "all" speak to one another in the universal voice of poetry. History still mars our words, and we will be transparent to one another only when history itself disappears. For as long as social relations are skewed, who speaks in poetry can never be a neutral matter.

The cultural space of diversity is mocked by the banishment from the *massed* media of those groups stigmatized as too inconsequential or out of tune to represent even "diversity"; it's torn to shreds when the tragic death of one white heterosexual teenage boy from AIDS is given a public acknowledgment equivalent to the tragic deaths of thousands of individual gay men.

I sometimes even wonder whether men can understand the voice of the women we live next to and from whose bodies we have come, since I hear every day the male version of the universal voice of rationality trying to control, as if by ventriloquism, female bodies. Though as men we have to make it clear that these men do not speak for us, do not represent us, but mock what men could be but too rarely are.

I wonder sometimes what sense it makes to speak of the possibility of communication among all the peoples of America as long as there are homeless who most of us have learned to cast outside the human circle of care and acknowledgment—unless it be on the Universal Broadcasting Networks's Rock Star and Child Celebrity Tribute to the Dispossessed, the Survivors of Racial Violence, and the Victims of Sexual Assault.

In a society with such spectacularly inequitable distributions of power, the very idea of public space has been befouled—not by the graffiti of the folk but by the domination of the means of communication by those dispossessed of their connection with just such folk. What can be decried as parochial patterns of reading is in fact an essential strategy for survival, to have a deep immersion in a contemporaneity and history that are difficult to locate and need to be championed.

The direction of poetic interest can better be directed outward, centrifugally, to the unknown and the peripheral, than toward a constant centripetal regrouping and reshoring through official verse culture's enormously elastic and sophisticated mechanism of tokenization that targets, splits off, and decontexualizes; essentializing the mode of difference and incorporating the product (never the process) into its own cultural space.

Too often, the works selected to represent cultural diversity are those that accept the model of representation assumed by the dominant culture in the first place. "I see grandpa on the hill / next to the memories I can never recapture" is the base line against which other versions play: "I see my yiddishe mama on Hester street / next to the pushcarts I can no longer peddle" or "I see my grandmother on the hill / next to all the mothers whose lives can never be recaptured" or "I can't touch my Iron Father / who never canoed with me / on the prairies of my masculine epiphany". Works that challenge these models of representation run the risk of becoming more inaudible than ever within mainstream culture.

There is no reason to suppose that poets working in opposition to the dominant strains of American culture should have any intrinsic interest in the narrow spectrum of official verse culture. If their work rejects the values of most of this culture, indeed finds these values part of a fabric of social constructions that maintains coercive economic and political hierarchies, then the idea that all sides should politely take an interest in aesthetic craftiness is absurd: on the one side, such interest is patronizing; on the other, self-negating.

The insidious obsession with mass culture and popularity, here translated into the lingo of a unified culture of diversity, threatens to undermine the legitimacy of working on a small, less than mass, and, yes, less than popular scale.

Within the emerging official cultural space of diversity, figures of difference are often selected because they narrate in a way that can be readily assimilated—not to say absorbed—into the conventional forms of the dominant culture. Difference is confined to subject matter and thematic material, a.k.a. local color, excluding the formal innovations that challenge those dominant paradigms of representations. Indeed, the political and social meaning of sound, vernacular, nontraditional rhythms—that is, those things that make a text a poem—are often discounted as negligible in the fetishizing of narrative and theme; formal values being left for a misconceived avant-garde that has been involuntarily decultured—deracinated, ungendered, and therefore removed from those contexts that give it sense.

To be sure, signature styles of cultural differences can be admitted into the official culture of diversity if they are essentialized, that is, if these styles can be made to symbolically represent the group being tokenized or assimilated. Artists within these groups who are willing to embrace neither the warp of mainstream literary style through which to percolate their own experience nor the woof of an already inflected, and so easily recognized, style of cultural difference will find themselves falling through the very wide gaps and tears in the fabric of American tolerance. Such artists pay the price for being less interested in representing than enacting.

Franz Kafka once asked, "What have I in common with the Jews, I don't know what I have in common with myself?" This can itself be understood as a Jewish attitude, but only if Jewishness is taken as multiplicitous and expressed indirectly. When Nicole Brossard makes a litany of the various shifting meanings *we* can have for her—we Quebecois / you Canadians; we women / you men; we lesbians / you heterosexuals; we poets / you prose writers, she raises a problem similar to Kafka's.

John Berger, writing recently of the spiritual regeneration of the new nationalisms of Central Europe and the Soviet Union, remarks, "All nationalisms are at heart deeply concerned with names . . . Those who dismiss names as detail have never been displaced; but the peoples on the peripheries are always being displaced. That is why they insist on their identity being recognized" [*The Nation*, May 7, 1990, p. 627]. But naming is never a singular act; what is once named may no longer exist when that name is repeated. It is not that I wish to dismiss names as details but to recognize details as more important than names, as always already peripheralized as names become packages through which a commodity is born. For even individuals are multiple, indeed, as Emmanuel Levinas remarks, "The mind is a multiplicity of individuals."

What represents a Jew or a white Protestant American or an African American, a male or a female? In poetry, it's less a matter of thematic content than the form and content understood as an interlocking figure—the one inaudible without the other; like the soul and the body, completely interpenetrating and interdependent. Formal dynamics in a poem create content through the shapes, feelings, attitudes, and structures that compose the poem. Content is more an attitude toward the work or toward language or toward the materials of the poem than some kind of subject that is in any way detachable from the handling of the materials. Content emerges from composition and cannot be detached from it; or, to put it another way, what is detachable is expendable to the poetic.

What poetry belabors is more important than what poetry says, for "saying is not a game" and the names that we speak are no more our names than the words that enter our ears and flow through our veins, on loan from the past, interest due at the dawn of each day, though not to the Collector who claims to represent us in the court of public discourse but to the Collector we become when we start to collect what belongs to us by right of our care in and for the world.

When we get over this idea that we can all speak to each other, I think it will begin to be possible, as it always has been, to listen to one another, one at a time and in the various clusters that present themselves, or that we find the need to make.

Artifice of Absorption

Meaning and Artifice

> *Then where is truth but in the burning space*
> *between one letter and the next? Thus the book*
> *is first read outside its limits.*
> —Edmond Jabès[1]

The reason it is difficult to talk about
the meaning of a poem—in a way that doesn't seem
frustratingly superficial or partial—is that by
designating a text a poem, one suggests that its
meanings are to be located in some "complex" be-
yond an accumulation of devices & subject matters.
A poetic *reading* can be given to any
piece of writing; a "poem" may be understood as
writing specifically designed to absorb, or inflate
with, proactive—rather than reactive—styles of
reading. "Artifice" is a measure of a poem's
intractability to being read as the sum of its
devices & subject matters. In this sense,
"artifice" is the contradiction of "realism", with
its insistence on presenting an unmediated
(immediate) experience of facts, either of the
"external" world of nature or the "internal" world
of the mind; for example, naturalistic
representation or phenomenological consciousness
mapping. Facts in poetry are primarily
factitious.

---

1. *The Book of Questions: Yael, Elya, Aely,* tr. Rosmarie Waldrop (Middletown: Wesleyan University Press, 1983), p. 7 [unnumbered].

Veronica Forrest-Thomson, in *On Poetic Artifice,*
notes that artifice in a poem is primarily marked
by the quality of the poem's language that makes it
both continuous & discontinuous with the world of
experience:

> Anti-realism need not imply, as certain French theorists might claim,
> a rejection of meaning. All that Artifice requires is that nonmean-
> ingful levels be taken into account, and that *meaning be used as a*
> *technical device* which makes it impossible as well as wrong for
> critics to strand poems in the external world.[2]

The artificiality of a poem may be more or less
foregrounded, but it is necessarily part of
the "poetic" reading of any document. If the artifice
is recessed, the resulting textual transparency
yields an apparent, if misleading, content.
Content never equals meaning. If the artifice is
foregrounded, there's a tendency to say that there
is no content or meaning, as if the poem were a
formal or decorative exercise concerned only with
representing its own mechanisms. But even when a
poem is read as a formal exercise, the dynamics &
contours of its formal proceedings may suggest, for
example, a metonymic model for imagining
experience. For this reason, consideration
of the formal dynamics of a poem does not necessarily
disregard its content; indeed it is an obvious

---

2. Veronica Forrest-Thomson, *Poetic Artifice: A Theory of Twentieth Century Po-*
etry (New York: St. Martin's Press, 1978), p. 132, italics added; subsequent citations
from Forrest-Thomson are from this text. This remarkably precocious book carries
Empson's criticism one step further than Empson was willing to go—into the realm
of what Forrest-Thomson calls the "nonmeaningful" levels of language, which she
sees as the vital future for poetry. Her considerations of Ashbery and Prynne are
particularly valuable, as is her critique of the flaws inherent in "confessional" po-
etry—she speaks of the "suicide poets", from whom she is at great pains to exclude
Plath. At times, Forrest-Thomson's work is frustratingly claustrophobic; but its un-
compromising, fierce, and passionate seriousness makes it an enormously moving
experience to read. Forrest-Thomson, whose *Collected Poems* were published in
1990 by Allardyce, Barnett, died in 1975 at the age of twenty-seven, after receiving
her Ph.D. from Cambridge.

starting point insofar as it can initiate a
multilevel reading. But to complete the process
such formal apprehensions need to move to a
synthesis beyond technical cataloging, toward the
experiential phenomenon that is made by virtue of
the work's techniques. Such a synthesis
is almost impossible apart from the tautological
repetition of the poem, since all the formal
dynamics cannot begin to be charted: think only
of the undercurrent of anagrammatical
transformations,[3] the semantic contribution of
the visual representation of the text,[4] the
particular associations evoked by the phonic
configurations. These features are related to the
"nonsemantic" effects that Forrest-Thomson
describes as contributing toward the "total image-complex"
of the poem (but what might be better called its total
meaning complex, since *image* may suggest
an overly visual orientation):

> The image-complex is the node where we can discover which of
> the multitude of thematic, semantic, rhythmical, and formal patterns
> is important and how it is to be related to the others. For the image-
> complex alone operates on all levels of sound, rhythm, theme, and

3. Steve McCaffery discusses how anagrams drove Saussure to distraction near the
end of his life when he was studying late Latin Saturnian verse: "Implicit in this
research is the curiously nonphenomenal status of the paragram. [It is] an inevitable
consequence of writing's alphabetic, combinatory, nature. Seen this way as emerging
from the multiple ruptures that alphabetic components bring to virtuality, meaning
becomes partly the production of a general economy, a persistent excess, non-inten-
tionality and expenditure without reserve through writing's component letters . . .
The unavoidable presence of words within words contests the notion of writing as a
creativity, proposing instead the notion of an indeterminate, extraintentional, differ-
ential production. The paragram should not be seen necessarily as a latent content or
hidden intention, but as a sub-productive sliding and slipping of meaning between
the forces and intensities distributed through the text's syntactic economy." "Writing
as a General Economy", in *North of Intention* (New York: Roof Books / Toronto:
Nightwood Editions, 1986), pp. 201–221; subsequent citations from McCaffery are
from this essay.

4. Johanna Drucker has been exploring this area in a systematic way. Her "Writ-
ing as the Visual Representation of Language" was presented at "New York Talk"
on June 5, 1984. See "Dada and Futurist Typography: 1909–1925 and the Visual
Representation of Language", Ph.D. diss., University of California, Berkeley, 1986.

meaning and from it alone, therefore, can be derived a sense of
the structure of any particular poem . . . Critical reading must never
try to impose meaning in the form of an extension of meaning into
the non-verbal world until the reader has determined by examining
the non-meaningful levels just what amount of meaning is required
by the poem's structure from each phrase, word, and letter. Only
when this is done can the critic hope to reach a thematic synthesis
which will make contact with the poem itself on its many levels and
not with some abstract, or indeed concrete, entity created out of
his own imagination. The reader must . . . use his imagination . . .
but he must use it to free himself from the fixed forms of thought
which ordinary language imposes on our minds, not to deny the
strangeness of poetry by inserting it in some non-poetic area: his
own mind, the poet's mind, or any non-fictional situation. [p. 16]

So there is always an unbridgeable lacuna between
any explication of a reading & any actual
reading. & it is the extent of these lacunas—
differing with each reader but not indeterminate—
that is a necessary measure of a poem's
meaning.

There is, however, something I find
problematic about Forrest-Thomson's account. It
seems to me she is wrong to designate the nonlexical,
or more accurately, extralexical
strata of the poem as "nonsemantic"; I would say
that such elements as line breaks, acoustic
patterns, syntax, etc., *are* meaningful rather than,
as she has it, that they *contribute* to the meaning
of the poem. For instance, there is no fixed
threshold at which noise becomes phonically
significant; the further back this threshold is
pushed, the greater the resonance at the cutting
edge. The semantic strata of a poem should not be
understood as only those elements to which a
relatively fixed connotative or denotative meaning
can be ascribed, for this would restrict meaning to
the exclusively recuperable elements of language—a

restriction that if literally applied would make
meaning impossible. After all, meaning occurs
only in a context of conscious & nonconscious,
recuperable & unrecoverable, dynamics.

Moreover, the designation of the visual, acoustic,
& syntactic elements of a poem as "meaningless",
especially insofar as this is conceptualized as
positive or liberating—& this is a common habit
of much *current* critical discussion of syntactically
nonstandard poetry—is symptomatic of a desire to
evade responsibility for meaning's total, &
totalizing, reach; as if meaning was a husk
that could be shucked off or a burden that could be
bucked. Meaning is not a use value *as opposed to*
some other kind of value, but more like valuation
itself; & even to refuse value is a value & a sort
of exchange. Meaning is no where *bound*
to the orbit of purpose, intention, or utility.

While this is a crucial distinction, its significance
for Forrest-Thomson's view is not as great as
it is in many more recent commentaries because
her terminology is intended to foreground artifice
as much as possible & for this reason she wishes
to cede as little as possible to the conventional
semantic arena—a decision that makes her book, if
flawed in this respect, so powerfully informative
in the first place.

Forrest-Thomson's account compares interestingly
with Galvano della Volpe's "dialectical paraphrase"
in his *Critique of Taste,* in which the ideological
paraphrase is specifically contrasted with the way
this ideological content is expressed in the work.
This method, says della Volpe, "is in a position to
avoid both formalism & fixation on context."[5]

5. Galvano della Volpe, *Critique of Taste,* tr. Michael Caesar (London: Verso,
1978), p. 193. Quoted by Jerome McGann in his Conclusion to *The Romantic Ideol-
ogy* (Chicago: University of Chicago Press, 1983).

The dialectic of della Volpe's "dialectical
paraphrase" involves the weighing &
measuring of the poetic artifice of the work. "Do
not forget," says Wittgenstein in a passage quoted
by Forrest-Thomson [p. x], "that a poem, even
though it is composed in the language of
information, is not used in the language game of
giving information." She adds that "form and
content are [not] identical, still less are they
fused . . . they must be different,
distinguishable in order that their relations may
be judged" [p. 121].

The hermeneutic rejoinders of della Volpe &
Forrest-Thomson are primarily aimed at discouraging
an exclusive emphasis on the overt ideology or
content of a poem, though they might equally apply
to exclusively formal readings. A poem composed in
the language of artifice & device is not
necessarily without content. What does
one make as a content paraphrase of this stanza
from P. Inman's "Waver" [*Abacus* 18, 1986]?

> it was only her curved say
> leaving till any more
> i want
> to write noise
>   a white
>   out of betweens,
>   think off-misted
>   (piled holster)
>   wouldn't say "fault".
>   stills by size
>   glass cattle
> (denominations between her work)
>   kints grasp
>   off than
>   cinder ink
>   dreadlocks pollen

> seems to any on
> draws as pang
> waiting for a keyboard
> "so much depends
> on starch"
> ute broils
> Keats with the wrong facts
> everything took place at all

In a sense, the procedure of dialectical paraphrase
must be reversed in reading this poem. An attempt
must first be made to elucidate the "nonsemantic"
elements of the poem ("to write noise / a white /
out of betweens"), but the reading should not stop
there ("piled holster"), as it all too often might.
This first survey must be dialectically contrasted
with how the noted devices might have been
used to different ends, what type of overall
architecture is constructed by the particular
sequence of devices ("curved say"), what semantic
associations can be attributed to the specific
"nonsemantic" elements & which ones are relevant
in the particular context of the poem. That is,
the devices must be differentiated from the image
complex to which they contribute. When I say that
della Volpe's procedure must be reversed in reading
"Waver", I mean that because the formal dynamics of
the poem are the most overt, identifiable feature,
they have the weight of "content" in a more
traditional poem ("Keats with the wrong facts");
just as the content threatens to naturalize
(Forrest-Thomson's term) the artifice of a more
conventional poem in an undialectical reading ("'so
much depends / on starch'"), so here the form
threatens to negate the content in an undialectical
reading ("kints grasp"); for this reason, "Waver"
destabilizes the polarities of form & content,
undermining the dialectic's value for thinking
about (as opposed to deciphering) the poem

("wouldn't say 'fault'"). By fully semanticizing
the so-called nonsemantic features of language,
Inman creates a dialectic of the recuperable &
the unreclaimable, where what cannot be claimed is
nonetheless *most* manifest.

The obvious problem is that the poem said in any
other way is not the poem. This may account for
why writers revealing their intentions or
references ("close readings"), just like readers
inventorying devices, often say so little: why
a sober attempt to document or describe runs so
high a risk of falling flat. In contrast, why not
a criticism intoxicated with its own metaphoricity,
or tropicality: one in which the limits of
positive criticism are made more audibly
artificial; in which the inadequacy of our
explanatory paradigms is neither ignored
nor regretted but brought into fruitful play.
Imagine, then, oscillating poles,
constructing not some better diadicism, but
congealing into a field of potentialities
that in turn collapses (transforms) into yet other
tropicalities. This would be the criticism of desire:
sowing not reaping.

Adapting Steve McCaffery's terms from "Writing as a
General Economy", the economy of reading suggested
here is not a utilitarian "restricted economy" of
accumulation (of contents, devices) but a "general
economy" of meanings as "nonutilizable" flow,
discharge, exchange, waste. An individual poem may
be understood as having a restricted or general
economy. Indeed, part of the meaning of a poem may
be its fight for accumulation; nonetheless, its
text will contain destabilizing elements—errors,
unconscious elements, contexts of (re)publication
& the like—that will erode any proposed
accumulation that does not allow for them.

McCaffery derives his idea of a general economy
from Bataille, whom he quotes:

> The general economy, in the first place, makes apparent that ex-
> cesses of energy are produced, and that by definition, these excesses
> cannot be utilized. The excessive energy can only be lost without
> the slightest aim, consequently without meaning.

McCaffery continues:

> I want to make clear that I'm *not* proposing "general" as an alter-
> native economy to "restricted". One cannot replace the other be-
> cause their relationship is not one of mutual exclusion. In most cases
> we will find general economy as a suppressed or ignored presence
> within the scene of writing that tends to emerge by way of rupture
> within the restricted [paragrams, as discussed in note 3], putting
> into question the conceptual controls that produce a writing of use
> value with its privileging of meaning as a necessary production and
> evaluated destination.

These "nonutilizable" excesses are related to
Forrest-Thomson's "nonsemantic domains", while
clearly being a conceptually larger category. In
this context, I would again argue against ascribing
to meaning an exclusively utilitarian function.
Loss is as much a part of the semantic process as
discharge is a part of the biological process. Yet
the meaning of which I speak is not meaning as we
may "know" it, with a recuperable intention or
purpose. Such a restricted sense of meaning is
analogous to the restricted senses of knowledge as
stipulatively definable. But let's look at how
these words are used or can be used:
You know what I mean & you also mean
a lot more than you can say
& far more than you could ever intend,
stipulatively or no.
It is just my insistence
that poetry be understood as epistemological

inquiry; to cede meaning would be to undercut
the power of poetry to reconnect us
with modes of meaning given in language
but precluded by the hegemony of restricted
epistemological economies (an hegemony that moves
toward the negation of nondominant restricted
economies as much as repressing the asymptotic
horizon of the unrestricted economies). As
McCaffery puts it, "such features of general
economic operation do not destroy the order of
meaning, but complicate & unsettle its
constitution and operation". They destroy, that
is, not meaning but various utilitarian &
essentialist ideas about meaning. To this point
it must be added that to speak of the nonutilizable
strata of a poem or a verbal exchange is as
problematic as to speak of nonsemantic elements—
for what is designated as nonutilizable
& extralexical is both useful & desirable
while not being utilitarian & prescribable.

These comments are partly intended as caution
against thinking of formally active poems as
eschewing content or meaning—even in the face of
the difficulty of articulating just what this
meaning is. That is, the meaning is not absent or
deferred but self-embodied as the poem
in a way that is not transferable to another code
or rhetoric. At the same time, it is possible
to evoke various contours of meaning
by metaphorically considering the domains made real
by various formal configurations.

Absorption and Impermeability

> *If we studied societies from the outside, it would*
> *be tempting to distinguish two contrasting types:*
> *those which practice cannibalism—that is which*
> *regard the absorption of certain individuals pos-*

sessing dangerous powers as the only means of neutralizing these powers and even of turning them to advantage—and those which, like our own society, adopt what might be called the practice of anthropemy *(from the Greek* emein, *to vomit); faced with the same problem, the latter type of society has chosen the opposite solution, which consists in ejecting dangerous individuals from the social body and keeping them temporarily or permanently in isolation, away from all contacts with their fellows, in establishments especially intended for this purpose. Most of the societies we call primitive would regard this custom with profound horror; it would make us, in their eyes, guilty of that same barbarity of which we are inclined to accuse them because of their symmetrically opposite behavior.*

—Claude Lévi-Strauss, *Tristes Tropiques*

The entire reality of the word is wholly absorbed in its function of being a sign.

—V. N. Voloshinov, *Marxism and the Philosophy of Language*

Ever wonder why one person can eat a meal of French toast and sausage, followed by a glass of milk, to little effect, while if you . . . Absorption problems.

—*Guide Amber à la Gastronomie*[6]

6. Claude Lévi-Strauss, *Tristes Tropiques*, tr. John and Doreen Weightman (New York: Atheneum, 1984), p. 388; V. N. Voloshinov [pseudonym of Mikhail Bakhtin], *Marxism and the Philosophy of Language*, tr. L. Matejka and I. R. Titunik (New York: Seminar Press, 1973), p. 14; Caudio Amber, *Guide Amber Gastronomie* (Graisse, N.Y.: White Castle Press, 1950), unpaginated.

In thinking about how to respond
to a request to do a reading of one of my poems,
I've found myself
thinking about "absorption" & its obverses—
impermeability, imperviousness, ejection,
repellence—both as a compositional question
& as
a reading value.[7] The terms began to consume
my imagination, a pataphysical extravaganza
of accumulating works & fields absorbed
into this tropic zone without benefit
of underlying unity of perspective. There seemed no
limit to what
the absorption/antiabsorption nexus could
absorb.

Thinking of Canada, where I initially presented my
speculations, the political metaphor kept erupting:
Canada does not wish to be absorbed into the U.S.
cultural orbit any more than Quebec wishes to be
absorbed by Canada; but then Quebec feminists may not
want to be absorbed by a male-dominated "free" Quebec.
Identity seems to involve the refusal to be absorbed
in a larger identity, yet the identity formed as
a result of an antiabsorptive autonomism
threatens to absorb differential groupings
within it. It's as if the very desire not
to be absorbed creates a new threat
of absorption—down to the individual divided
against itself—its nonsocial "identity"
at odds with its social "selves".[8]

---

7. Michael Fried's *Absorption and Theatricality: Painting and the Beholder in the Age of Diderot* (Berkeley: University of California Press, 1980) was my starting point for these considerations. I discuss issues related to absorption in "Film of Perception" (see especially the discussion of movies that begins the section) and "On Theatricality" in *Content's Dream: Essays 1975–1984* (Los Angeles: Sun & Moon Press, 1986).

8. Nick Piombino makes this distinction in "Writing, Identity, and Self", *The Difficulties* 2:1 (1982).

& then there are the biological senses
of absorption & excretion: the body's narration.
Steve McCaffery pointed out
that having an infant around
for the first time had had its effect:
I had been changing a half-dozen superabsorbant
diapers a day, ever in fear
that they would not be superabsorptive enough
& spillage would result. So *this*
is the answer to that
persistent & irritating question: Has having a child
affected your writing?

Moreover, the nature of absorption as a dynamic
of reading needs to be understood as a key element
in any ideologically conscious literary criticism.
This can be taken as the central polemic of
Jerome McGann's *Romantic Ideology*.[9] The
uncritical absorption of a poem of William
Wordsworth, for example, entails an absorption
of Romantic ideology that precludes an historically
informed reading of the poem. In order for a
sociohistorical reading to be possible, absorption
of the poem's own ideological imaginary must be
blocked; the refusal of absorption is a
prerequisite to understanding (in the literal sense
of standing *under* rather than inside). Indeed,
absorption may be a quality that characterizes
specifically Romantic works. This is suggested by
McGann when he discusses the "romantic" rationale
behind a persistent preference for a version of Keats's "La
Belle Dame sans Merci" that substitutes "Oh what
can ail thee, knight-at-arms" for the more
ambivalent or ironic "Ah what can ail thee,
wretched wight" (where *wight* means both brave &
base as well as being deliberately archaic).

9. See note 5 above. I discuss this work more fully in "McGann Agonist", *Sulfur*
15 (1986).

"By 'romantic' here I mean simply that [the preferred]
text does not distance itself the way the [other]
text does. The former is a more self-absorbed and
self-absorbing text, whereas the latter is more
self-conscious and critical."[10]

Insofar as I make a distinction between the
absorptive & antiabsorptive, these terms
should not be understood as mutually exclusive,
morally coded, or even conceptually separable.
Absorption & antiabsorption are both present
in any method of reading or writing, although
one or the other may be more obtrusive or evasive.
They connote colorations more than dichotomies.

From a compositional point of view
the question is, What can a poem absorb?
Here, think
of a text as a spongy substance, absorbing
vocabulary, syntax, & reference. The idea
of a poem absorbing these elements is meant
to provide an alternative to more traditional
notions of causal narration or thematic
relevance as producing a unified work.
A poem can absorb contradictory logics,
multiple tonalities, polyrhythms. At the
same time, impermeable materials—or moments—
are crucial musical resources for a poem,
though not all impermeable materials will work
to create the desired *textural* space.
There are relative degrees
or valences of impermeability that can be angled
against one another to create
interlinear or interphrasal "gaps" that act
like intervals in musical composition. Pushing
further, impermeable elements may fuse together

10. McGann, *The Beauty of Inflections* (New York: Oxford University Press, 1985), p. 40n35.

Inasmuch as an authentic rendering—a rendering made with extreme artistic skill—will give you more the sense of having been present at an event than if you had actually been corporally present, whereas the reading of the most skillful of literary forgeries will only leave you with the sense that you have read a book the artistic rendering is the more valuable to you and therefore the greater achievement. I once heard a couple of French marine engineers agreeing that although they had traversed the Indian ocean many times and had several times passed through, or through the fringes of typhoons, neither of them had ever been in one till they had read Conrad's "Typhoon" . . .

To produce that or similar effects is the ambition of the novel today . . .

The fact is that with Elizabeth English became a supple and easily employable language and, making the discovery that words could be played with as if they were oranges or gilt balls to be tossed half a dozen together in the air, mankind rushed upon it as colts will dash into suddenly opened rich and easy pastures. So it was, for the rich and cultured, much more a matter of who could kick heels the higher and most flourish tail and mane than any ambition of carrying burdens or drawing loads.

In the end, however, what humanity needs is that burdens should be carried and provided that things get from place to place the name of the carter or horse is of very secondary importance. If it is the fashion we will go down to the meadow and watch the colts cavorting: but all the while we are aware that the business of words as of colts or of the arts is to carry things and we tire reasonably soon of watching horse-play! For if I say: "I am hungry," the business of those words is to carry that information to you, and if you read the "Iliad" it is that the art of that epic may make Hecuba significant to you . . .

The struggle—the aspiration—of the novelist down the ages has been to evolve a water-tight convention for the frame-work of the novel. He aspires—and for centuries has aspired—so to construct his stories and so to manage their surfaces that the carried away and rapt reader shall really think himself to be in Brussels on the first of Waterloo days or in the Grand Central Station waiting for the Knickerbocker Express to come in from Boston though actually he may be sitting in a cane lounge on a beach of Bermuda in December. This is not easy . . .

It is for instance an obvious and unchanging fact that if an author intrudes his comments into the middle of his story he will endanger the illusion conveyed by that story—but a generation of readers may come along who would prefer witnessing the capers of the author to being carried away by stories and that generation of readers may coincide with a generation of writers tired of self-obliteration. So you may have a world of Oscar Wildes or of Lylys. Or you might, again, have a world tired of the really well constructed novel every word of which carries its story forward: then you will have a movement toward diffuseness, backboneless sentences, digressions, and inchoatenesses.[14]

These marvelous passages deserve fuller &
closer attention than I propose to give them.
In any case, they speak well for themselves.
But it is useful to understand that Ford's
antiaestheticism (he grew up in a household where
Swinburne was a frequent guest) is related to
the Vorticist pronouncements of his friend Ezra
Pound (direct treatment, no word that does not
contribute), to which, inevitably, I shall return.
Ford here makes the classic case for a transparent
language that in no way interferes with the
reader's absorption in the story being told; he
dismisses any form of opacity or self-consciousness
or formal play as hindering this readerly
absorption. It is striking that this position is
consonant with, rather than opposed to, powerful
currents within early modernism; he means by
his remarks to negatively target

14. Ford Madox Ford, *The English Novel: From the Earliest Days to the Death of Joseph Conrad* (Philadelphia: J. B. Lippincott, 1929), pp. 62–63, 70–71, 86, 148–149; recently reprinted by Carcanet. This work was especially prepared for Lippincott's "The One Hour Series". In his wonderfully digressive and ornately self-conscious preliminary remarks, Ford writes, "I should like to observe for the benefit of the Lay Reader, to whom I am addressing myself—for the Professional Critic will pay no attention to anything that I say, contenting himself with cutting me to pieces with whips of scorpions for having allowed my head to pop up at all—to the Lay Reader I should like to point out that what I am about to write is highly controversial and he should take none of it too much *au pied de la lettre*" (p. 31).

Dickensian character-typing as much as literary
ornamentation, stilted "verse" diction
(the dominant form of magazine verse at the time),
& experimentation. While writing this
humorous & close-to-parodic study, Ford marshals
his arguments to support Conrad; but
it should be remembered that, for Ford, the
"Master" would always be James, & James
was not the master of transparency but of Artifice.
(I hope I need not reiterate
that Conrad's writing consciously
employs artifice fully as much as Oscar Wilde's
& that readers are likely to be conscious of, &
to appreciate, the artifice of both writers.
Ford's study is indeed a brief
for the greater technical control required to
achieve the effects of Flaubertian artifice.)
In any case, what Ford fails to account for
in his giddy study is that impermeable textual
elements may actually contribute toward
absorptive effects, & that such textures
may be particularly vital at a time when readers
are skeptical of the transparency effect, whether
it is used to reveal unmediated inner states or
external narrative spaces.

By *absorption* I mean engrossing, engulfing
completely, engaging, arresting attention, reverie,
attention intensification, rhapsodic, spellbinding,
mesmerizing, hypnotic, total, riveting,
enthralling: belief, conviction, silence.

Impermeability suggests artifice, boredom,
exaggeration, attention scattering, distraction,
digression, interruptive, transgressive,
undecorous, anticonventional, unintegrated, fractured,
fragmented, fanciful, ornately stylized, rococo,
baroque, structural, mannered, fanciful, ironic,
iconic, schtick, camp, diffuse, decorative,
repellent, inchoate, programmatic, didactic,

theatrical, background muzak, amusing: skepticism,
doubt, noise, resistance.

Absorptive & antiabsorptive
works both require artifice, but the former may hide
this while the latter may flaunt
it. & absorption may dissolve
into theater as these distinctions chimerically
shift & slide. Especially since,
as in much of my own work, antiabsorptive
techniques are used toward
absorptive ends; or, in satiric writing (it's a put
on, get it?), absorptive means are used
toward antiabsorptive ends. It remains
an open question, & an unresolvable
one, what
will produce an absorptive poem & what will
produce a nonabsorptive one.

These
textual
dynamics
can
be
thought
about
in
relation
to
the
reader
&
to
the
structure
of
the
poem.

On Fordian absorptive terms, the reader
(a.k.a. beholder) must be ignored, as in
the "fourth wall" convention in theater, where what
takes place on the stage is assumed to be sealed
off from the audience. Nothing
in the text should cause self-consciousness
about the reading process: it should be as if
the writer & the reader are not present.
As Diderot puts it, also (if unwittingly) articulating
the dilemma of the role assigned to women in
sexist society, *"It is the difference between a
woman who is seen and a woman who exhibits
herself."*[15] This distinction is
a fiction; texts are written to be read or heard,
that is, exhibited; but the degree the "teller"
or "way it's told" are allowed to come
into focus affects the experience of "what"
is being told or "what" is
unfolding. Nor is poetry,
by nature emphasizing its artifice,
immune from this dynamic. For poems
do not necessarily make the beholder conscious
of his or her role as a reader, nor can such
self-consciousness be obliterated only by
presenting highly visualizable scenes of sea
voyages or Homeric adventure.

---

15. Quoted by Fried, p. 97; italics added. Diderot's remark epitomizes the double bind of women being defined by a male gaze: to be seen as a woman one must be passive, while to stare back (as in Manet's *Olympia*) is to exhibit oneself, to become a whore. This implicitly valorizes the woman as subject, absorbed in the world as opposed to acting on it. As Nicole Brossard made clear at the New Poetics Colloquium in Vancouver, discussing her *Journal intime* (Montreal: Editions Herbes Rouges, 1984), the subjective space is treacherous for a woman since it risks accepting the subjectification of women in the model described by Diderot. Brossard's response is to write something called an "intimate journal", a diary (the traditionally accepted form of women's writing) that refuses the primary terms of that form, refuses, that is, to absorb the gaze of the reader but rather deflects this gaze onto the artificial/actual process of self-construction: "ma vie qui n'est qu'un tissu de mots" [my life which is only a tissue of words] (p. 15). This transformed, you might also say evacuated, journal requires the name *poetry*.

Many nineteenth-century lyric poems involve a self-
absorbed address to a beloved, the gods, or
the poet her/himself: an address that, because
it is *not* to the reader but to some presence
anterior or
interior to
the poem, induces readerly absorption
by creating an effect of overhearing in contrast to
confronting.

Absorption can be broken
by any direct address
to the reader, whether as in
a how-to book ("now go get that leaky poem"), an
instruction manual ("stop here and complete the
test questions"), a sermon ("I'm calling
on you, not your neighbor, not the Jew Boy
next door, not them playdough inverts"), the Ten
Commandments ("I/thou"), or just by asking
you to look at the period at the end of this
sentence & pointing — he does this here
out that it's about the size of your macula.—"Who
are you calling a macula!" Don't get huffy. Don't
get "huffy". Why just yesterday (but when was
today, dear reader?) Bob Perelman was saying "I'm
also using more repetition, deictics [words that
point, like 'this' word but which word is *this*
word 'this' or this], speechlike elements which posit
a co-presence of 'speaker & listener', i.e., writer
and reader." Perelman quotes from "Cliff Notes":
"It can't be the knobs' fault because this is back
before knobs" & from "Let's Say":

> A page is being beaten
> back across the face of 'things'.
> . . . . .
>
> and the you and I spends its life
> trying to read the bill

alone in the dark
big wide streets lined with language glue

Perelman comments:

> The reader and the writer, "the you and the I," are such languages
> transforming into pulp language, non-languages and back, de-
> graded, exploded, overburdened systems of public & private ad-
> dress. There's no inner escape from our environment, where such
> powerful emblems of coercion as USA TODAY constantly conflate the
> initials U.S. with their editorial staff and with "us," so that "we"
> read that "we" are buoyed by the progress of the Salvadoran army
> or that "we" are attending more ballgames than ever this summer.[16]

Or, as he writes in "Binary": "Finally the I
writing / and the you reading (breath still misting
the glass) / examples of the body partitioned by the
word" [*The First World*, p. 47].

Absorption is blocked by misting
this glass, or by breaking it, or
by painting on its surface. Any

---

16. Bob Perelman, "Notes on *The First World*", *Line* 6 (1985), 101, 108–109;
this talk was originally presented at the New Poetics Colloquium in Vancouver. The
poems quoted by Perelman in his talk, as well as the citations that follow, are from
The First World (Great Barrington, Mass.: The Figures, 1986). —"If only the plot
would leave people alone", Perelman writes in "Anti-Oedipus" (p. 20). His passion-
ate refusal to be housed by the poem, his insistence on breaking loose from the social
hypnosis that deadens response, nonetheless cannot readily be understood as prevent-
ing absorption, despite its striking awareness of itself as a poetry & its forthright
address to the reader. For Perelman has created poetry that is funny, political, engag-
ing—and does not distance itself from the reader in ways we have grown accustomed
to. In a recent interview Perelman was careful to put off the suggestion that because
his poems do not employ causal unity (are not "little short stories"), they are there-
fore not coherent. "China", a work in *The First World*, "coheres grammatically,
thematically, politically in terms of tone. It's certainly not something that throws you
off the track, like playing trains as a kid, whipping from side to side until someone
falls off—it's not that." This last image of a train flipping the tracks is precisely a
description of the effect of the antiabsorptive on reading. Interview by George Hart-
ley, conducted in Berkeley in 1986, quoted in "Jameson's Perelman: Reification and
the Material Signifier", a draft chapter of Hartley's dissertation (University of New
Mexico); not included in the chapter of the same name in Hartley's *Textual Politics
of the Language Poets* (Bloomington: Indiana University Press, 1989).

typographic irregularity,
any glitch in expected
syntax, any
digression . . .
Nicole Brossard makes this a theme
in *A Book,* where the process
of creating the fiction is explicitly put
as the role of the reader:

> The event is seen from a distance and out of context. All that is
> happening is this reading being done, the only real thing, causing
> a few muscles to move imperceptibly and making one conscious of
> his own breathing . . . To be aware of what happens at the very
> instant the eyes focus on the hand holding the book, on the book
> and the words it is made up of . . . The words are yours . . . The
> game is over. The book too. The manuscript is no more . . . Time
> passes slowly, so slowly. Someone is reading. And gently closing the
> object.[17]

Another way of acknowledging, or calling attention
to, the reader/writer relationship is
the Brechtian device of captioning, or the use of
marginal titles, as in the digressive &
picaresque novels of the eighteenth century, or in
Coleridge's "The Ancient Mariner", or
more recently, in Lyn Hejinian's *My Life.*
Beyond this works that ask the reader to do
something, such as those poems by Jackson Mac Low
that have accompanying instructions, make use
of a primary antiabsorptive technique. The Coleridge
poem usefully underlines the difficulty of identifying
antiabsorptive means with antiabsorptive ends.
McGann persuasively argues in "The Ancient Mariner:
The Meaning of the Meanings" that the interpretive
glosses inserted by Coleridge into his poem serve

17. Nicole Brossard, *A Book,* tr. Larry Shouldice (Toronto: Coach House Press, 1976), secs. 19, 91, 98, 99.

to *reconcile* the readers of his time to otherwise
patently alien material (pagan superstition &
early Catholic legend); that is, his hermeneutic
interventions effectively enabled the reader to
absorb, by discovering a continuity with, diverse
& discordant historical & ideological
perspectives. As McGann points out, Coleridge
envisioned his project as reducing "all knowledge
to harmony", where harmony is understood as being
created by the "higher" light of his own Broad
Church Protestantism.[18]

Bruce Andrews' recent work explores
a different technique for using the presence
of the reader antiabsorptively. Andrews'
audience-directed confrontational language,
with its aggressive street slang & scatological
language, peppered with second-person accusations
provoking questions ("Isn't nature bored with your
devotion?" "Hey, Fuckhead") & first-person
deprecations ("Mash me to a pulp"), invoke & assault
the reader with the exploitive, racist, sexist
underside of our collective syntactic & metaphoric
practices. Andrews makes obtrusive
the social & ideological nature & function
of language habits in which we are
ordinarily so absorbed as to ignore
or repress. Rather than absorb
the reader in the poem, the poem radiates
out, projectile-like, against
placid ear, pseudosensitive
appropriateness, *politesse*—"contesting
the social ground" without abandoning a commitment
to the social constitution of meaning.
For Andrews, as for Perelman & Brossard,
the resistance to absorption is a

18. See McGann, *The Beauty of Inflections*, part 3, chap. 1, especially pp. 152–155, 160–161, and 166–169.

political act; in "I Guess Work the Time Up",
"Confidence Trick", & "Shut Up", Andrews has
produced an antiabsorptive writing more socially
refractive than aesthetically impermeable.[19]

Direct address to the audience can, in contrast,
be used to *further* absorptive reading, as in
David Antin's attempt, in his talks/monologues,
to revitalize poetry by focusing its address
on a live audience, & more subtly by disarming
reader or audience skepticism by acknowledging
their presence as well as his own. Here's
how he starts one work, which, like most of his
recent poetry, is based on a transcript
of a performance that, as writing, simulates
the immediacy (*urgency* as he puts it) of
in-person communication:

> ive called this talk *tuning*   and you probably have no very good
> idea of what i am going to talk about . . .   though i have a
> considerable notion of the terrain   into which i tend to move
> and the only way im going to find out whether it was worth doing
> or not   is when i hear what ive got   which has been my
> way of entrapping myself   and the reason ive chosen to entrap
> myself rather than to prepare in advance   a precise set of
> utterances   has been that i felt myself   ive written things
>   before this   in the natural vacuum that is the artificial
> hermetic closet that literature has been in for some time   and
> the problem for me   is in the closet confronting a typewriter
> and no person   so that for me literature defined as literature
>   has no urgency   it has need of address   there are too
> many things   no there are not too many things there are only
> a few things you may want to talk about but there are too many
> ways you could talk about them   and no urgency in which way

19. At the New Poetics Colloquium in Vancouver, Andrews read from *I Don't Have Any Paper So Shut Up (or Social Romanticism)* (Los Angeles: Sun & Moon Press, 1991), a work related to, and written just after, "Confidence Trick". In Vancouver Andrews also read excerpts from "Total Equals What: Poetics and Practice", published subsequently in *Poetics Journal* 6 (1986).

you to choose talk about them   there are too many ways to
proceed   too many possibilities for making well crafted
objects   none of which seem particularly necessary.[20]

Let me turn again
to consideration of the internal structure
of a poem, putting aside, for a moment,
the poem's relation to the reader.
One approach to creating a poem that absorbs
the attention is through the unity of its
elements: the *causal* necessity of every element
& relationship being strikingly & instantaneously
apparent. Diderot, speaking of painting (but
the idea translates), called for the elimination
of all incident, however appealing, that did not
contribute *directly* & indispensably to the most
dramatic & expressive presentation of the subject
that could be imagined: "A composition cannot
afford any idle figures, any superfluous accessory.
The subject must be one."[21] This is echoed,
well over a century later, in Pound's Imagist
& Vorticist dictums against the extraneous & idly
ornamental. Indeed, the metaphors of speed &
vortex in the Italian Futurism of Marinetti
& the Vorticism of Pound were related to
the absorptive, unifying power of dynamic energy;
the fast car unified the landscape by virtue
of its power, in the Imagist poem "Emotion seizing
up some external scene or action carries it intact
to the mind; & that *vortex purges it of all
save the essential or dominant dramatic qualities,*
& it emerges like the external original."[22]

20. David Antin, *Tuning* (New York: New Directions, 1984), pp. 105–106.
21. Quoted by Fried, p. 84. In the present instance, quoting part of Diderot's
French might qualify as appealingly superfluous: "aucune figure oisive, aucun acces-
soire superflu. Que le sujet en soit un." Ls so he does it
22. Ezra Pound, "Affirmations—As for Imagisme" (1915), *Selected Prose, 1909–*
1965, ed. William Cookson (New York: New Directions, 1973), p. 375; italics
added.

Moreover, something like Diderot's credo still
has a powerful hold on quite diverse practices
of contemporary poetry. I would interpret
Allen Ginsberg's latterday insistence on breath
& clarity, & the focus that meditation can bring,
as an attempt to hone in on the essential
& separate out the beclouded. Louis Simpson, speaking,
like Ginsberg, for a large number of practitioners, decries
obscure syntax or vocabulary, advocating the articulation
of the voice of the "common man", which necessarily
requires, to achieve the effect, the causal unity
of elements. While Antin, approaching the issues
in a different way from Ginsberg & Simpson,
nonetheless has spoken of "goodness
of fit" as a criterion not adequately replaced in poems
(& paintings & movies) that rely on juxtaposing
highly disparate materials. He contrasts this
with the goodness of fit in "discourse",
such as his own talks, where there is a more
organic progression.[23]

Causal unity is often motivated by a desire
to create more absorbing, "effective"
poems. The problem is that often
it doesn't work; the devices employed
create poems that seem phony
or boring or
uncompelling. One reason
for this pragmatic failure
is that much contemporary American
poetry is based on simplistic
notions of absorption through unity, such
as those sometimes put forward by Ginsberg
(who as his work shows

---

23. See David Antin, *The Principle of Fit*, 2 (Washington, D.C.: Watershed Tapes, 1980); Antin expressed his distrust of jump cutting and other forms of radical juxtaposition in a talk at the Guggenheim Museum in the late 1970s. See also Louis Simpson's various comments in *What Is a Poet?*, ed. Hank Lazer (Tuscaloosa: University of Alabama Press, 1986).

knows better, but who has made an ideological
commitment to such simplicity) & Simpson
(whose case is less complex). In contrast, Antin's
thinking about these issues is determinately
sophisticated & his practice shows it—
the work suggests
new possibilities for pursuing the concerns
he articulates.

Causal unity is by no means the only approach
that has been used to create absorptive works.
Metrical versification traditionally has been used
for this purpose: the regular recurrences of sounds
& beats lulling—or pulling—the attention
inward. At present, however, this strategy
may backfire on pragmatic grounds since such
works run a high risk of being tediously
repetitive & witlessly contrived, that is,
nonabsorbing: dull while wanting to be
bright. Conversely, metricality & other
traditional prosodic devices, especially when
foregrounded, can be potent antiabsorptive
techniques (& were traditionally used as such
by many English poets prior to the rise of
Romanticism). A sestina, in almost anybody's
hands, seems artificial. In this sense,
some of the most inert & lobotomized poetry
of our time uses such devices to accent its archaism,
its formality, its Verse Ethos, or worse still,
to trivialize the whole endeavor (as in Vickram
Seth's "verse novel" *The Golden Gate,*
widely praised for touching on the issues
of poetic artifice—yet this work is without feeling
for poetic devices or able to do anything with them
save evacuate them of their possibilities
to mean or to sing.[24]) In contrast,

---

24. "There is no form of platitude which cannot be turned into iambic pentameter
without labor. It is not difficult, if one have learned to count up to ten, to begin a

Swinburne was perhaps the last poet in English
who was able to fully realize the possibilities
inherent in the conflict between the absorptive
& artificial in the use of elaborate formal prosodic
structures; for in the extremity of his rimes
& syntaxes, he inhabited a unique domain
on the borderline between the rhap-
sodic & the theatrical.

Forrest-Thomson makes this point with great acuity,
praising Swinburne for having created

> an artificial world both continuous & discontinuous with the world
> of experience. It is a world which simplifies and exalts but also, and
> by the same token, parodies . . . Swinburne is aware that expansion
> of the level of meaning & imposition of Naturalisation are inevitable
> constituents of the process of reading poetry and must be allowed
> for in the process of writing it. He is further aware that in making
> such allowances one can find ways of making a poem transcend its
> initial Naturalisation and impose its own world of imaginative pos-
> sibilities, simply because it has made technical allowances for the
> reader's initial realistic expansion/limitation. [pp. 118 and 121]

Poetry is often distinguished from other forms
of writing by the fact that it marks its artifice
by its line breaks or, if prose format, by virtue
of prosodic devices usually not foregrounded
in other types of prose. Helen Vendler, in her introduction
to *The Harvard Book of Contemporary American Poetry,*
writes:

> While the novel, unstoppable, wants to keep reeling us into its
> labyrinth, the unjustified margin of poetry pulls us up, *even if gently,*
> at the end of each line. (Even the prose poem, by its sheer density,
> forces an interruption on us at the end of each sentence, a practice
> that would be fatal to the novel.) [This may explain why the works

---

new line on each eleventh syllable or to whack each alternate syllable with an ictus."
Pound, "Affirmations", p. 375.

that have caused critics to invent the "death of the novel" are
probably the ones most alive.] . . . The symbolic strength of poetry
consists in giving presence, through linguistic signs, *to absent real-
ities,* while insisting, by the very brilliance of poetic style, on the
linguistic nature of its own being and the illusionistic character of
its effects.[25]

First off, one might wonder, why give presence to
"absent realities" & not to absent unrealities,
or why not give absence to (obliterate)
present realities, & so on; but this takes us
too far afield (which is the point). For despite
the many problems with this passage, it still
suggests that the anthology includes poems that
display their linguistic self-consciousness
in a variety of antiabsorptive ways. But this
is not the case since for Vendler the "interruptions"
of poetry are so "gentle" as hardly to be
noticed at all; they are polite
& discrete, to be *seen*
& not heard. As Vendler puts it,
"When we first read a poem we read it
illusionistically; later we may see its art."
Vendler's selections, insofar as they
do display linguistic self-consciousness, are
restricted to doing so in terms of discursive
stylistic practices. Disjunction
is almost entirely absent from the poems selected.
By antiabsorptive it should be apparent that I
do not mean what Vendler has in mind; I'm talking
about *real* disruption that prevents an initial

25. Helen Vendler, Introduction to *The Harvard Book of Contemporary American
Poetry* (Cambridge: Harvard University Press, 1985), pp. 2, 17, italics and brackets
mine; later quotes from pp. 9, 13, 17. *The Harvard Book of Contemporary Ameri-
can Poetry*—including "contemporary" poems by Stevens, who was born in 1879
and died thirty years before the book was published—is the only recent anthology of
American poetry that my local public library has acquired. For more on official verse
culture see Marjorie Perloff's astute commentary on the Vendler anthology, "Of
Canons and Contemporaries", *Sulfur* 16 (1986), and Rae Armantrout's "Mainstream
Marginality", *Poetics Journal* 6 (1986).

"illusionistic" reading. It becomes clear,
however, why Wallace Stevens & the John Ashbery
of "Self-Portrait in a Discur(v)sive Mirror"
are the best examples of Vendler's thesis since
they have both created remarkable works within
the domain she focuses on. These works
are so aesthetically convincing
that it may be hard for some readers to accept
alternate prosodic methods.

Vendler is very much under the spell of
realist & mimetic ideas about poetry. In this
sense, she still has much to learn from Stevens &
Ashbery. She writes that poets "attempt that
accuracy—of perception, of style",
discounting Wilde's
observation that reality is shaped by art,
& not the other way around
(& what does accuracy have to do with it
anyway?). But perhaps
the most irritating thing about
Vendler's manner of argument is that it is always
referring to what "all" poems do, making it
impossible for her to even consider that some poems
may come into being just because they don't do what
some other poems have done. Vendler says
she hopes readers will be provoked by some of the
anthologized poems to say—"'Heavens, I recognize
the place, I know it!' It is the effect every poet
hopes for." I would hope
readers might be provoked to say of *some* poems,
"Hell, I don't recognize the place or the time or
the 'I' in this sentence. I don't know it."

Donald Wesling argues, in *The Chances of Rhyme:
Device and Modernity,* that one of the features of
the "modernity" that developed in the West after
1795 was an attempt to "naturalize" artifice
(in Forrest-Thomson's sense) by *emotionally
necessitating* & removing from the foreground

the devices that are an inevitable part of poetic
composition, thus setting in motion a fecund
paradox or contradiction that persists to the
present.[26] In Wesling's
account, English neoclassicism
as practiced by the Augustans in the period
immediately preceding this "major prosodic
break" was even more rigidly
naturalizing of devices, but for these writers
there was a natural symmetry between the rhetoric
of rule-bound devices & reason. Paraphrasing
Edward Bysshe's *Art of English Poetry* (1702),
Wesling notes that "sound repetitions are to come
at stated intervals, like perfect chimes: any
unpredictability or sense of sound would be 'harsh,'
or 'rough,' an uncivil prosody". Indeed,
any antiabsorptive use of rime was to be "expunged"
under the principle that "rhyme was completely
natural, assuming couplets were the mind's true
order". However, the break
Wesling locates at 1795 is not so much a rejection
of the value of naturalization as a radical change
in what was assumed to be natural, specifically
a substitution of an "organicist" conception
of form for a "rhetorical" one:

> Post-Romantic writers are suspicious of literary form in its guise of
> ornamental rhetoric, and this has made the history and role of the
> device central in modern poetics. Rhyme, the instance chosen here,
> is not disappearing . . . but rather is being *wrenched* as far as
> possible into *personal meaning*.

The naturalizing of devices such as rime fits
into Vendler's paradigm, as just discussed.
I would contrast this naturalizing of the

26. Donald Wesling, *The Chances of Rhyme: Device and Modernity* (Berkeley:
University of California Press, 1980); later quotes from pp. 54, 56, 73, 81, 98, 108,
118, 121, 133.

antiabsorptiveness of devices to the use of
antiabsorptive techniques for absorptive ends
since that process foregrounds device,
you might say acknowledges "deviceness" or "devicehood",
rather than attempting to contain
or "derhetorize" it. Wesling's book locates
these contradictory impulses as basic, since
"under the historical conditions of modernity,
poetry and commentators alike are enmeshed
in a contradictory structure of thought
where the highest twin values are
the corporality and the transparency"
—I would say the impermeability & the absorbability—
"of the medium of language". Wesling's
own account reflects the contradiction.

Wesling presents a useful discussion of sound
as an inherently antiabsorptive dimension of poetry,
quoting, albeit critically, Harry Lanz's *1931*
description of the "transparency effect" in *The
Physical Basis of Rime: An Essay on the Aesthetics
of Sound:*

> in ordinary speech, in prose, we entirely forget about the physical
> existence of words as signs or sounds. Meaning, ideas, is what we
> *get for* it. With their physical reality forgotten . . . the words become
> transparent . . . fully resolved into what they mean. Poetry is called
> upon to save the physical element of words and bring it to our
> attention in the name of art. Thus sound, the music of words,
> acquires an independent artistic value which is largely indifferent to
> the meaning or the sense of it.

Lanz, like Forrest-Thomson, is mistaken to claim
sound as independent of, rather than constitutive
of, meaning; or perhaps is mistaken to assume
that meaning is a strictly utilitarian concept.
Wesling speaks of the different period styles
of the "dissociative" or "divestive" function
of poetic devices in referring to Sigurd Burckhardt's

comment that poetry's goal—which can never be completely,
only "proximately" achieved—is to drive "a wedge
between words and their meanings, lessen as
much as possible their designatory force and thereby
inhibit our all too ready flight from them to
things they point to"; I would rather say
that the "all too ready flight" of normative
discursive practices is what drives the wedge, but
then sound can no more be divided from its meaning
than a body can be split off from its soul.
As Wesling judiciously comments, "sound and
sense in literary composition determine each other
reciprocally, no place more evidently than in
rhyming practice". Or as Alan Davies has it,
"The sound sense isn't in the diction. It's
in the thought."[27] Nonetheless,
Wesling is uncomfortable about the too
ostensibly antiabsorptive use of device:
"poetic devices, and the labor
they imply, do seem highly obtrusive
in the failed poem"; he seems to disallow
that a "good" poem might choose
not to "balance" what he calls "aesthetic
and cognitive principles". Still Wesling's
view is that

> since 1795 there has been no comparable attempt [to that of the
> English neoclassical poets] to restrict the subversive, independent-
> of-things nature of the language medium [by boycotting puns and
> confining rhymes]; rather an exaggeration of it, almost a
> logomimesis . . . Modern use of the device [of rhyme] may be said
> to force its artificiality and irrationality into the light.

But it seems to me that a good deal of the "canonical"
poetry subsequent to 1795 has been prized precisely
for its strategic resourcefulness in enabling

27. Alan Davies, "Unadorned ca73", *Signage* (New York: Roof, 1987), p. 60.

the continued naturalization of devices (for
example, as Romantic reconciliation) while
much heterodox writing has been discounted, by
critics such as Vendler, for its too obtrusive
"wordness". Moreover, official verse culture
of the last 25 years has engaged in militant
(that is to say ungenerously uniformitarian)
campaigns to "restrict the subversive,
independent-of-things nature of the language"
in the name of the common voice, clarity, sincerity,
or directness of the poem, & specifically
in the highly problematic equating, as in
the passage from Wesling, of the "irrational"
& the "artificial".
It is the repressing of,
rather than the acknowledging of,
devicehood that violates the claims of reason,
all the more so when reason finds itself
at odds with rationality.

Yet despite these significant complications,
it still makes sense to think of rhapsodic
odes, rapturous lyrics, the song & ballad
traditions, & the like, as emphasizing
a seamless, self-enclosed continuity con-
sistent with an absorptive effect. Subject
matter will often contribute; for example,
ecstatic poems of religious or romantic
experience/devotion are self-absorbed or
self-canceling rather than self-conscious.

Nor is a poem necessarily unabsorbing because
it is short. Rather, there is a potential
for a kind of metonymic enactment
of absorption, with the poem
completely caught up in
its own internal acoustic & semantic
dynamics: absorbed sound or
completely saturated sound. These features,
though they may accentuate

artifice & opacify
subject matter, are nonetheless
primary techniques for absorptive writing.
For the power of sound "itself" is
as great as sound's ability to evoke
an image; those poetries that have tapped
into this power have, in refusing to let words
become transparent, made them potent.

This is related to
the *spellweaving*
& *spellbinding* functions of
nonoccidental,
nonoriental poetries, such as those collected in
Jerome Rothenberg's *Technicians of the
Sacred,*
especially if considered in the light
of Andrew Welsh's distinction, in *The Roots
of the Lyric:
Primitive Poetry & Modern
Poetics,*
between "song melos" (externally imposed
meter) &
"charm melos" (internally derived from sound &
rhythm patterns).
Charm melos depends on
"artificial", jaggedly rhythmic
prosodic elements to create a centripetal
(or vortical)
energy in the poem that is
able to capture & hold the attention (not
just conscious attention, but the imagination
or
psyche). The power of charm melos is *technical*
in the precise sense of Rothenberg's title: the
superficially antiabsorptive elements
(disjunction,
repetition, accentuated stresses, nonlexical "scat"
sounds) are the basis for this

souped-up poetic
engine. McCaffery describes this magical
doubling of the antiabsorptive & absorptive this
way: "Semiotically viewed, the shaman drum
is a profound contradiction; it is both itself &
the very means of transcending that self."[28] (This
is a familiar enough transformation in
rock & roll, where the
disbelieving hear loud, repelling
noise & the
initiate is totally engrossed: "I want to get lost
in your rock & roll, & drift away.")
McCaffery continues:

> At the Shaman's initiatory seance, the drum acts self-creatively, its
> sound carrying a distinctly centripetal value drawing into itself the
> environmental spirits around it, destroying context by drawing con-
> text into its own constitutional elements, becoming by absorbing
> the energic forces around it. In this state the drum is a self-generating
> sign with the capacity of drawing powers into itself and shutting
> them in . . . Behind all Shamanistic drum use is the sense of drum
> as instrumental in connecting with a universal centre, a term that
> should not be taken topographically but emotionally as denoting
> the sacred space that ecstasy inhabits. The Shamanistic Centre is,
> in fact, a highly charged gap or metope between signs in a cosmic
> syntax; to reach a centre is to enter that space as an ecstatic vortex.

For Robert Kelly, charms propose a *method:*

> (spells as the hidden content of our literature, aversions of the evil
> thing, securing of the good by: music. Song moving reality to bring
> into harmony the irreducible needs & urgent tenors of our condition.

28. Steve McCaffery, "Drum Language and the Sky Text", *Alcheringa* 3.1 (1977),
81; as subsequently revised by the author (manuscript, 1986).

The old german *zauberspreche,* the anglo-saxon charms propose a
method. If music answers.)[29]

& his "spel V" invokes the power of song
to absorb the singer into it as in turn, a turn,
the song is absorbed into the singer:

now the meadow drinks
now drink I

cup, good cup be full

Think here
again
of the surrealist project
in which the aim was to mine more deeply
into the unconscious & the dream
state than normally possible with conventional
writing practices. The
odd juxtapositions & strange syntax
of surrealist poetry was not an attempt to creatively use
inattention; on the contrary, Breton
rejected those poets whom he felt were pursuing
such Dadaist or constructivist programs. Surrealism,
as expounded by Breton, is the most radically
absorptive poetry imaginable; its
quest is not to foreground artifice but to reveal
"surreality". Nonetheless its procedures
involved using antiabsorptive
techniques to reach
this "deeper", more absorbing reality.

The invention of *zaum* poetry by the Russian
futurians Velimir Khlebnikov & Alexei

29. Robert Kelly, *Thors Thrush* (1962; reprint Oakland: Coincidence Press, 1984),
unpaginated; "spel V" is part of this work. There is a Tibetan saying to the effect
that *the sacred is sound* (entoning the lower notes is believed to bring one closer to
the sacred). The practice of mantra chanting is relevant as well: written on the page,
a mantra would appear like a concrete poem; performed it may become hypnotic.

Kruchenykh is also relevant. Zaum,
which has been translated as *beyonsense*
& *transrational,* is made up of what Khlebnikov
called "language situated beyond the boundaries
of ordinary reason". It uses words not found
in any dictionary, derived—in Khlebnikov's practice—
in a quasimathematical way, by joining
various root syllables in "unrestricted
combinations, which represents the voice at play
outside of words". While the resulting poetry
may seem opaque or antiabsorptive, Khlebnikov
believed that zaum was a major breakthrough
toward the creation of a universal—what I
would call "transabsorbable"—language.

> What about spells and incantations, what we call magic words, the
> sacred language of paganism, words like "shagadam, magadam,
> vigadam, pitz, patz, patzu"—they . . . form a kind of beyonsense
> language in folk speech. Nevertheless an enormous power over
> mankind is attributed to these incomprehensible words and magic
> spells, and direct influence upon the fate of man. They contain
> powerful magic . . . The prayers of many nations are written in a
> language incomprehensible to those who pray. Does a Hindu un-
> derstand the Vedas? Russians do not understand Old Church
> Slavonic . . . In the same way, the language of magic spells and
> incantations does not wish to be judged in terms of everyday com-
> mon sense. Its strange wisdom may be broken down into the truths
> contained in separate sounds: *sh, m, v,* etc. We do not yet under-
> stand these sounds . . . But there is no doubt that these sound
> sequences constitute a series of universal truths passing before the
> predawn of our soul.[30]

30. Velimir Khlebnikov, "On Poetry", *Collected Works,* vol. 1: *Letters and Theo-
retical Writings,* tr. Paul Schmidt, ed. Charlotte Douglas (Cambridge: Harvard Uni-
versity Press, 1987), p. 370. The quotation immediately following is from "Our Fun-
damentals" in the same volume, p. 385.
    In "The Poetics of Sound", originally in *Technicians of the Sacred* and reprinted
in *Pre-Faces & Other Writing* (New York: New Directions, 1981), pp. 144–145,
Jerome Rothenberg provides a relevant commentary on an aborigine rain chant—
"Dad a da da / Dad a da da / Dad a da da / Da kata kai": "Sounds only. No mean-
ing, they say, in the words of the song, or no meaning you can get at by translation

According to Khlebnikov, national/rational
languages prevent the possibility of universal
communication: "Beyonsense language is thus
the universal language of the future, although
it is still in an embryonic state. It alone
will be able to unite all people. Rational languages
have separated them."

A related use of antiabsorptive modalities
for absorptive ends is suggested by Michel
Leiris:

> I don't believe that I have ever seen anyone captivate their audience
> the way Cab Calloway did. I have never seen anyone who was able
> to put an entire hall of people in a state verging on trance the way
> Cab Calloway did at La Salle Pleyel. Perhaps it was in part his scat
> singing that created such a powerful effect on his audience. I adore
> scat singing. It has a dizzying, giddy effect on you. [31]

In another context, Leiris describes a startling
use of antiabsorptive techniques to increase
the power of an absorptive experience, quoting
Michelet—"The ability, above all, to believe
every lie." Leiris contrasts two types of spirit
possession ceremonies in the Zar cult of Ethiopia,
based on his field experience. In one,
the participants seem fully aware of the fraudulence
of the possession, that it is a lie:

---

into-other-words; & yet it functions; the meaning contained then in how it's made to
function. So here the key is in the 'spell' & in the belief behind the 'spell'—or in a
whole system of beliefs, in magic, in the power of sound & breath & ritual to move
an object toward ends determined by the poet-magus. Said the Navajo chanter . . .
'The words have no meaning, but the song means' . . . Such special languages—
meaningless &/or mysterious—are a small but nearly universal aspect of 'primitive-
&-archaic' poetry. They may involve (1) purely invented, meaningless sounds, (2)
distortion of ordinary words & syntax, (3) ancient words emptied of their (long
since forgotten) meanings, (4) words borrowed from other languages."

31. Michel Leiris, "Jazz", interview ed. and tr. Michael Haggerty, *Sulfur* 15
(1986), 103.

> Alongside those cases where the lie seems preponderant and where
> it would be proper to speak of *acted theater,* there are cases in
> which the reality of the possession is not in doubt ⌣ . ⋅ which
> correspond to what may be called *lived theater.* Seen another way,
> this may in fact be acted theater but with a minimum of artifice
> and free of any intention to impose on the spectator.[32]

Acted theater & live theater (based on "ecstatic
techniques") resonantly rhyme with absorption &
theatricality. What is remarkable is not so much
the distinction, but the striking observation
Leiris makes about the greater effect of the antiabsorptive
acted theater:

> In a general way, then, it is probable that if the theater as such
> possesses a certain virtue of *katharsis* or "purgation" of the passions
> . . . then from this perspective how much greater must be the virtue
> of a theater where the person, far from remaining confined to
> passivity or losing itself in pure play, is completely engaged and
> even in some degree able to invent for itself the scenes whose
> protagonist it becomes.

There is, then, a considerable history
of using antiabsorptive techniques
(nontransparent or nonnaturalizing elements)
(artifice)
for absorptive
ends. This is an approach
I find myself peculiarly
attracted to, & which reflects my
ambivolence
(as in wanting multiple things)
about absorption & its converses.
In my poems, I
frequently use opaque & nonabsorbable

32. Leiris, "Acted Theater and Lived Theater in the Zar Cult", tr. James Clifford,
Sulfur 15 (1986), 115 and, just following, 117; first set of italics added.

elements, digressions &
interruptions, as part of a technological
arsenal to create a more powerful
("souped-up")
absorption than possible with traditional,
& blander, absorptive techniques. This is a
precarious road because insofar
as the poem seems
overtly self-conscious, as opposed to internally
incantatory or psychically
actual, it may produce
self-consciousness in the reader
destroying his or her absorption by theatricalizing
or conceptualizing the text, removing
it from the
realm of an experience engendered
to that of a technique
exhibited.
This is the subject of much of my
work.

These reflections suggest that absorption
can be achieved without transparency, causal
unity, or traditional metrics;
that abandoning these devices
may be necessary to
capture a reader's attention.

But why dwell on *capturing* (the theatrical
economy)? From the look on the faces of the
people on the bus & the beach, today's
bestsellers routinely "spellbind", just like
it says on the covers. How, exactly, does
this differ from the spellweaving charms
just discussed? For one thing,
the more intensified, technologized
absorption made possible by
nonabsorptive means may get the reader
absorbed into a more ideologized
or politicized space; if not to say,

less programmatically,
one that really *can* engross: not
ersatz but, at last, the real
goods.

Still, the image of spellbinding fictions
that hype the most mundane of
literary deteriorata, & the nexus of
suspicions that has arisen in reaction
to this type of work, has
usefully led some writers to try to create
nonabsorbable or antiabsorptive works.
For these writers,
there has been a useful
questioning of what we are normally
asked to be absorbed into &
an outright rejection of any accommodation
with or assimilation into this "bourgeois"
space. Moreover, spellbinding doesn't have a
monopoly on creating meaning or pleasure
& may (I like Dashiell Hammett too)
inhibit both. The use of nontransparent
& nonunified modalities may produce far
more resonant music & content than
otherwise possible, just as it may produce works that are boring
& didactic. For many readers
& writers, the limits on what
can be conveyed absorptively are too
great, & the products of such
approaches are too misleading. For such
writers, the project is to wake
us from the hypnosis of absorption.

This century has seen an explosion
of nonabsorptive forms, which together comprise
a significant investigation
of the possibilities for poetry
—both absorptive & impermeable.
It would be difficult to map even a
small portion of these traditions,

which spread out over many languages
&, importantly, into the
translation practices within & among
many languages. The range
of writing made available in English
in the past hundred years, from the
poetries collected in *Technicians of the Sacred*
to *The Greek Magical Papyri*[33]
to "lost" diaries of women from every walk of life,
to hundreds of specialized-language publications (from
surfing to genetics to computers),
has sharpened an awareness of the interrelation
of cultural distance & opacity as played out in language.
To be absorbed in one's own immediate language practices
& specialized lingo
is to be confronted with the foreignness
& unabsorbability of this plethora of
other "available" material;
the ideological strategy of mass entertainment,
from bestsellers to TV to "common voice" poetry,
is to contradict this ever-present other reality through
insulation into a fabricated "lowest" common
denominator that, among its many guises, goes under
the Romantic formula "irreducible human values".

Some antiabsorptive traditions within twentieth-
century poetry could be traced back to
Stein (while *The Making of Americans,* written in
the "continuous present", suggests a *neoabsorptivity,*
& the early portraits & related works have a

---

33. *The Greek Magical Papyri in Translation, including the Demotic Spells,* vol. 1: *Texts,* ed. Hans Dieter Betz (Chicago: University of Chicago Press, 1986). As a typographic, pictographic, lexical, indexical, and syntactic extravaganza, this work suggests, without necessarily intending to, the richness of "antiabsorbiana" that can be found in scholarly translations of obscure and occult material. This book is close to the sort of text Armand Schwerner parodies/honors in *The Tablets:* "PGM L. 1–18: . . . out of . . . and if their principal (lots?) should [fall] on the side of [the lots] of 'Tyche' or 'Daimon' [it is good?] for a spell (?) concerning sorcery / —the same principal (tosses?) of the lot producing the same results, with 'Tyche' or 'Daimon' being an excellent toss." (p. 283) The book also contains pages of spells using beyonsense magical words such as Khlebnikov discusses.

rhythmic quality that relates them to charm melos,
the denser sections of *Tender Buttons* & the word-
to-word halting in *How To Write* are
great achievements of antiabsorptive writing);
Pound's *Cantos* (the use of collage &
fragmentation, graphic material, the inclusion of
printer's & other errors, the disruptive presence
of a legion of references outside the poem);
Zukofsky's "Poem beginning 'The'",
with its numbered citations
of different quotations, &
assorted other found material;
Joyce's *Finnegans Wake;*
Duchamp's prose levy's en Anglais;
Dadaism in North America;
ee cummings for his typ,,OgRAPHic(((,,
in()ventio.,.ns;
Lettrism & other visual poetries, from
Apollinaire's *Calligrammes* to De Campos &
Gomringer to Ian Hamilton Finlay.
. . . to name a few . . .

In the contemporary context, the pursuit
of antiabsorptive or impermeable textuality is
pervasive, whether frontally proclaimed or
ambivolently situated.[34]

---

34. Some examples: The typographic visions of Johanna Drucker's letterpress
bookwork extend the poetics of lettrism and futurist book art into the present. Tina
Darragh has consistently worked with complex visual arrangements, elaborate pun-
ning, puzzles, & procedures in an effort to interrogate (in a buoyantly funny way)
the structures of language. David Melnick's *Pcoet,* made up almost entirely of non-
standard words, & his *Men in Aida,* a homophonic translation of the *Iliad,* are
intensely musical works that use an invented syntax in one work & invented words
in the other not to formulate a transrational or universal language, as proposed by
Khlebnikov, but to create a world as local & specific as possible, in which a height-
ened awareness of the pleasure of words is its own sensuous reward. Frank Kuen-
stler's densely mosaicked *Lenz* proceeds, for the most part, by splicing two words
together with a period and placing these pairs in paragraph sequences: "purr.Force
leica.Misanthrope deanna.Dearborn" (New York: Film Culture, 1964; p.63). In con-
trast, Michael Gottlieb's "Phlogiston" disrupts lexical identities by intercollocating
the letters of capitalized and lower-case phrases: "L I KoEn e already K N EfWr o
m" (*Roof* 6, 1978; p. 40). Clark Coolidge's early works developed several antiab-

A dense or unfamiliar vocabulary
can make a poem hard to absorb, not only by calling
attention to the sound qualities of its lexicon
but also by preventing any immediate processing
of the individual word's meaning. At some point,
the appropriate reference source may be consulted—
but this is by no means the only way to hear
or understand the work. There is, however, in
postwar North American poetry, a prejudice against using
an obscure vocabulary for its own sake,
partly because so much emphasis has been placed
on a "speech" orientation that tends to encourage
a plainer vocabulary, & partly (though paradoxically)
because dialect has been constantly marginalized
as a serious poetic project (that is, insofar
as a dialect drifts incommensurably from the prestige
dialect that is "standard American English").
Apart from the extensions
of zaum & the use, in a number
of works written primarily in the seventies, of frag-
mented words (ing, ment, ility, uble, iplious, ure),
recent antiabsorptive techniques have tended
to use syntactic and graphemic rather than lexical
invention & so follow in the tradition of Stein's
& Williams' more *lexically* conventional practices—
conventional, that is, compared with
late Joyce or Abraham Lincoln Gillespie.
Still you don't have to know Scots
to hear the music of Hugh MacDiarmid's
A Drunk Man Looks at Thistle;
it may be singularly instructive
to read that work closely with much of the
vocabulary left opaque—before taking up a more

---

sorptive styles. In *Suite V,* two words are juxtaposed at the top & bottom of each
page (for example, "dots" & "mats"), leaving the page mostly blank; while some of
the poems in *Ing* consist of configurations of word parts, numbers, articles, & iso-
lated words & phrases. "On Once" begins: "no in took/ than mar// their/ than the/
thinks// a su/ (he of)// the awd con// is solu// no non/ of the/ of using// but a// a but/
a Rug// 'Schillan'" (New York: Angel Hair Books, 1968; unpaginated).

lexically informed reading. & this is the attraction
rather than limitation to reading, or hearing,
such Jamaican "dub" poets as Michael Smith.
Basil Bunting's *Briggflats* is probably
the English-language poem of this century
to most richly realize the musical depths
of an opaque, but not invented, lexicon.
Nor is such an "uninformed" reading
of *Briggflats* foreign to Bunting's poetic
purposes. In "The Use of Poetry" he says that
poetry's power to evoke emotion is unrelated
to any utilitarian idea of the meaning or ideas
a poem conveys; rather the emotion is
aroused by the sound of the words:

> My own contribution, such as it is, has been to see what poetry
> can borrow from the devices and form music has developed since
> the two arts seemed to separate towards the end of the seventeenth
> century . . . poetry is to be heard, to be read aloud or sung . . . We
> lose very little by not knowing what the words mean, so long as
> we can pronounce them.[35]

Bunting continues, "I've tested that by reading
to class. I've read them German, Italian, Persian,
and Welsh, and so far as I could judge,
they got as much out of it as they did
from many English poems."
Of course, what is a foreign
language or an incomprehensible
dialect to one reader is native
to another. Dialect writing
is generally related to a nationalist cult-
ural program & aims
at acknowledging the pre-
vailing vernacular as a
means of establishing a group

35. Basil Bunting, "The Use of Poetry", *Writing* 12 (1985), 36–43.

identity. Dialect poetry is not
often intended to be anti-
absorptive or opaque to its initial
readers. Yet,
inevitably, the effect of group particularization
of language is to make it strange
to outsiders fully as much as
to make it familiar to insiders.
Insofar as English-language poets pursue
their dialectical differences in a radically de-
centering way, then all of us will confront
—more often than some of us now do—"foreign"
Englishes & no dialect will be held above
the others as common coin. Such
a development in English-
language poetry is welcome: the inherent difficulties
are more than compensated for by the knowledge
that comes from respecting differences.
What I suggest is unusual in postwar North
American poetry is the use of an obscure,
but not invented, vocabulary.
Briggflats rides the cusp
of this possibility: we can imagine
a small community of readers for whom this
lexicon might be familiar, yet Bunting's
primary audience has always been
readers for whom his vocabulary is opaque
& this is inextricable from the poem's power &
particular music.

This series of references bleeds
into an interrelated group
of poems, in prose
formats, whose syntax spirals
outward in an open-
ended way.[36] Such "imploded-sentence"

36. Among other works I am thinking of Coolidge's *Quartz Hearts* & *Weathers;*
Christopher Dewdney's *Spring Traces in the Control Emerald Night;* Peter Seaton's

works can be contrasted
with another prominent tendency
in current poetry—the serial
ordering (juxta-
position) of more
syntactically orderly,
"tightly" structured sentences
in so-called "new-sentence"
writing.

Clark Coolidge's improvisatory extensions
of the line refuse the closure of the subject/verb/object
sentence; refuse, that is, the syntactic ideality
of the complete sentence, in which each part
of speech operates in its definable place so that
a grammatic paradigm is superimposed on the actual
unfolding of the semantic strings. In imploded-
sentence poetry, meaning flows durationally—
horizontally—by means of the linear continuousness
of the sweeping, syncopated rhythms. While in
the complete/closed sentence, attention is deflected
to an abstracted, or accompanying, "meaning"
that is being "conveyed", in the imploded sentence
the reader stays plugged in to the wave-like
pulse of the writing. In other words, you keep
moving through the writing without having to come
up for ideational air: the ideas are all inside
the process. This, again, suggests
that a surface *disruption* of syntactic ideality
can expand the total prosody of the poem, whose rhythms
engage as they envelop, much as John Coltrane's
opening up of a tune—or opening up
beyond any background reference to a
tune (this could be called "ascension")—intensifies

The Son Master, Crisis Intervention, & *Piranesi Pointed Up;* James Sherry's *Popular Fiction;* George-Therese Dickenson's *Tranducing;* Jerry Estrin's *In Motion Speaking;* Abigail Child's *From Solids;* Lynne Dreyer's *White Museum;* the prose works in Diane Ward's *Never Without One;* & a number of Steve Benson's performance transcriptions.

rather than distances or ironizes
the musical sweep of his compositions. Here's
Coolidge, talking about jazz improvisation in the
liner notes to a Rova Saxophone Quartet album:

> To sound is to resist rested definition, to leave oneself outward into
> a trend where the fissures and masses spring a feeling free of its
> telling . . . To improvise: to know *in,* and only while undergoing,
> the process of doing. To perceive only in the motion of an act, in
> the movements of practicing that act . . . Thus, as in the definition.
> "not foreseen" because only experienced in the movement and
> passing along with it . . . Though improvisation sometimes feels like
> a matter of . . . moving vast fragile masses, bales of sound, or
> ducking (or absorbing) that projectile coming around again . . .
> where musics become a reality beyond "tune" "beat" etc.[37]

In Peter Seaton's poems the eclipsing
of a hard-to-absorb syntax with the absolute
current & dynamism of compositional flow
reaches majestic proportion. As Larry Price notes,
Seaton's work collapses the operant distinction
between reader & text (a distinction
that is a prerequisite for the differentiation
of absorption & impermeability)
by "reconstituting writing 'below'" its normally
understood function as exchange, "in its
materiality as language".[38] The aesthetic
wholeness & integrity of Seaton's work
demonstrate the necessity for expression
& the rewards if accessibility is not used
as a justification to compromise this necessity—
a compromise that may *block* access.
The fever of truth, of conviction—
"dreams for flesh"—
puts to rest any lingering notions of a mutual

37. Clark Coolidge, "Rova Notes", in *Sulfur* 17 (1986), 129–134.
38. Larry Price, "Aggressively Private: Contingency as Explanation", *Poetics Journal* 6 (1986), 80–86.

exclusivity of absorption & impermeability:
they fit, Seaton shows, like a body & a soul,
like words & their meaning.

But to continue circling
the parabola ("we keep coming
back and coming back . . ."
to the vision of dis-
placement at the site of
enactment, procurement,
debasement, trans-
substantiation, fulmination,
culmination . . .):

McCaffery's *Panopticon* is perhaps the exemplary
antiabsorptive book.[39] The first twenty pages
are printed on a grid background, a visual trope
for the refusal of these pages to be absorbed
by the reader. A man's torso
with a cutaway view
of the digestive system adorns
the cover & six of these opening
twenty pages. After a halftitle
page, the first three recto pages feature
a quote from Plato's *Symposium*
in English; an ad for
acne cream in Spanish; & a brief scenario about a
woman playing an aging movie star starring in a
film called *The Mark* being photographed
reading a novel called *The Mind of
Pauline Brain*. The next recto
page features a large picture of McCaffery
staring at the reader,
together with the book's title, author,
& press. The pages that
follow feature two Latin epigraphs & a page

39. Steve McCaffery, *Panopticon* (Toronto: blewointmentpress, 1984), unpagin-
ated.

with the handwritten designation "plates 21–29", but
of course there are no plates. Then come
three pages of prose continuing, or more accurately
displacing by varying, the scenario
already commenced. At this
point, a page announces "Part III: The Mind
of Pauline Brain"; flipping to the end of the book,
the reader finds that the last section is designated
"Part I: The Mark". *Panopticon*
makes use of just about
every possible antiabsorptive device: several
pages summarize "a book entitled
Panopticon"; the middle
section of the work has a separate text running in
the bottom third of the page, which is shaded
gray; a number of pages are all caps; a number
have two separate strands of meaning on alternating
prose lines, one
designated by caps & the other by upper/lower
case. At
one point, *The Mind of Pauline Brain*
is described as noteworthy "less for its verbal
content than for [its] superb illustrations" of
anatomical dissections; this suggests
that *Panopticon*'s value is as a dissection
of the book & that the title's
image represents the multiple scannings
that make this possible & mark
its break from the single-focus opticon
of conventional narrative. But the title
also has an ominous ring, since the panopticon is
an image of surveillance & control, referring
to a prison built radially to allow
one centrally placed
guard to see all
the prisoners. As McCaffery writes,
in a statement that is
intermixed with other material several times in the
book:

THE TEXTUAL INTENTION PRESUPPOSES READERS WHO KNOW THE
LANGUAGE CONSPIRACY IN OPERATION. THE MARK IS NOT IN-
ITSELF BUT IN-RELATION-TO-OTHER-MARKS. THE MARK SEEKS THE
SEEKER OF THE SYSTEM BEHIND THE EVENTS. THE MARK INSCRIBES
THE I WHICH IS THE HER IN THE IT WHICH MEANING MOVES
THROUGH. A TEXTUAL SYSTEM UNDERLIES EVERY TEXTUAL EVENT
THAT CONSTITUTES "THIS STORY" HOWEVER THE TEXTUAL HER-
MENEUSIS OF "THIS STORY" DOES NOT NECESSARILY COMPRISE
A TOTAL TEXTUAL READING. THE TELEOLOGY OF "THIS MARK
BEFORE YOU" DOES NOT SIGNIFY PER SE BUT RATHER MOVES
TOWARDS A SIGNIFICATION. HENCE THE MOST IMPORTANT FEA-
TURE OF "THIS MARK" IS NOT ITS MEANING BUT THE WAY IN
WHICH "THAT MEANING" IS PRODUCED . . . THAT WE SPEAK IN
ORDER TO DESTROY THE AURA OF LISTENING. THAT THE MARK
UNDERMINES THE MEANING IT ELABORATES.

The "mark" is the visible sign of writing.
But reading, insofar as it consumes &
absorbs the mark, erases it—the words disappear
(the transparency effect) & are replaced by
that which they depict, their "meaning". Thus
absorption is the "aura of listening" destroyed
in this writing: Antiabsorptive
writing recuperates the mark by making it opaque,
that is, by maintaining its visibility
& undermining its meaning, where "meaning" is
understood in the narrower, utilitarian sense
of a restricted economy. To make a movie
of the "mark" is to theatricalize it, exactly
the contrary of creating, as in conventional narrative
in film or writing, the conditions for the mark
to be absorbed (repressed or erased).
In a similar way, to make a play of the mind
& call it "brain", as in *The Mind of Pauline Brain,*
suggests that mind/brain dualism is a theatricalization
of the conditions of human being; the brain
& the mark are superseded by what they engender—
mind & meaning; *Panopticon* reverses this process
by acknowledging the material base of mind & meaning,

marking the return of what has been repressed:
brain & mark. *Panopticon,* then, is
the novelization of the movie *The Mark* based on
the play *The Mind of Pauline Brain,* which has been
adapted from a novel called *Panopticon;* or then
again, *The Mark* is the play . . .

To speak of a radically impervious text
is to speak oxymoronically—absorbency & repellency
are relative, contextual, & interpenetrating
terms, not new critical analytic categories.
The unreadable text is an outer limit for poetry;
in practical terms, the complete shutout
of the reader's attention is subverted
by most ostensibly antiabsorptive texts, partly
by some readers' "paradoxically" keen interest
in impermeability, & partly by the writer's need
to be readable, even if only by herself or himself.
The nonabsorbable text often turns
out to be eminently performable, as in
the performances of McCaffery or Mac Low.
Antiabsorptive does not necessarily mean nonentertaining—
on the contrary. Devices, whether absorptively
or antiabsorptively employed, are in themselves
conventionalizing & readers can be expected
to enjoy a device that ruptures the "commodification"
of reading insofar as this fulfills
their desire for such a work &, likewise, to
be bored to irritation by a device meant to soothe
or entertain.

Similarly, the ideal
of a radically absorptive text
is reduced
to an absurdity as
when, in Robert Wilson's
Life and Death of Joseph Stalin,
an actor shrieks out the text
of the most absorbing possible
human experience: "It was like being burned

alive in a fire!
Ahhhhhhhhhhhahhhhhhahhhhhhhhhhhh!"
Excruciating pain obliterates all self-
consciousness by capturing
one's entire attention (think
of Artaud screaming); this suggests
the value of a little tempering
absence &
or postponement.

Translating Zukofsky's formula for poetry
(lower limit, speech; upper limit, music)
I would suggest that
poetry has as its outer limit, impermeability
& as its inner limit, absorption.

Unfamiliarization
is a well-tried
antiabsorptive
method; Brecht's
*verfrem*dumdum*den* effect
explicitly sets
this as its
goal. But
unfamiliarization
is significantly
distinguishable
from impermeability.
Brecht used his techniques
in conjunction with a
[bracketed]
subject matter
& this subject
matter tended
to be in
the form of
melodrama,
a form which
exaggerates
absorptive dynamics.

Brecht wished
the spectator to look
at the plot
. without
being caught up
in it; but
he also counted on this
process of critique
as *itself*
holding,
& even intensifying,
the audience's attention.
Nor
did he eliminate
the absorbing
qualities of the
melodrama
"underneath":
What will happen to Polly Peachum?
In effect, Brecht doubles
the attention
of the spectator
in his hyperabsorptive
theater, bringing
to mind
Leiris' observation
that the most
compelling
theater
distances itself
from the veridicality
of what it
enacts
so that
the spectator,
rather than being
passive,
has something to
do

& so can become
maximally
engaged.
This suggests
that the critical
reader needs something
to engage
her or his
critical attentions
& that what may
appear
antiabsorptive
in one context
contributes to
a
fuller engagement
with a work
in another.
In
this way, the
distinction
between the two
terms
breaks
down.

It's worth noting again that Ford specifically
excludes melodrama & Dickensian character-typing
from his model because these compromise the reader's
belief in the reality of the story. For Ford,
to be entertained by scoffing at the characters,
or being made aware of their fictitiousness,
prevents the "deeper" absorption of the Flaubertian
novel; but insofar as the theatrical is understood
as the converse of the absorptive, it's apparent
that it has the upper hand as entertainment—
whether that be as charade, caricature, or farce.

Bruce Boone's metacommentaries, in *My Walk with Bob
& Century of Clouds,* provide an interesting

example of a critique of absorptive narrative: he
continually breaks off in his recounting of
seemingly autobiographical stories to comment on
the way he has told the story & some of the
political implications of the story & its
style of telling. But Boone's interruptions also
function, like Brecht's framing devices, to situate
the reader at an alternative vantage point, an
additional attentional field, rekindling interest
in a narrative that might not hold the interest
without this *supplement*.

Similarly, the programmatic structure of Ron
Silliman's *Tjanting* or *Ketjak* is explicitly present
at all times but it acts as a semipermeable
membrane that does not preclude absorption
in the various subject matters of the text
but rather doubles one's attentional focus: *in
& beside*. The absorption is diffused but constant
on the Brechtian model, but without the melodramatic
underlayer. Something comparable to that
underlayer, however, *is* present
in *Sunset Debris* in the form of the recurring sexual
content of the subject matter & the patterned
insistence of the every-sentence-a-question
structure; here the reader is whirled
into a powerfully woven fabric
while never losing sight of its constructed
quality. This is something like the experience of
reading Barrett Watten's "trilogy" (as I connect
them) *Plasma/Parallels/X, 1-10, & Complete Thought*.
In these works the visually intense, urgent
sentences ("I see a tortoise drag a severed head to
the radiator") are frequently absorbingly
arresting in content & effect ("The essence of
poison is the power to soothe: the citizens spit
flames of a rationalism they don't understand")
while not being mediated by an *obtruding* structural
plan. The reiteration of paradigmatic syntactic

structures, together with the patent variation
of formats from poem to poem within each book, &
the frequent use of stanzaic formats that isolate,
or frame, short sections of the work (for example
single sentences or sentence pairs), reveals an
unmistakable ectoskeletal structure; as with
Silliman, a semipermeable form. Watten writes
in *Total Syntax,* "Distance, rather than
absorption, is the intended effect."[40] This
is produced, in part, by the taut, membranous
surface structure that becomes increasingly insistent—
vivid—as one reads each work; yet this bracketing
process, as practiced by Watten, seems to recharge,
more than diffuse, the potency of the reading
experience. Silliman puts it this way:

> No, the reader does not have a participatory role in a work that is
> truly absorptive. Yet a work that is thoroughly nonabsorptive (in the
> sense of opaque to the point of repelling the reader) disempowers
> the reader in just the opposite direction. What *is* needed is the
> capacity for a work that will empower the reader, while making
> him/her conscious of the dangers of absorption/domination/passivity
> implicit in the process itself.[41]

This double concern is present in many recent works. Lyn
Hejinian's *The Guard* opens this way:

> Can one take captives by writing—
> "Humans repeat themselves."
> The full moon falls on the first. I
> "whatever interrupts."
> . . . . .
> Such hopes are set, aroused
> against interruption. Thus—

---

40. Passages quoted are from Barrett Watten's "Plasma", *Plasma/Paralleles/X* (Berkeley: Tuumba, 1979), unpaginated; "Real Estate", *1–10* (Oakland: This Press, 1980), p. 31; *Total Syntax* (Carbondale: Southern Illinois University Press, 1985), p. 64.

41. Silliman is responding to the Vancouver presentation of this work as well as subsequent discussions of it in a letter to me dated September 12, 1986.

in securing sleep against interpretation.
Anyone who could believe can reveal
it can conceal.

The Guard guards against the domination
of the reader; the line is a guardrail, an
interruption, disturbing sleep by requiring
interpretation but in order to safeguard—
"secure"—sleep. "If the world is round
and the gates are gone . . ."
Hejinian explains:

> The word "captives" refers to several things. First, and most im-
> portant, to capturing the world in words. I want to explain to myself
> the nature of the desire to do so, and I wonder if it is possible. The
> poem opens with a challenge to the poem itself and raises the lyric
> dilemma.

The dilemma of absorption might be called a dilemma
of belief ("the seance of session"): what is lost
if one reveals the grounds of belief & what is
lost if one conceals them.[42]

Such considerations as these
do not resolve my fascination with absorption
& impenetrability, which seem to cut to the heart
of my most intimate relations with language.
I find I
enact in my work an oscillating pull
in both directions, cutting into & out of—
en(w)rapment/resistance, enactment/delay, surfeit/
lack, but my suspicion of such polarized terms
introduces a third element of skepticism
about these binary divisions.

42. Lyn Hejinian, *The Guard* (Berkeley: Tuumba Press, 1984); all quotes except
the prose extract are from the first page of this book. At the New Poetics Collo-
quium in Vancouver, Hejinian read from and discussed *The Guard*—see "Language
and 'Paradise'", *Line* 6 (1986); the prose extract is from p. 91 of this text.

The sexual analogy
seems inescapable: an interruptiveness
that intensifies & prolongs desire, a postponement
that finds in delay a more sustaining pleasure &
presence. That is, an erotics of reading &
writing, extending from Barthes's descriptions
of the pleasures of the text (which is an erotics
of absorption) to Bataille's more troubling coupling
of repellence & transgression with rapture.
In Bataille's analysis, disgust & nausea
are necessary preconditions for the most intense
feelings of sexual pleasure that result from
transgressing the inhibitions that create
repellence. Bataille specifically connects
these sexual dynamics with poetics.
Transgression, in his account, may be the paradigm
case of using antiabsorptive (socially disruptive,
anticonventional) techniques for absorptive
(erotic) ends:

> The whole business of eroticism is to destroy the self-contained
> character of the participators as they are in their normal lives. [It]
> offers a contrast to self-possession, to discontinuous existence, in
> other words. It is a state of communication revealing a quest for a
> possible continuance of being beyond the confines of the self . . .
> Obscenity is our name for the uneasiness which upsets the physical
> state associated with . . . the possession of a recognized and stable
> individuality . . . religious eroticism is concerned with the fusion of
> beings with a world beyond everyday reality . . . Eroticism always
> entails a breaking down of the established patterns . . . of the
> regulated social order basic to our discontinuous mode of existence
> as separate individuals. But in eroticism . . . our discontinuous mode
> of existence is not condemned [but] *jolted* . . . What we desire is
> to bring into a world founded on discontinuity all the continuity
> such a world can sustain . . . Poetry leads to the same place as all
> forms of eroticism—to the blending and fusion of separate objects.
> It leads us to eternity, it leads us to death, and through death to

continuity. Poetry is eternity; the sun matched with the sea [la mer
allée avec le soleil].[43]

Bataille's account opens
a way of
understanding
a radical ambivolence
that lies
at the heart
of writing & reading.
Learning to read & write
is not a mechanical operation
but a social,
& in Bataille's sense
erotic,
experience. ("What
was your first textual experience?")
Many poets I know
had, like myself, "learning"
difficulties
in this area: I would call them
resistances—a dread,
or refusal, of submission
to a rule-governed wor(l)d,
the inscription of "regulated social order"
into language.
I would not adopt the Lacanian
description of this process: we emerge from
"amniotic fluid [in]to semiotic fluidlessness";[44]
there is no
"pre-Symbolic"
stage but there are different
modes of relationship

43. Georges Bataille, *Erotism: Death & Sensuality*, tr. Mary Dalwood (San Francisco: City Lights Books, 1986), pp. 17–19, 25. Italics added: "jolts of melody".
44. From my "Blow-Me-Down Etude", *Rough Trades* (Los Angeles: Sun & Moon Press, 1991), p. 104.

to language
that are
constantly potentially copresent & constantly
potentially blocked
off.

Fear of submission yet desire to be submerged—
the cycle has no resolution, no force of conclusion
because the risk of submergence in language is
that you may lose contact with the very materiality
that made it so endlessly fascinating in the first
place.

> what if I were to scream
> "I am the light and the way"
> //the poem would recede
> and look like a prop
> //we focus on the phrases
> & guess what will come next
> in order to be surprised
> //I'd guess you too'd distrust
> the dominant subject just
> because it implies prediction
> just where you desire
> escape—the kind of escape that clouds
> experience on becoming lakes
> //. . . And to have enough
> things knocking against
> one another, a subject broad
> enough in application that
> the thing won't resolve and
> still have many resolutions
> but it won't resolve once and for all[45]

Escapism has perhaps been given a too-short shrift
in the repulsion from what we are commonly asked

45. David Bromige, poem read at Ear Inn, New York, October 11, 1986. The final
seven lines are Steve Benson's contribution to this collaboration with Bromige.

to escape into: out of the frying pan & into
the omelet (of conviction's embalming).
There is, as well, a kind of puritanism
that will embrace the pleasures of the text up to
a point only.
But escape can be an image of release from captivity
in a culture that produces satisfactions as a means
of exploitation or pacification. The problem
with "escapist" literature is that it offers no escape,
narratively reinforcing our captivity.
To escape, however, if only
trope-ically, is not a utopian refusal
to encounter the realpolitic of history: it is a
crucial dialectical turn that allows imaginal place
outside history as we "know" it,
in order to critique it,
an Archemidian point of imaginative
construction, in which we can be energized,
our resources shored. The utopian, ecstatic
is not a refusal of history
but an envisionment of the indwelling
potentialities of history
that must be envisioned—audibly embodied—
in order to occur. The political
response is not to rule out escape but to
repeatedly ask who/what is captured—
& to what/where. As Susan Howe illuminates
in her discussion of captivity narratives,
once captured, by what seemed from outside
as everything to be feared, all that is
destructive, one may never be able to return
or may not wish to.

Absorbed into what, where?
Not necessarily a deeper sur-reality
or even an "other" reality.
Perhaps this is also the nature of shamanistic
practices—"acted theater" in Leiris' sense—an
understanding that is inhibited by the need

to always project an *other*
by constantly casting such practices in religious
& magical terms.
—We never leave reality but neither do we ever
exhaust it.

Something powerfully absorptive is needed to pull
us out of the shit, the ideology in which we slip—
mind altering as the LSD ad used to put it. &
poetry does have a mission to be as powerful as
the strongest drug, to offer a vision-in-sound
to compete with the world we know so that we can find
the worlds we don't. But we don't
in fact escape ideology: no other
perhaps not even different: but an alternate point
of perspective, a supplemental attentional
focus/unfocus. Paradise, as hell,
inheres: there are no limits that language cannot
reach.

The hermeneutics of suspicion
(it used to be called skepticism)
that denies knowledge
because it must be mediated by "codes"
makes a game of fashion
out of exposing the sign systems
that make up language;
but the antiabsorptive obsession
of recent poetry can be under-
stood quite differently.
The antiabsorptive does not so much prevent
absorption as shift its plane
of engagement—forcing
a shift in attentional focus.
Quoting the opening of Andrews'
Jeopardy, which frames
each word on a separate line—
"Words/were/what/were/whole/what/wasted/
words/want/waiting/whose/travel/there—/
tips/threats/necessary/noise/nothing/needed/

noise/noise/not/order . . ."[46]—
Nick Piombino notes:

> Here, thoughts absorb energy from each other, racing the mind
> towards ever greater rates of absorption, while simultaneously the
> meanings move away from each other with equally great force,
> increasing enormously the possibility of several realities acting upon
> each other simultaneously. What is placed in jeopardy, I think, is the
> ordinary meaning of meaning itself.[47]

Piombino, in his essays, makes a sustained attempt
to chart the psychic dynamics at work in
reading & writing poetry; because he does not
concentrate on aesthetic effect or formal process
as ends in themselves, his investigations insist
on a rethinking of the nature & function of the poetic
process, acutely reviving the sense
that poetry has *functions*. This is nowhere
more apparent than in the application of his re-
searches to the dynamic of absorption & dis-
rupture:

> Since the poet is as vulnerable to the spell of accepted reality as
> anyone else, she or he must somehow find a way to concentrate
> the attentional beam on areas of experience that were hitherto . . .
> not apprehendable . . . the poet must find some way of directing
> the gaze of consciousness onto literally inconceivably complex and
> entangled linkages between various modes of experience . . . Al-
> though indeterminacy is one way to describe the oscillation (or
> discontinuity) that underlies the perceptual process, this blur is ac-
> tually one state in the focussing of the attentional beam . . . These
> oscillations may form an exchange of energy so great as to cause a
> shift in magnitude of attentional focus . . . the poetic state of
> consciousness . . . makes possible an expansion of the absorbability

46. Bruce Andrews, *Jeopardy* (Windsor, Vermont: Awede Press, 1980); reprinted
in a less interesting horizontal format in *Wobbling* (New York: Roof Books, 1981),
pp. 90–93.
47. Nick Piombino, "Subject to Change", *Temblor* 5 (1987), 127–131.

of experiential data by the attentional mind. Intense wakefulness is
stimulated by an oscillation of types of mental attention-reverie,
obsessive attention to detail, symbolic transpositions . . . Such a
conception of poetics would be a call for actuality over reality,
actuality consisting not only of the area of experience now available
to the attentional focus, but all actualities which can be felt and
sensed in the total experiential process.[48]

"Poetry is like a swoon
with this exception:
it brings you to your senses."[49]
The oscillation of attentional focus,
& its attendant blurring,
is a vivid way of describing
the ambivolent switching, which I
am so fond of, between absorption &
antiabsorption, which can now
be described as redirected
absorption. The speed
of the shifts ultimately becomes a metric
weight, & as the pace picks
up, the frenzied serial
focusing/unfocusing enmeshes
into a dysraphic whole—not
totality—an *alchemical*
"overlay and blending"
as Piombino notes,
forming what he terms a
"combinatorial" or, in Forrest-Thomson's words,
an "image-complex".

The re-
di-
rection

48. Nick Piombino, "Currents of Attention in the Poetic Process", *Temblor* 5
(1987), 120–131. Both cited Piombino essays are in *Boundary of Blur* (Los Angeles:
Sun & Moon Press, 1991).
    49. As the Klupzy Girl virtually puts it in my *Islets/Irritations* (New York: Jordan
Davies, 1983), p. 47.

of at-
ten-
tion-
al
focus
can
as use-
ful-
ly be
located
in the
shift
of at-
tention
from the
rhet-
orical
effect
(the thing
said/de-
picted)
to the
rhetoricity.
For instance
the way
Stein,
or Cree-
ley, makes
possible an
attention
to each
word,
one word—
or even syllable—
at
a
time.
Robert Grenier's
work is made up

of iso-
lated, discontinuous units, framed
so as to
necessitate
that the read-
er stop & re-sound
each element
while at
the same time integrating
this
into the series
of which any unit is
a
part. As
in
A Day at the Beach:
a *day* becomes a *place*
in which perfectly realized
articulations of each moment
move
from one to the
next:
"Morning" glows with a lush
"foliage" of vowels "in the blue sky
seeping"; "Midday"
settles, placid & rippling—
"all of the yellow flowers of the sour grass closed";
"Afternoon/Evening" dis-
closes "melody /
not versus".[50] In contrast,
in Grenier's *Phantom Anthems*
the complexity of the syntax
creates an especially puzzling "combinatorial"
or *complex*
requiring,

50. Robert Grenier, *A Day at the Beach* (New York: Roof Books, 1984), unpaginated.

again, to sound
it out, so a kind of
disabsorptive "charm".

The repetitions in the poetry of Leslie Scalapino
also create a kind of disabsorptive charm:
the slight, accented, shifts in similar statements
operate as gradually shifting scans of the field of
perception, where this perceptual reiteration
gradually, processionally, discloses more & more,
so that the outer shell of any momentarily fixed
perception gives way to a depth-full field of
"actuality". Scalapino correlates shifts
in syntactic patterns with shifts
in attentional focus. Using a language
sometimes bordering on
sociological observation, the details
that Scalapino reveals
have the intensity of the obviously
factual while continually showing
themselves, within
the echo chamber that is each
work, to be hidden truths, clues
to how a life is understood through the unfolding
of specific details, obscured or repressed, brought
to light by
the probing of memory, perception, & invention.
Yet, finally, it is the rhythm created
by permutating the attentional beams, the chordal
patterns created by her serial scannings,
that create the musical coherence
that takes the work beyond
any distancing or dislocating
devices that serve to build
it. The refusal to be absorbed
in any single focus on a situation
gives way to a
multifocused absorption that eerily
shifts, as an ambiguous figure,

from anxious to
erotic to diffident
to hypnotic.

The drama of absorption & interruption is a theme
played out, with a staggeringly literal precision,
in Beckett's *Krapp's Last Tape*.[51] As he listens
to his tape, Krapp falls into a state of rapt self-
absorption, suggesting revery. Krapp's
"listening posture" ("leaning forward, elbows on
table, hand cupping ear toward machine") mimes
a recurrent image in painting of a completely
engrossed reader or writer bending over a book or
page. In many ways this picture of Krapp,
hovering over the tape recorder, is a primary image
of reading, & by extension writing. What *Krapp*
seems to show is that the constant interruptions
created by turning the tape off & on, sometimes
rewinding or fastforwarding in between, make
the experience all the more intense: again, an
antiabsorptive technique used for absorptive ends.
Indeed, the very jagged moments when the tape is
abruptly turned off—moments in which the
listener's absorption may seem to be
ruptured—only serve to heighten the dramatic power
of the play. Beckett's incisively spliced
dislocations have a spellbinding
theatrical effect. What Krapp keeps putting off &
on is a "vision" of sexual & spiritual union, of an
absorption that he cannot sustain, nor does he wish
to recover, but which is all the more overwhelming
because it must end. The play ends with an
uninterrupted playing of a section cut & recut
until then:

> I said again I thought it was hopeless and no good go-ing on . . .
> Let me in. *(Pause.)* We drifted in among the flags and stuck. The
> way they went down, sighing, before the stem! *(Pause.)* I lay down

51. Samuel Beckett, *Krapp's Last Tape* (New York: Grove Press, 1960), pp. 9–28.

across her with my face in her breasts and my hand on her. We lay
there without moving. But under us all moved, and moved us,
gently, up and down, and from side to side. *(Pause. Krapp's lips
move. No sound.)* Past midnight. Never knew such silence. The earth
might be uninhabited . . . Perhaps my best years are gone. When
there was a chance of happiness. But I wouldn't want them back.
Not with the fire in me now. No, I wouldn't want them back. *(Krapp
motionless staring before him. The tape runs out in silence.)*

For Krapp, to make absorption audible, visible
is one step beyond "being" absorbed, one step
beyond the false hopes, the vain
resolutions. But to be able to live in
"actuality" is to take
infinite pleasures in the materials at hand:
"Nothing to say, not a squeak. What's a year now?
The sour curd and the iron stool. *(Pause.)* Revelled
in the word spool. *(With relish.)* Spooool!
Happiest moment of the past half million."
This is the "fire" Krapp will not exchange
for the carrot of ersatz escapism: hearing all
the *oooo*s he needs, reveling in the word,
& world, made opaque that it may be apprehended.

The lessons I draw from Leiris' comments on "acted
theater" & Piombino's reflections on shifts of
attentional focus are similar: that the power of
making aware, which necessarily involves a
disruption of a single plane of attention or
belief, results in a hyperattentiveness
that has its own economy of engagement.
Defamiliarization, though an antiabsorptive
technique, registers a failure of response to the familiar &
the need to be shocked in re-cognition: that the
familiar & the expected cannot command
attention, do not absorb the faculties. This is
to say that the experience of everyday life
can be diffuse, uncompelling, slack, & that an alternative
is desired. Or else, we turn away
from that experience, bland as it may sometimes be,

.because it exposes us to a repulsive
venality too horrible to be absorbed by, or
to have doled out in palatable po(r)tions: this
is the banality of evil, low-calorie absorption
for the person in a hurry.

The suspicion about & rejection of absorptive
writing is partly & importantly a response to
attempts to absorb
readers in an eminently palatable, amusing stasis.
"If only the plot would leave people alone" writes
Perelman. One may wish an end to this
monotonizing of experience: not to be further
submerged in it, as in the deadening cyclic
narrativity of those most diverting of contemporary
absorptive genres, the TV series. Or perhaps
the simplistic reduction
of everyday life, the distractions of reading
"entertainments"—the fastread magazines &
fictions & verse—absorb only listlessly, tonic
for the insomniac but not the stuff of sleep;
fueling the banality of everyday life,
not reflecting its elusive actualities.

It is a different, more difficult, less
fashionable project to create a poem that can absorb
its readers in something other than static—
call it ec-static, or u-topia, or say
it is the unnameable that writing constantly
names. To do this requires something strange & jolting,
& whether the surge is jagged or pulsing, it does
well, in Dickinson's words, to "stun . . . with bolts
of melody".

"Next to us all this twirls in spin rapt as
reverie as much as sight, sound, sign. Repelled
or riveted, the consciousness of seeing clumped
with signs fills out or insists on absence."[52]

---

52. "The Taste Is What Counts" in my *Poetic Justice* (Baltimore: Pod Books, 1979), p. 47.

PL 735 .T77 1983

PS 3552 .E7327 P64

(over)

yuu ludwn
tenors
appearing
fiddler tunes

Article Author:

Article Title:

Item Barcode:

Copy Number:

Call Number: HT1108.Z5 S2513 2006

Shelf Location: Uafro

Request date: 11/17/2014 12:24 PM

Print Queue: Hillman Ground Floor

Callslip Request #:

Callslip Request

Today's antiabsorptive works are
tomorrow's most absorbing ones, & vice
versa: the absorbable, accommodationist devices
of today will in many cases fade into arcanity.
The antiabsorptive, insofar as it is accurately
understood as essentially transgressive, is
historically & contextually specific. Understood
as a dynamic in the history of a work's reception,
absorption & repellency will shift with new contexts
of publication, new readers, & subsequent formal &
political developments. For this reason,
the acknowledgment from the first of a work's
status as artifice may better prepare it
for its journey through time. As Stein pointed out,
genuinely "contemporary" works will first seem odd,
but it is this oddness that gives them the character
to endure. & the oddness,
eclipsed by the distance of years passed
& the familiarity of repetition, fades. David Melnick's
Men in Aida may one day seem no more strange
than Verdi's *Aida*—both composed in a foreign
language, but once we know the score,
it's pure song. & once
we get used it, *Panopticon* sings as well—
what seemed to be hesitations & disruptive repetitions
become rhythmic cues, syncopated stops, strobe
lighting (if you'll forgive, & why should you?,
another psychedelic allusion).

Yet it's not that contemporary works will one day
be more understandable than they are now
but that they will be understood *differently*.
Works that proceed in an
unexpected way may submerge
readers in many disorienting pages
before rhythms dawn
amidst dense-packed
words. This is a
question of *attunement* to which
the passage of

time is not a party. A social value of poetry
may be
to provide opportunities to
tune ourselves
up
so that we can hear
the tunes of our fellows
(of all sexes)
& of the earth & sky.

The *intersection*
of absorption & impermeability is precisely
flesh,
as Merleau-Ponty uses this term
to designate the intersection of the visible
& the invisible. This
is the philosophical interior
of my inquiry—that absorption & impermeability
are the warp & woof of poetic composition—
an intertwining or chiasm whose locus
is the flesh of the word. Yet writing re-
verses the dynamic Merleau-Ponty out-
lines for the visible & the invisible:
for it is the invisible of writing
that is imagined to be absorbed
while the visible of writing usually goes unheard
or is silenced. The visibility of words
as a precondition of reading
necessitates that words obtrude impermeably into
the world—this
impermeability makes a reader's absorption
in words possible. The *thickness*
of words ensures that whatever
of their physicality is erased, or engulfed, in
the process of semantic projection,
a residue
tenaciously in-
heres that will not be sublimated
away. Writing is not a thin film

of expendable substitutions that, when reading, falls
away
like scales
to reveal a meaning. The tenacity of
writing's thickness, like the body's
flesh, is
ineradicable, yet mortal. It is
the intrusion
of words into the visible
that marks
writing's own absorption in the world.
To literally put words into Merleau-Ponty's mouth:
The thickness of writing between
the reader & the poem is constitutive for the poem
of its visibility & for the reader
of the outer limit of his or her absorption
in the poem; it is not an obstacle
between them, it is their means
of communication. The thickness of writing,
far from rivaling that of the world,
is on the contrary the sole
means it has to go to the heart of things
by making itself part
of the material world, absorbed
by it.[53]

53. The last two sentences of the stanza are based on this passage from Merleau-Ponty: "It is that the thickness of flesh between the seer and the thing is constitutive for the thing of its corporeity; it is not an obstacle between them, it is their means of communication . . . The thickness of the body, far from rivalling that of the world, is on the contrary the sole means I have to go into the heart of the things, by making myself a world and by making them flesh." From "The Intertwining—The Chiasm", chap. 4 of *The Visible and the Invisible,* ed. Claude Lefort, tr. Alphonso Lingis (Evanston: Northwestern University Press, 1968), p. 135. A *chiasm* is a decussation or x-shaped crossing or intersection. This is its meaning in anatomical nomenclature as well; for example, the *optic chiasm* is the crossing point of the fibers from both eyes, where they connect to the brain.

Merleau-Ponty elucidates the meaning of *flesh* in these words: "it is that the look is itself incorporation of the seer into the visible, quest for itself, which *is of it,* within the visible—it is that the visible of the world is not an envelope of quale [a pellicle of being without thickness], but what is between the qualia, a connective tissue of exterior and interior horizons—it is as flesh offered to flesh that the visible has its aseity [self-origination] [. . .] whence vision is question and response . . . The

Absorption & its many con-
verses, re-
verses, is at heart a measure
of the relationship between
a reader &
a work: any attempt to isolate
this dynamic in terms exclusively of
reading
or composition
will fail on this account.
As writers—
& everyone inscribes
in the sense
I mean here—
we can
try to intensify
our relationships by considering
how they work: are we putting
each other to sleep

---

openness through flesh: the two leaves of my body and the leaves of the visible world . . . It is between these intercalated leaves that there is visibility . . . the world, the flesh not as fact or sum of facts, but as the locus of an inscription of truth: the false crossed out, not nullified" (p. 131; only bracketed ellipsis added).

It's interesting to juxtapose a passage from Jerome Rothenberg's opening up of the concept of "deep image" in his 1960 essay "From Deep Image & Mode: An Exchange with Robert Creeley": "So there really are two things here, conceivable as two realities: 1) the empirical world of naive realists, etc. (what Buber and the hasidim call 'shell' or 'husk'), and 2) the hidden (floating) world, yet to be discovered or brought into being: the 'kernal' or 'sparks'. The first world both hides and leads into the second, so as Buber says: 'one cannot reach the kernal of the fruit except through the shell'; i.e. the phenomenal world is to be read by us: the perceived image is the key to the buried image: and the deep image is at once husk and kernal, perception and vision, and the poem is the movement between them. Form, then, must be considered as emerging from the act of vision: completely organic . . . Form . . . is the pattern of the movement from perception to vision: it arises as the poem arises and has no life outside the movement of the poem, i.e. outside the poem itself. (This implies too that the experience of the poet, unlike that of the mystic, is patterned and developmental, i.e. expressive; *the mystic, so I'm told, may not even be said to be seeking a vision of reality, but absorption within it—silence rather than speech.* But mystics are close to visionary consciousness and are often poets themselves.)" *Prefaces & Other Writings,* pp. 57–58; italics added.

Compare this with Creeley, writing in *In London:* "The so-called poet of love / is not so much silent as absorbed. / He ponders. He sits on / the hill looking over." *Collected Poems* (Berkeley: University of California Press, 1982), p. 454.

or waking each other up;
& what do we wake to?
Does our writing stun
or sting? Do we cling to
what we've grasped
too well, or find tunes
in each new
departure.

In the Middle of Modernism
in the Middle of Capitalism
on the Outskirts of New York

A dizzying, contradictory, incommensurable thicket of theorizing has recently cropped up on the topic of postmodernism. What is perplexing is not that different commentators disagree about the value of given artworks or cultural phenomena but, in sharp contrast, that no consensus exists as to whether the umbrella term (we know it's raining but ceci n'est pas une *para*pluie) applies to a particular historical period or can be characterized by any delineatable stylistic features. For example, prominent proponents and opponents of postmodernism suggest that the term designates the whole arena of contemporary sociohistorical cultural developments corresponding to, for some, the period Ernest Mandel defines as Late Capitalism and, for others, simply that same period of time without reference to economic determinants; still others see postmodernism as a condition or epistemological perspective, unbounded by historical period or objective economic correlatives, that reaches back to Laurence Sterne or Gertrude Stein while excluding (indeed, being in opposition to) most present cultural production. There is no agreement on whether postmodernism is a period, a tendency within a period, an aestheticophilosophical category transcending, indeed deploring, periodization, much less exactly who or what would constitute the definition of the term even if one of these options were elected. Then again, each medium's practitioners and commentators define postmodernism in their own terms, often with little connection to its application to other media: thus in the visual arts the imagined "absorption", even dominance, of avant-garde modernism is considered a necessary prerequisite for postmodernism, while in poetry the continued marginality of radical elements of early modernism still conditions the discourse about that art form and suggests a very different set of meanings for "postmodern". Finally, and this cannot be generalized much beyond literary studies, the poetries of the different Indo-European languages have very different histories; as a result, studies within French culture do not easily translate into American issues. Moreover, the intensifying discussions of postmodernism bring into sharper view the fact that there is no single definition of modernism, which is seen by various commentators as beginning with Augustine (though perhaps Plato's late dialogues should really be added), or with the Enlightenment's break with medieval scholasticism, or in English literature with Romanticism's rejection of Augustan formalism, or, finally, with a set of a dozen conflicting genealogies within the current century, differentiated by art medium, aesthetic theory, politics, and reception.[1]

It is almost as if the debate on postmodernism itself embodies the worst features of its putative subject: all stable categories seem to be constantly, if unintentionally, thrown in the air; essays cross purposes with an unconscious and almost unfathomable deliberateness; and attention is deflected from substantive issues of the meaning of various concrete cultural, social, and artistic formations/works onto the simulated concern for topological coding and categorization that risks relying on reductive *and repressive* concepts of sameness.

This categorical homogenization has particularly disastrous consequences for any consideration of the roles and meaning of specific rhetorical/aesthetic techniques. That is, the "same" artistic technique has a radically different meaning depending on when and where it is used: techniques must always be understood in context rather than as some universal cipher of "devicehood" Juxtaposition of logically unconnected sentences or sentence fragments can be used to theatricalize the limitations of conventional narrative development, to suggest the impossibility of communication, to represent speech, or as part of a prosodic mosaic constituting a newly emerging (or then again, traditional but neglected) meaning formation; these uses need have nothing in common; neither can such techniques be identified

---

1. The literature on postmodernism is extensive and immediately opens onto the vast arena of modernist studies. This response focuses especially on Fredric Jameson's essay, "Postmodernism, or the Cultural Logic of Late Capitalism", in *New Left Review* 146 (1984); references to this essay are given subsequently in the text. Andreas Huyssen, in *After the Great Divide: Modernism, Mass Culture, Postmodernism* (Bloomington: Indiana University Press, 1987), provides a far more positive assessment of postmodernism, but one informed by concerns related to Jameson's. See the endnote appended to this essay.

with all uses of "fragmentation" or collage in the other arts. Nor is the little-known painter who uses a neo-Hellenic motif in her work necessarily doing something comparable to the architect who incorporates Greek columns into a multimillion-dollar downtown office tower. But it is just this type of mishmashing that is the negative horizon of those discussions of postmodernism that attempt to describe it in unitary socioeconomic terms—a decontextualizing and leveling that flattens rather than heightens the distinctness and meaning(s) of specific works and therefore can itself be characterized as a sort of "bad" postmodernism.

In his postmodernism essay, Jameson stresses that his conception of postmodernism is based on an historically periodizing account of the global effect of multinational capitalism. That is, he sees postmodernism not as one optional style among many available but as "the cultural dominant of the logic of late capitalism" [p. 85]. Jameson starts with an overgeneralization: that the works of the modernists are completely assimilated by the culture and now seem to artists "like a set of dead classics" [p. 56]. He then describes the "deconstruction of expression" as evidenced in the movement from "high-modernist" (?) Vincent Van Gogh to "*the* central figure in contemporary visual arts," Andy Warhol (a kind of postmodern hyperbole that sacrifices critical distance for dubious leveling). This movement is evidence of "the emergence of a new kind of flatness or depthlessness, a new kind of superficiality in the most literal sense", which Jameson also characterizes as the "waning of affect" and the replacement of the "depth" of Munch's *The Scream* with a multiple play of surfaces in postmodernism [pp. 60–62]. He relates this development to the "fragmentation of the subject", which in turn results in the "well-nigh universal practice . . . of pastiche" [pp. 63–64]. In this process, "real history" is threatened by the "breakdown of the signifying chain", a situation that is mimed in the "schizophrenic fragmentation" of postmodern art.

Jameson seems to take the high ground when he warns against moralizing about different postmodernist objects because this would tend to distract from the globalizing panorama of his approach, as if we are trapped in postmodernism and no matter what we do we just get further inside its grip—a further play on his own phrase "the prison house of language", as if language, rather than the specific uses that women and men make of it, were the prison.[2] But we can act, and we are not trapped in the postmodern condition if we are willing to differentiate between works of art that suggest new ways of conceiving of our present world and those that seek rather to debunk any possibilities for meaning. To do this, one has to be able to distinguish between, on the one hand, a fragmentation that attempts to valorize the concept of a free-floating signifier unbounded to social significance, that sees no meaning outside conventional discourse and only arbitrary codicity (convention's arbitrary formalism) within it; and, on the other hand, a fragmentation that reflects a conception of meaning as prevented by conventional narration and so uses disjunction as a method of tapping into other possibilities of meaning available within language. Failure to make such distinctions is similar to failing to distinguish between youth gangs, pacifist anarchists, weatherpeople, anti-Sandinista contras, Salvadoran guerrillas, Islamic terrorists, or U.S. state terrorists. Perhaps all of these groups are responding to the same stage of multinational capitalism. But the crucial point is that the *responses* cannot be understood as the same, unified as various interrelated symptoms of late capitalism. Nor are the dominant practices the exemplary ones that tell the whole story.

From the point of view of the poetry to which I am committed, I can see little relevance in "postmodernism" as a label. "The futurist moment" in literature, to borrow Marjorie Perloff's term for the years immediately preceding the First World War, set in motion a set of radical modernist concerns that are still relevant to current poetic and political practice, just as they are still unacceptable to the official cultural apparatus.[3] I say this despite the fact that the term "modern-

2. Fredric Jameson, *The Prison House of Language* (Princeton: Princeton University Press, 1972).

3. See Marjorie Perloff, *The Futurist Moment: Avant-Garde, Avant Guerre, and the Language of Rupture* (Chicago: University of Chicago Press, 1987). An excellent anthology of radical modernist poetry is *Revolution of the Word: A New Gathering of American Avant Garde Poetry, 1914–1945*, ed. Jerome Rothenberg (New York: Seabury Press, 1974).

The official cultural apparatus, as it applies to American poetry—what I've called "official verse culture"—is most clearly revealed in the publishing and reviewing practices of the *New York Times, New York Review of Books, New Yorker, American Poetry Review*, and a number of old-line literary quarterlies; by the Pulitzer

ism" has to some degree been appropriated by the antimodernist literary canon makers from the New Critics to Helen Vendler. Many of the New Critics, like Vendler, constructed their own partisan map of High Modernism, purged of the more formally radical and avant-garde directions not only among excluded poets but, significantly, within the poets canonized. It is this type of gutted modernism, which frequently transforms itself into outright antimodernism, that may lead some critics to cede "modernism" as a project to its most politically and aesthetically conservative commentators and consequently to suggest that the avant-garde and modernism are antithetical.[4]

By "modernist" I am referring to a break from various ideas about narrative and description to a focus on the autonomy and self-sufficiency of the medium that implicitly challenges any idea of language as having one particular "natural" mode of discourse. This challenge represents a significant break from the naturalist rhetorical assumptions of both Augustan and Romantic poetry. The understanding of language as an entity, with properties of its own, rather than as an instrument that could be used neutrally and transparently to "transmit" a pregiven communication, shook the fundamental as-

---

Prize, the National Book Awards, and the Guggenheim and MacArthur Fellowships; by the poetry lists of the major trade publishers; by such presenting organizations as the Poetry Center of the 92nd Street Y in New York and the American Academy of Poets; and by the poets on the tenured faculties of the major U.S. universities. While the type of work supported by these institutions is diverse, and subject to a variety of pressures that encourage such diversity, the bulk of this verse tends to be blandly apolitical or accomodationist, neoromantic, and (often militantly) middle-of-the-road or, as it is now called, "suburban". Moreover, what is most striking is not the relatively unsystematic quality of the inclusions but the systematic nature of what is—with important strategic exceptions—excluded: almost all of the formally active poetry developing out of New American Poetry contexts, the many divergent small-press tendencies, and the poetry of gays, blacks, and hispanics, as well as the variety of "ethnic" poetries that reject standard English as their dialect (categories that should be seen as overlapping rather than as distinct).

4. Perloff lucidly addresses this issue in *The Dance of the Intellect: Studies in the Poetry of the Pound Tradition* (Cambridge: Cambridge University Press, 1985), particularly in "Pound/Stevens: Whose Era?" and "Postmodernism and the Impasse of the Lyric". Perloff argues that Pound and Stevens, just as Stein and Eliot, suggest *contradictory* modernisms. Thus critics like Vendler and Bloom appear to have misrepresented modernism in their preoccupation with late Romantic lyric; yet if late Romantic lyric is to be named modernist, then the radical innovations of the modernist period by Stein, Pound, Joyce, or Woolf would need to be called postmodernist. Within literary studies, this meaning of postmodernism is common and needs to be critically distinguished from the more recent use of postmodernism in visual arts criticism. For a discussion of "avant-garde" versus "modernism" see the endnote below.

sumptions of nineteenth-century narrative realism—both as an artistic
and a critical practice. Jameson, in his essay, laments the loss of "real
history" in *post*modernism, but what the early modernist writers
showed was that the history of narrative historiography was a product
of a specific rhetorical mode, a simulacrum if you will, blinded to its
own rhetorical status by an unacknowledged positivism *insofar as it
claimed scientific status*. What modernist writing revealed was not a
loss of History but a crisis in the representation of history. Its great
contribution was to begin to explore ways in which the "cognitive
mapping" that Jameson usefully calls for could be undertaken by
seeking new ways to confront, *enact,* and transform the "real" while
insisting that the real is not a fixed external but a construction of the
social/economic/ideological spheres understood as an interdependent
whole.⁵ But there is a danger of history being "lost", lost in the denial
of these newer methodologies in a retreat to the hegemony of social
science together with an insistence on the loss of "critical distance"
in the nonscientific spheres (which Jameson sees as an essential char-
acteristic of postmodernism).⁶ The problem of cultural distance affects

5. Jameson ends his essay by pointing to the need for "new maps" to chart the
cultural space of the postmodern period. "An aesthetic of cognitive mapping [will
seek] to endow the individual subject with some new heightened sense of its place in
the global system . . . the new political art—*if indeed it is to be possible at all*—will
have to hold the truth of postmodernism . . .—the worldspace of multinational capi-
tal—at the same time at which it achieves a breakthrough to some as yet unimagina-
ble new mode of representing this last, in which we may again begin to grasp our
positioning. . .and regain a capacity to act and struggle *which is at present neutral-
ized* by our spatial as well as social confusion" [p. 92, italics added].
    6. Jameson writes that "no theory of cultural politics current on the Left today has
been able to do without one notion or another of" critical distance [p. 87]. But the
"new space of postmodernism" has abolished not only "critical distance" but "dis-
tantiation" in general. As a result, "even overtly political interventions . . . are also
somehow secretly disarmed". In this way Jameson manages to make Adorno look
optimistic; but one of the anomalies of his argument is that he seems not to take
these bleak words too much to heart. For if Jameson believed this argument, he would
be forced to assess his own work as undifferentiatable from the postmodern space he
decries—and even that assessment would have to be understood as without critical
distance. But Jameson appears to exclude the social sciences from the "de-distanc-
ing" dominant of postmodernism, and indeed his whole argument rests on the cru-
cial "Archimedean" role of an *historical* and economically informed analysis, such as
Mandel's and his own. Indeed, Jameson turns to Althusser's differentiation between
science and ideology, affirming that while we may not be able to represent "the
world and its totality", we nonetheless can have abstract, scientific knowledge of this
totality [p. 91]. The loss of critical distance, then, appears to be a virtually insur-
mountable problem not for the *critics* of culture, but only for the *producers* of cul-
ture, whose work is *"distorted and unreflexive"* [p. 88].

all modes of discourse, historical and aesthetic. Nor does this problem need to fatally impair the ability to assert values or act with justice in art or in politics.

For the Left, especially, it is vital to be able to identify those elements of contemporary culture that have been negatively described by commentators like Jameson as postmodern. In their distrust of traditional modes of authority, postmodernist works may express a positive social value, but insofar as they reject the possibility of new forms of socially grounded meaning, such postmodernism appears to undercut the potential for any transformational political interpretation or action. However, in this arena of postmodern negativity, it is necessary to distinguish between an expressive pessimism and an opportunistic "antipolitical" cynicism in which values are strictly market values, determined by the specific needs of fashion, celebrity, and a targeted audience.[7] Both of these manifestations share a similar evaluation of the loss of a fixed, authoritative, transcendental set of values, though for one the response is that of multinational capital—to cash in and have a party—and for the other the response is a deep despair at the passing of a world that once seemed to have a purpose that now seems irrevocably lost.

Yet the bracketing of the "transcendental signified" or the "death of God" does not entail a meaningless world—for these are realities of a modernist dialectical materialism as much as of a negative postmodernism. That is, once the hollow legitimacy of capital and kings has been exposed, the truths of the human world can begin to be *made*. And the cognitive mapping of this collective struggle to make, not consume, history will falter if it relies on the simulacra produced

7. William Burroughs and Andy Warhol might serve as exemplary of each category. This is especially true if Warhol is viewed as *not* being ironic, a currently popular view in postmodern art circles. In many ways, such a de-distancing of Warhol is grotesque, but it does give rise to the specter of "simulated" Warhols (and Burroughses for that matter) that end up giving Warhol an unsuspected depth. Another form of expressive pessimism can be found in recent German art, as in the very powerful work of Joseph Beuys, Georg Baselitz, or Anselm Kiefer. The remarkable collaborative team of Komar and Melamid is also worth mentioning here. Komar and Melamid, who are Soviet emigrés, paint in a technically brilliant form of Zhadonovite socialist realism, tinged with, among other things, surreal genre scenes reminiscent of German Romanticism. For example, there is a marvelous portrait of Lenin, deep in a forest, kneeling down by a river apparently to look at an animal ("Lenin in Zurich"). There are also "official" portraits of Stalin, and one of Reagan as a centaur, all done with high gloss and high drama, fit for a state hall.

by trying to exorcise the "tropicality"—to use Hayden White's related argument[8]—out of sociohistorical accounts and critiques by making them fit into the bourgeois, liberal, patriarchal space of a rhetoric-free discourse that aspires to be unitary, causal, linear, dialect-neutral, imperious/impersonal, unambiguous. Not that inverting or negating these qualities is a *sufficient* condition for the sort of cognitive mapping required. For what is needed is the ability and willingness to distinguish between the *necessary* and the *sufficient* use of alternative compositional strategies, to take positions and make distinctions *within* what is too easily written off in toto, or embraced en masse, as postmodern. The pernicious fallout of postmodernism understood as an all-permeating cultural condition is that we are asked to either take it or leave it, or asked to imagine that there is no difference whether we do or do not . . . But seeing these *differences* is the source of our social power to intervene, to agitate, to provoke, to rethink, to take sides—using all the formal and cultural rhetorics at our command.

Finally, it is worth noting that a number of the discussions of postmodernism, including Jameson's, mislead by comparing profitable postmodern artworld commodities to, in their own time, obscure and noncommercial modern artworks. (Significantly, Jameson's postmodern examples are all highly successful men whom he identifies as dominant.[9]) In contrast, the more useful comparison would be to

8. In *Tropics of Discourse: Essays in Cultural Criticism* (Baltimore: Johns Hopkins University Press, 1978), Hayden White argues that the metaphoric structures and tropes (trope-icality) of the narrative forms used by historians are always value-laden. Since there can be no value-free narrative choices, historical and social scientific methodologies have more in common with literary studies than is often assumed. An excellent collection of works emerging out of this approach—which has something in common with Jameson's cognitive mapping—is *Writing Culture: The Poetics and Politics of Ethnography*, ed. James Clifford and George E. Marcus (Berkeley: University of California Press, 1986). In his introduction, Clifford suggests that the "critical distance" that has been lost in the new ethnography is *better* lost since it does not mask the interest-components of its discursive practices.

9. Certainly men have been the dominant, but by no means exclusive, force in the canonized visual art of this century, as in the past. According to the Women's Caucus for Art, New York Chapter, "Far more than 50 percent of New York artists are women [while] only 2 percent of the artists showing regularly in major galleries are woman artists" (1987). At the same time, a number of phallocentric and misogynous features of modernism have been exposed by feminist criticism, and this has no doubt supported the value of some postmodern perspectives. A perverse twist on this situation is the idea—which has established some fair measure of commercial and critical cache—that the "gaze" of the "other" (women) has entered into the art con-

those works of the "modern period" that had commercial success in their time but are now aesthetically discounted (either by the market, by the official cultural apparatus, or by active artists) or, alternately, to compare uncommercial modern-period works to commercially unviable works of the present period.

One of the sharp contrasts between modernist writing and High Modern architecture—which particularly accentuates the incoherence of seeing postmodernism in these two fields as continuous—is precisely the dramatic difference in their histories of reception. Much modernist writing was virtually invisible while High Modern architecture became a primary showcase of the major industrial corporations. Indeed, modernist writing established a tradition of resisting the market imperatives of Capital through the formation of alternative publishing and distribution networks that were able to separate themselves from the increasing multinational corporatization of publishing—thus transforming what in many ways was a necessity into a strategy. This tradition of alternative social organizing continues into the present, transformed by a great deal more political self-consciousness and commitment. This may help to explain why, at the formal level, High Modernism in architecture can be characterized as unitary, unembroidered, and without irony or ambiguity—that is, the very opposite of the qualities that could be ascribed to modernist writing with its emergent range of collage, parody, appropriation, irony, and even pastiche.[10]

I am arguing, then, that a political account of contemporary art must, in the first instance, account for the specific social and economic

---

text in forms considered marginal—photography and performance rather than painting and sculpture. Thus a few women working in these so-called marginal media (specifically Cindy Sherman, Barbara Kruger, and Jenny Holzer) are lavished with praise, while the resourceful and considerable work of women sculptors and painters continues to be ignored, now on the high ground that women articulate their otherness best when they stay away from the dominant forms—which are presumably best left to the mastery of men. Thus institutional modernism dealt the first blow, and now postmodernism tries for the knockout. See Craig Owens, "The Discourse of Others", in Hal Foster, ed., *The Anti-Aesthetic* (Port Townsend, Wash.: Bay Press, 1983).

10. Linda Hutcheon provides a sharp dissent to Jameson's critique of postmodern architecture in "The Politics of Postmodernism: Parody and History", *Cultural Critique* 4 (1986–87). Her *A Poetics of Postmodernism* (New York: Routledge, 1988), published after my essay was completed, offers one of the most thoughtful proposals for what postmodernism could mean in a positive way.

factors that shape the context within which a given artwork exists. The meaning of specific works is constituted not only by the intrinsic features visibly inscribed on the face of a canvas, page, stage, video monitor, or contact sheet, or audibly inscribed in a magnetic tape or compact disc, but also in the way the work situates itself in the context of its market or nonmarket, its readers or viewers, the history of its medium, and the political and social climate contemporaneous to its creation. The same technique used for a sure sell in one medium, or in one moment, may assure a sure marginalization in another: in the one case this may signify postmodernism's empty gesture, in the other *resistance*.

In the current New York visual art world, what tends to be promoted by the motor of fashion are the most simple, trivializing—consumable—formal developments; ones that most give credence to the negative features of postmodernism articulated by Jameson and others: for it is this lack of complexity in confronting the methodological legacies of modernist thought that gives legitimacy to the charge of postmodernist depthlessness, what Jameson accurately describes at the "waning of affect": *all technique, no substance*.[11] (As if affect itself were not the product of a particular constellation of techniques.) This waning, however, is not the product of what artists do, or might, create but rather of the market forces that economically reward and promote such work over and above an enormous amount of other (possible and actual) work. This, emphatically, is not to say

---

11. One of the most commercially and critically successful recent tendencies in the New York art world involves the simulation of previous art styles in such a way that their codes are alleged to be exposed while their meaning has been evacuated. Thus Peter Halley's "neo-geo" paintings, which were prominently featured in the 1987 Whitney Biennial, are intentionally bland day-glo imitations of minimal color-field paintings; this work is supposed to represent the "cells and conduits" of postmodern existence, though it brings to mind life inside the corporation more than life on the very hot and unsimulated New York streets. This may suggest the destination such work has. It has certainly proved highly collectible. Another painting at the Biennial seemed to be simulated Dada (confrontation without the confronting). The sometimes energetic and imaginative Julian Schnabel had a huge canvas completely covered with a wornout piece of tarp, over which is attached a silk banner enscribed with the word "virtue". Or consider Sherrie Levine's much-discussed photo series produced by having a commercial lab make copies of Walker Evans' famous photos of tenant farmers, which Levine then signed—an instance of appropriation *without intervention* that, the weighty critics insist, is supposed to show us that originality is a bogus, and even bourgeois, concept. But *ownership*, of course, thrives with high pricetags attached to these simulated works.

that all commercially successful art is compromised or directly sup-
portive of this system, since the system demands a certain amount of
heterogeneity in the form of a wide range of tokens.[12] The typical
scenario of exclusion, however, takes a disturbing turn when com-
mentators unsympathetic to the postmodern fashion machine none-
theless attend only to the already-visible, already-promoted work,
thus increasing its dominance while pushing even further to the mar-
gins those artworks that contest—in a be*wild*ering variety of ways—
the prevailing aesthetic. A related tactic, as I have already suggested,
is to give a postmodern interpretation to works that can more usefully,
and legitimately, be understood as antipathetic to the values being
ascribed to it. Jameson, in his depiction of a particularly resourceful
form of poetic cognitive mapping as "schizophrenic disjunction", risks
doing just this: he comes close to mistaking the diagnosis for the
disease, as if when the voice of reason finally sounds we won't be
able to recognize it because it sounds so different from what we've
grown used to.[13]

These brief considerations suggest that the depthlessness of post-
modernism is as much a specific product of the art market and
associated culture industries as it is a reflection of the zeitgeist: our
culture has a depth that far exceeds its dominating objects. To find
alternatives to depthlessness we must look outside the centers of

12. There are other directions that suggest the vitality of the visual arts in ways
not adequately accounted for by either the detractors or the promoters of postmod-
ernism. In sharp contrast to the axes of negativity and simulation already sketched, it
is instructive to think of such visual artists as Philip Guston, Jake Berthot, Robert
Colescott, Agnes Martin, Malcolm Morley, Alice Aycock, Nancy Spero, Mimi Gross,
Eva Hesse, Lawrence Weiner, Louise Bourgeois, Pat Steir, Arakawa and Gins, David
Reed, or Elizabeth Murray—to restrict the list to a few well-known individuals, each
of whose quite different work would seriously deepen discussions of the contempo-
rary cultural period just because they do not offer the reductive solutions of those
artists selected as the avatars of market postmodernism. My close association with,
and active commitment to, the paintings of Susan Bee make her work my most active
example. For a further discussion of this issue, see my essay, "For M/E/A/N/I/N/G"
in *M/E/A/N/I/N/G* 1 (1986).

13. See Jameson's misreading of Bob Perelman's poem "China" as an instance of
"schizophrenic fragmentation"—an aesthetic that he feels characterizes "so-called
Language Poetry" in general (pp. 71–72). For a number of alternative readings
of the diverse field of poetic activity Jameson is referring to here, see *The
L=A=N=G=U=A=G=E Book,* ed. Bruce Andrews and myself (Carbondale:
Southern Illinois University Press, 1984); *In the American Tree,* ed. Ron Silliman
(Orono, Maine: National Poetry Foundation, 1986); *"Language" Poetries,* ed. Doug-
las Messerli (New York: New Directions, 1987), and *"43 Poets (1984)",* which I
edited for *boundary* 2 (14:1/2, 1987).

fashion and promotion—just as we must look outside the major political parties and major media to find alternative and oppositional political discourses.[14] When this happens, the cognitive mapping that Jameson calls for will be understood not only as a future project but as one with a *real history* and a real present.

Endnote: What Is Divided?

Huyssen's *After the Great Divide* is one of the more useful books to appear on the subject of postmodernism. But, like so much of the debate surrounding this misunderstood—and perhaps not understandable—term, Huyssen hinges his remarks on a highly contestable definition of modernism.

For Huyssen, postmodernism is characterized by the breakdown in the distinction between high art and popular culture (which he sees as a repudiation of the purism of modernism) and by a loss of faith in the power of avant-garde art (and more generally *modernization*) to bring about a better future through technology. Huyssen, however, is too ready to accept Peter Burger's distinction between modernism and the "historical avant-garde" (dada, early surrealism, the postrevolutionary Russian avant-garde), which in practice are so intricately intertwined as to defy strict separation. (See Burger's *Theory of the*

---

14. Unfortunately, in many discussions of cultural trends the only artists mentioned are those who have been validated by the market and who therefore may have some "name" recognition. This mars my own examples of visual artists in the notes just preceding. What rarely is investigated is the makeup of the "mass" of artists whose names never become tokens of art-critical discourse but who nonetheless are *producing* the art of our time. (The Whitney's 1987 Biennial catalog estimates—the figure seems high—that there are 60,000 visual artists in New York alone.) A recent survey of 900 applicants for New York's statewide art grants is revealing. About 90 percent of the applicants—from all art disciplines—considered their primary occupation to be artists. Seventy percent of the artists defined a professional artist as someone who "spends a substantial amount of time creating art"; 93 percent of the respondents who viewed themselves as professional artists rejected the marketplace definition (I make my living as an artist, I receive some income from my work as an artist, I intend to make my living as an artist). Gross income *from art* was low: 42 percent earned less than $2000 per year, 66 percent earned less than $6,000, and 92 percent earned less than $20,000. Gross household income for 56 percent of this group was between $10,000 and $30,000 and 75 percent of these claimed one or two dependants. These statistics are based on Joan Jeffri, Joseph Hosie, and Robert Greenblatt, "The Artist Alone: Selected Highlights", *FYI* 3:2 (New York: Center for Arts Information, 1987).

Avant-Garde, tr. Michael Shaw [Minneapolis: University of Minnesota Press, 1984].)

In Burger's terms, the avant-garde's project was to disrupt the norms of bourgeois "institution art" (including those reflected in modernism) by breaking down the distinction between art and life through the embracing of technology and progress. In contrast, modernism attempted to keep art and life separate and, through radical development of the autonomy of the art object, to create new ways of "representing" and producing meanings—essentially extending the project of late nineteenth-century aestheticism (art for art's sake, pure art). Modernism, in this account, posed no obstacle to its elevation to the status of institution art.

Burger's schema is reductive since it equates modernism with its critical *reception* by, for example, some "formalist" criticism. Indeed, from a formalist perspective, modernism was the embodiment of the Hegelian movement of art's "advance". In this sense, progress was a common agenda of some avant-garde *and* modernist theory. In contrast, many modernist/avant-garde artists rejected or had no interest in "progress". Gertrude Stein, for instance, perhaps English literature's most radical theorist of modernism, spoke of contemporeity, not progress. Furthermore, regardless of what individual artists or theorists have written about progress or disruption, the works themselves often tell a quite different story; at a minimum, many can be usefully interpreted without reference to their putative positions on these issues. Indeed, *a* central modernist project was the disruption of habitual patterns of thought and perception—just the patterns constantly being reinscribed by the culture industry. In this light, the avant-garde and modernism are fractions of the same dialectical movement.

It is the dizzying undecidability of distinctions like avant-garde *versus* modernism that makes discussions of postmodernism so frustrating. The labels constantly disintegrate into each other and seem to prove their opposite. Huyssen cannot shore his terms against this tide.

Huyssen sees the American pop, beat, and "alternative" art of the 1960s (his examples range from Cage to Ginsberg and Burroughs and Kerouac to Warhol and Johns) as the first stage of postmodernism, since all this work breaks with modernism in three ways that echo the strategies of the historical avant-garde: postmodernism blurs the distinctions between high art and popular culture, it makes icono-clastic attacks on institution art, and it possesses a "technological optimism". "Perhaps *for the first time* in American culture," Huyssen says, "an avantgarde revolt against a tradition of high art and what was perceived as its hegemonic role made sense" [p. 103, italics added].

These generalizations break down on close inspection, especially if the different media are considered separately. Warhol always aspired to represent the culture industry while assuming, rather than contest-ing, the mantle of institution art; and he is in no way optimistic, technologically or otherwise. Burroughs is among the most techno-logically pessimistic writers of the century. Cage and Schoenberg share a highly formal sense of musical structure that suggests as many continuities between them as discontinuities; as a result of their formal investigations, both have been foolishly attacked, but with equal vehemence, for their inaccessibility and for their rejection of the formally conventional features of popular culture. Johns "aestheti-cized" popular iconography into blue-chip high-art works that were almost immediately successful in the market and, soon after, as insti-tution art (which is not to say that his work was in any sense undeserv-ing of its success, just that it cannot be used as an example of work that posed greater obstacles to becoming institution art than the modernist work that immediately preceded it).

In contrast, the ascent to institution art of the abstract expression-ists, and other American modernists of the 1950s, was *slower and more militantly opposed,* and a number of the artists were more iconoclasticly anti-institution art, than several of Huyssen's sixties postmodernists. In any case, the whole edifice falls apart if you don't buy the distinction between avant-garde and modernism, since the supposed revolt represented by what Huyssen calls "avantgarde Pop" was not necessarily against modernism per se but against specific, and often radically reductive, critical mappings of modernist art. To argue, as Huyssen does, that pop art was more avant-garde than abstract expressionism and to make this a basis for postmodernism is not only unconvincing, it empties the aesthetic content from particular works in a grand sweep of cultural criticism. Furthermore, it ignores the socioeconomic analysis that would see pop less as a revolt against a sanctified modernism than as a necessary new fashion or trend re-quired to keep the art market productive. (In any case, no general conclusions about the *value* of an artwork can be drawn from its commercial success or failure; indeed, highly contestatory works may gain wide public—or commercial—credence without losing their oppositional force, or they may not. Yet this type of generalizing is encouraged by Huyssen's analysis.)

Huyssen is quick to point out that the distinction between avant-garde and modernism makes more sense from a European perspective than from an American one; but this is because he believes that, until the 1960s, American high art was not firmly entrenched enough to require an avant-garde. This is a problematic reading of the history of American culture and especially egregious in terms of literature, which is often Huyssen's specific field of reference. It's hard not to think of many of the American modernist poets, such as Williams, Pound, Riding, Stein, Zukofsky, Hughes, Brown, or Oppen as not being consciously in opposition to an entrenched literary establishment. In contrast to Huyssen's account, the "avant-garde" is perhaps best understood as being variously constituted by a fusion of one of a number of political and social aspirations found *within* modernist art—socialist, utopian, anarchist, conservative, fascist. In any case, it needs to be emphasized that Burger's historical avant-garde is an odd lot of individuals and groups who share much less than the label suggests: these movements must be considered within their specific geographic and sociopolitical contexts, or else neofascist Italians fetishizing machines will be equated with French leftists fascinated by the unconscious. Worse, German artists' attitudes about the mass culture of Weimar end up being equated with the aspirations of Russian artists for a *new* socialist culture, which are then equated with pop's fascination with American popular culture—*as if mass culture were a unitary phenomenon.*

Yet it is striking that in the most penetrating chapter in his book, "Adorno in Reverse", Huyssen makes a convincing case that Adorno's "modernism" can only be understood as a *fusion* of avant-garde and modernist concerns. Adorno advocated modernism on the political-ideological ground that the autonomous artwork was able to avoid the grip of administered culture. For Adorno, the political imperative was to insist that art and mass culture be kept separate: a concern that is no less relevant in the 1987 of Philip Johnson and *Amerika* (the TV miniseries) than it was in the 1937 of Albert Speer and Leni Riefenstahl. For art can be political by articulating something broken off from—for example—the postmodern nightmare Jameson depicts. Alternatives can, and must, be envisioned and enacted. Art is never pure in the sense of escaping the ideological. Rather, art may provide different approaches to representing or critiquing the ideological. In this context, Huyssen valuably suggests that Adorno's crucial point is that the social realm is always the subject of art, whether explicitly or implicitly.

Time Out of Motion:
Looking Ahead to See Backward

> *It is only an auctioneer who should admire all schools of art.*
> —Oscar Wilde

Millenial Ballad (after Wilde)

Each Cent'ry kills the thing it loves
By Each let this be heard
Some do it with a guillotine
Some with a genocide
Some do it with threshing machines
Some with atomic bombs

Yes, each period kills the thing it loves
But each century does not die

An enormous gulf separates us from the English-language poetry of the last decades of the nineteenth century. We do not speak or hear the same language: not just in the sense that all languages shift through time, but that American English, in the final decades of the last century, was invaded from without and, in the process of absorbing elements alien to it, irrevocably changed, cutting the umbilical cord to its putative English mother and seceding—in words a hundred years after the deed of 1776—from its Island-bound British father.

The immigrants of 1880–1900 radically subverted the language environment of the northeast and midwest as non-English speakers began to settle here at an almost geometrically escalating rate. By 1900, according to Peter Quartermain's assessment, about one quarter of the white U.S. population either did not speak English or learned it as a second language—while in the mid-Atlantic states and New

England perhaps only one person in four was a native speaker of English.[1] Such facts are important because I understand language not as an indifferent system for describing an independently external reality but as the perceptual and conceptual unconscious of reality. Changes in language affect reality just as they reflect social and historical developments. For American poetry of the twentieth century, there is no more important fact than the fundamental alteration of the language base—who was speaking and how they spoke—that occurred in the 1880s and 1890s; indeed, it is perhaps that period's most lasting legacy for our literature.

The subversiveness of second-language speakers and writers is not necessarily great; it can be contained by tightly controlled conventions for correct diction, pronunciation, and syntax—aberrations actively repudiated and their perpetrators socially (and therefore economically) shunned. Having learned an immaculate French, one becomes (almost) a Frenchman. In America, the reverse has been the rule: far from colonizing the foreigners' consciousness, the foreigners colonized English. Island English—the language of the English people—was no longer the common yardstick but only one of a number of inflected variants of a decentered confederacy.

Fifty years ago, Gertrude Stein said much of what I am saying in her lecture "What Is English Literature?":

> the poetry of England is so much what it is, it is the poetry of the things with which any of them are shut in in their daily completely daily island life. It makes very beautiful poetry because anything shut in with you can sing . . . As I say description of the complete the entirely complete daily island life has been England's glory. Think of Chaucer, think of Jane Austen, think of Anthony Trollope, and

1. In 1882, only about a fifth of new immigrants spoke English; about one third spoke German. In 1900, 38 percent of the total U.S. population was foreign born or first generation (probably doubling the figures for 1850). By 1910, probably one third of the U.S. population did not speak English or spoke it as a foreign language. If the south is left out of these statistics—significantly for white southern writing, non-English immigrants played a minimal role in the south—the prevalence of non-English speakers in America is even more dramatic. See Peter Quartermain, Introduction to *Dictionary of Literary Biography*, vol. 45: *American Poetry, 1880 to 1945*, lst series, ed. Quartermain (Detroit: Gale Research, 1986). Quartermain also provided me with additional compilations and observations based on Census Bureau reports and *Reports of the Immigration Commission* (1907–1910).

the life of the things shut up with that daily life is the poetry, think
of all the lyrical poets, think what they say and what they have.[2]

Of course Stein did not cite demographics; but her personal history
is the history of nonnative English speaking. As Quartermain docu-
ments, Stein, William Carlos Williams, and Louis Zukofsky—three
poets who created a ground for twentieth-century poetry—all learned
English as a second language.[3] Zukofsky grew up in a Yiddish-speak-
ing New York neighborhood, while Williams probably learned Span-
ish and English simultaneously. Stein's family moved to Vienna before
she was one, where she had a Czech tutor and an Hungarian governess
and probably spoke her first words in German; from four to six, she
lived in Paris; the family then moved to Oakland. Stein spent her
adult life listening to and speaking French while writing English. (One
might add that Charles Reznikoff, like Zukofsky, grew up in a Yid-
dish-speaking household.)

To come to a language as a second tongue, to rethink and relearn
the world in new and strange sounds, may inhibit a natural or un-
conscious acceptance of the relation of words to things. It may bring
home the artificialness of any language—that, as Veronica Forrest-
Thomson notes, language is both continuous and discontinuous with
the world, a thing that for a poet can be as plastic as transparent: the
translucency that illumines words when they are heard as sound as
well as sense; the realization that we can shape, and are shaped by,
the words we use.[4] Stein, Zukofsky, and Williams did not assume an

2. Gertrude Stein, *Look at Me Now Here I Am: Writing and Lectures, 1909–
1945*, ed. Patricia Meyerowitz (Baltimore: Penguin, 1971), pp. 34–35.
3. Peter Quartermain "Actual Word Stuff, Not Thoughts for Thoughts", *Cre-
dences* 2:1 (1983), 114.
4. Veronica Forrest-Thomson, *Poetic Artifice: A Theory of Twentieth Century Po-
etry* (New York: St. Martin's Press, 1978), p. 118. James Clifford discusses some of
these issues in respect to both Conrad and Malinowski—"both Poles condemned by
historical contingency to a cosmopolitan 'European' identity [and pursuing] ambi-
tious writing careers in England"—in his essay "On Ethnographic Self-Fashioning:
Conrad and Malinowski" in *Reconstructing Individualism*, ed. Thomas C. Heller,
Morton Sosna, and David E. Wellbery (Palo Alto: Stanford University Press, 1985),
rept. in Clifford's *The Predicament of Culture* (Cambridge: Harvard University Press,
1988), pp. 92–113, but see especially pp. 92–3 and 95–6; my citations, however, are
from Clifford's manuscript for this essay. "Conrad accomplished the almost impossi-
ble feat of becoming a great writer (his model was Flaubert) in English—a third
language he began to acquire at twenty years of age. It's not surprising to find his

Island English but invented their language word by word, phrase by phrase. In distinguishing the poetry of these three writers from more conventionally Island-oriented practices, I would make a contrast between *etymologic* English and *associational* English. Etymologic writing is symbolic and connotative, while associational writing involves a lateral glissade into *mis*hearing, sound rather than root connections, dialect, "speech" in Williams' sense.[5] Extending this metaphorically to prosody, metered verse with regular rhyme schemes would be etymologic, while free verse with irregular off-rhymes would be associational.

What Stein, Williams, and Zukofsky created is sometimes called American English, but this is a nationalist misnomer for an English-language writing for which Island English is no imperial sovereign but one of many tonguings, an English-language literature that does not evolve from Chaucer through other Island writers but has many roots in English and non-English; though the literature of the English people has a special fascination, it makes us feel a part of its daily island-life succession, like children looking at the painted ponies of a

---

writing permeated by a sense of the simultaneous artifice and necessity of cultural, linguistic conventions. His life of writing, of constantly *becoming* an English writer, offers a paradigm for . . . ethnographic subjectivity" in Malinowski. Clifford goes on to read *Heart of Darkness* "as an allegory of writing and of grappling with 'language' and 'culture' in their emergent twentieth century definitions"; it's worth noting that Conrad's experiences in the Congo, which form the basis for *Heart of Darkness*, occurred in the 1890s. Conrad was born in 1857; his first novel was published in 1896; *Heart of Darkness* was published in 1902.

5. I base this distinction on some remarks of Quartermain's in *Credences*, pp. 111 and 121: "Laura Riding acutely remarked in *Contemporaries and Snobs* that 'None of the words Miss Stein uses have ever had any experience. They are no older than her use of them . . . None of these words has ever had any history.' I think that applies equally well to both Williams and Zukofsky . . . Neither Williams nor Zukofsky play around with or rely on the connotations of words, so that there is a difference indeed between Eliot's 'multifoliate rose' in 'The Hollow Men' and Williams' 'rose.' Eliot . . . is close to the English tradition, playing for the connotations, moving towards the symbolic. Williams and Zukofsky are struggling to establish the American. 'I'm of this time,' Zukofsky wrote . . . 'my elders rather end off something European'". Of course no writing can ever be purely "associational" or "etymologic": these are *tendencies* reflected both in poetics and poems. Zukofsky, for example, plays both ends against the middle, and Stein's rose is both a punningly associational resounding of a literary symbol and a resurrection of it (a rose is arose). Another extension of this distinction would be the contrast in structural metaphor, if not textual practice, between *Finnegans Wake* and *Tender Buttons*. "Etymologic" and "associational" can as usefully be considered attitudes toward form as toward lexicon.

twirling carousel or going for a ride and later maybe building or buying a carousel concession.

When you look back a hundred years to the poetry that was being written in America, you find an odd lacuna. Much of what is called nineteenth-century American literature was over. Poe and Hawthorne, Thoreau and Emerson were dead; Whitman and Melville were in their final years: those who had taken the Island out of English, secession upon secession, finding out what might be a new England or a Manhattan, still had not completely succeeded in seceding.

By the 1880s and 1890s there was little poetry being written in America that now attracts the interest of the work immediately preceding it and following it: the eye of a hurricane in which the language itself was tumbling and turning.[6]

In one sense, the most significant event for poetry in America's last *fin* of *siècle* was the posthumous, and *sense*ored, first publication of Emily Dickinson's poems in 1890, a publication greeted with hostile reviews despite the editors' efforts to remove what might offend the ears of an Island-oriented audience. Dickinson achieved a greater textual eccentricity and self-sufficiency than any other nineteenth-century American writer; her work looked and sounded least like standard English, so it is altogether appropriate that it should emerge at a time of great transition for the language.[7]

---

6. In reimaging the relation of "our" fin de siècle with "theirs", I'm thinking here of American poets born between the mid-1830s and the mid-1850s or poetry that emerged most fully in the eighties and nineties. An interesting exception is Stephen Crane (1871–1900), who wrote poetry that in its directness of image marks an important break with English verse. The most popular poet of this period was Eugene Field (1850–1895).

7. "She built a new poetic form from her fractured sense of being eternally on intellectual borders, where confident masculine voices buzzed an alluring and inaccessible discourse, backward through history into aboriginal anagogy. Pulling pieces of geometry, geology, alchemy, philosophy . . . and philology from alien territory, a 'sheltered' woman audaciously invented a new grammar grounded in humility and hesitation. HESITATE from the Latin meaning to stick. Stammer. To hold back in doubt, have difficulty speaking. '*He* may pause but *he* must not hesitate'—*Ruskin*. Hesitation circled back and surrounded everyone in that confident age of aggressive industrial expansion and brutal Empire building. Hesitation and Separation. The Civil War split America in two. *He* might pause, *She* hesitated. Sexual, racial, and geographic separation are at the heart of Definition. Tragic and eternal dichotomy— if we concern ourselves with the deepest Reality . . . The omnivorous gatherer was equally able to reject. To find affirmation in renunciation and to be (herself) without. Outside authority, eccentric and unique . . . What is the communal vision of

If Dickinson can be said to have fashioned an idiolect, her work's publication in 1890 is also consonant with the liveliest poetic practice of the period, one quite distinct from Island-oriented literature: dialect writing. While English was at this time absorbing the effects of the language of new European immigrants, it had had plenty of time to be transformed by the cultural traditions, as they manifested themselves in English, of blacks and native "Americans", as well as the unique speech and writing patterns of these groups and of rural whites. Jerome Rothenberg and George Quasha, in their anthology *America: A Prophecy,* document poems of two writers of the period who use a radically nonstandard syntax and vocabulary based in part on regional dialect—Lafcadio Hearn's collage of New Orleans street cries that move from sound-associational English ("Cha-ah-ahr-coal!") to French ("Charbon! Du charbon, Madame!") and Jacob Carpenter's North Carolina obituaries ("he wars farmer and made brandy / and never had Drunker in family"). Obviously these examples only scratch the surface of such material.

Given this context, the black dialect poetry of Paul Dunbar seems all the more remarkable and speaks directly and significantly to a number of current preoccupations of English-language poetry. In Dunbar's dialect poetry, the sensuous pleasure in the sounds of the spoken language of a community is used to express the pleasures of the shared communions of a people poor in material possessions only. His local popularity among presumably nonliterary audiences attests to this poetry's specific origins in time and place; the aesthetic failure of his nondialect poetry is an equal mark of the source of his work's power. Dunbar's dialect poems achieve a perfect symmetry of form and content, extolling the paradise in the daily—words' dominion, not verbal tokens—over and above the postponed utopia of Redemption Day; as in "When De Co'n Pone's Hot" he compares the prayers, sermons, and songs of the church service unfavorably to the epiphany,

---

poetry if you are curved, odd, indefinite, irregular, feminine. I go in disguise. Soul under stress, thread of connection broken, fusion of love and knowledge broken, visionary energy lost, Dickinson means this to be an ugly verse. First I find myself a Slave, next I understand my slavery, finally I re-discover myself at liberty inside the confines of known necessity." Susan Howe, *My Emily Dickinson* (Berkeley: North Atlantic Books, 1985), pp. 21–22, 28, 117–118. Howe's discussion of "sovereignty" (pp. 79ff) is related to my discussion of imperial Island standards.

not in a symbolic English hearth, but in the particular smell of daily bread:

> But dem wu'ds so sweetly murmured
> Seem to tech de softes' spot
> When my mammy says de blessin'
> An' de co'n pone's hot.[8]

"Wu'ds tech" in sound's ascent; Island secession is complete and the here (spelled ear) and now (spelled *now*) of this world (pronounced "worl"/whirl) begins:

> Why won't folks gin up dey planin',
> An' jes' be content to know
> Dat dey's gitten' all dat's fu' dem
> In de days dat come an' go?
> Why won't folks quit movin' forward?
> Ain't hit bettah jes' to stan' . . .[9]

Of course, one hundred years ago was also the time that the first of the last great American Island-oriented writers, Henry James, was in his bloom, transforming by that most exquisite of implosions all that Island English had meant or would ever mean again, so that the syntax of his work is an elegy for all that could no longer be, a plunging deep into an infinite regress of nuance, shades of gloss and glosses of shade, till in the last and greatest works all contact with that daily island life transubstantiated into crystallized reflections: the sublime artifice of infinite pains so like in excess, and unlike in temper, his contemporary Swinburne (the one so far inside Island English as

---

8. *Complete Poems of Paul Laurence Dunbar* (New York: Dodd, Mead, 1913), p. 57. Dunbar was born in 1872; his poems began appearing regularly in 1895; he died in 1906.

9. Dunbar, "Foolin Wid De Seasons", p. 139. The reference here is to the "almanac" farmer who is always thinking of the next season and never living in the present one. Read politically, this poem may seem profoundly conservative, but that would be to misread its pointedly political rejection of utilitarian displacement as ameliorative reconciliation.

to have bored a black hole in it, the other oscillating between that hole and the other side).

Historical periodicity is like a viper sucking up a living context into its dry, timeless air. What relations have we to fragments of a past from which we are disconnected, without living root of transmission—foreign, lost? The violence of every generalization crushes the hopes for a democracy of thoughts: each paradigm excludes or forgets in disproportion to what it may elucidate. The nineteenth century never ended, or each day, as today, is its middle, end, beginning. A portion of the best is always lost, that which seems obscure or is obscured: those forgotten in their fleeting fame or total want of it; or that which never came into material existence. "In the case of painting, we pay for the failures," Viktor Shklovsky has written. "A Rubens or a Rembrandt is so expensive, not because it took so long to paint but because its value covers the cost of the failures of many painters"—failures of recognition as well as art.[10] There is no spirit of an age but incommensurable coexisting spirits; looking back, some may give us greater pause because they serve our purposes, because they tell something of where we are heading, more perhaps than where we have been: the mirror of 1886 is 2085. I wonder when I hear *fin de siècle* if it could mean the end of centuries not in an apocalypse but in a slow dissolve of utilitarian ideas of sequence. Artists are not before their time, precursors, but their time is inadequately described by the soap opera of the causal narrative closure of both formalist and traditional historical literary criticism. The past is our living present: we breathe it with our ears and exhale it through our eyes. The trial and death of Oscar Wilde is not only an event of the final years of the last century but hangs over us now like Damocles' sword.

Wilde incited riot in the house of English Literature. A gay Irish poet, he put on the manners of official English culture as a means of blasting away at its false pieties, its self-serving Enlightenment rationality and its Victorian sexuality. "The first duty in life is to be as artificial as possible," he wrote.[11] For his transgressions, more spiritual

10. Viktor Shklovsky, *Mayakovsky and His Circle*, tr. Lily Feiler (New York: Dodd, Mead, 1972), p. 144.
11. "Phrases and Philosophies for the Uses of the Young" (1884), *The Artist as Critic: Critical Writings of Oscar Wilde*, ed. Richard Ellmann (New York: Random

and ideological than sexual in the narrowest sense, we witness like a recurring nightmare the imperial fist of English society smashing yet another in a succession of rebel poets. Certainly he was not alone among poets of his time in his Mental Fight.—I have a vision of the Three Horsemen of England's eighties and nineties returning to lead a *fin de* millennium parade of "Nowhere" down Chicago's Lake Shore Drive: William Morris, brandishing a handcarved sword with swirls instead of edges; Oscar Wilde, bejeweled with a crown of gilded thorns; and Algernon Swinburne, reclining in a small horsecart sipping pure spirits from a crystal flask. Lewis Carroll is writing the proclamation, and out of the shadows Gerard Manley Hopkins intones an ecstatic benediction. Henry James covers the event for the BBC via a satellite video feed to his Boston suite.

The contemporaneity and relevance of Wilde, Swinburne, and Morris, as of Dunbar, increase as we head toward 2001. "What lies before me is my past," Wilde writes in *De Profundis;* the crucial word here is *lies.*[12] Wilde was a master antipositivist, and his *Decay of Lying* is a necessary and not outdated antidote to the emotional realism and ideologically repressed earnestness that makes up the bulk of today's magazine verse. Wilde's credo was that life imitates art, not the other way around. Swinburne, in his overdetermined assonance and alliteration, his dazzling and idle formal pyrotechnics, and Baudelairean sense of subject, literally brought English Island poetry to the end of the line. The artificiality that American poetry achieved, in part reactively, Swinburne's poetry realized by endogenous means, as an indwelling potential not in imperial Island English but in the traditions of the literature of the English people. Both Wilde and Swinburne spoke of the primacy of sound, a sound that overpowers and transforms sense. Their commitment to artifice—not easily understood by the motto "art for art's sake"—reflected the idea of a language that does not depict a separate external reality: art produces continually new Reals. Wilde said he wanted to create what is not, rather than represent what is. For Swinburne, the flow and rhythm of words

---

House, 1969), p. 433. Wilde (1854–1900) was sentenced to two years' hard labor in 1895 for "commiting acts of gross indecency with other male persons"; he never recovered from the effects of the imprisonment and other public humiliations.

12. "De Profundis" (1897), in *The Portable Oscar Wilde,* ed. Richard Aldington (New York: Viking, 1946), p. 564. The citation from Wilde in the next paragraph is from the same page.

eclipsed any fixed picture, like waves rolling over a sandcastle, dissolving and absorbing all images in the ebb and flow of an oceanic language constantly devouring the present into its eternal pastness; the living presences of the past existing not as allusion but as mythos. It is no wonder that Swinburne champions Blake and Whitman in the same breath.

The utopian impulses in Wilde and Swinburne are more explicitly narrated by Morris, who took the transformation of art and poetry to be a central part of the struggle for socialism. All three made art that was not in the service of morality or religion, but by its form realized the innate potentials of human beings. "We call ours a utilitarian age, and we do not know the uses of any single thing," said Wilde. And Swinburne: "The pure artist never asserts; he suggests and therefore his meaning is totally lost upon moralists and sciolists—is indeed irreparably wasted upon the run of men who cannot work out suggestions."[13]

The pleasure of life *is* art, according to Morris; and the greatest enemy of art is the system of Commerce and Fashion that produces both unnecessary things and a slavish compulsion to possess them. *Work* for art's sake was his sense; the pleasure in daily work that he imagined was the experience of the artisans who collectively created Europe's medieval architectural legacy. These views lead Morris, variously, to the romantic medievalism of *The Earthly Paradise;* to his commitment to handcraft and his polemical critique of the deadly drabness of nineteenth-century English industrial design and architecture; to revolutionary socialism; and, significantly, to a militant environmentalism in many ways similar to our present-day ecology movement and the program of Germany's Greens. For Morris, leisure and idleness, as well as pleasure, were central components of any civilization worthy of the name. His insistence that there must always be "*waste* places and wilds in it"[14] suggests most acutely the originality of his position and his rejection of more utilitarian forms of social progress. Morris' refrain in *The Earthly Paradise,* "the idle

---

13. Algernon Charles Swinburne, *William Blake: A Critical Essay,* (1868; reprint New York: Benjamin Bloom, 1986), p. 103. Swinburne, who was born in 1839, died in 1909.

14. "Art and Socialism" (1884), in *Political Writings of William Morris,* ed. A. L. Morton (New York: International Publishers, 1973), p. 128; italics added. Morris' dates are 1834–1896.

singer of an empty day", has been taken as oddly inappropriate for so prolific an artist. But idleness and emptiness are crucial notions for Morris, and his immensely popular early poetry was meant to serve as a respite from the toil of alienated labor; both the reading and the writing of poetry were to be an activity of pleasure ("joyance" is Morris' word, a Coleridgean term that would do nicely to translate Barthes's *jouissance*). Indeed, the poems become a means of transport to another world not inevitably correlated to this one: "a shadowy isle of bliss / Midmost the beating of the steely sea, / Where tossed about all hearts of men must be."[15]

Morris vowed early to conduct a "Crusade and Holy Warfare against the age"; for all their irreconcilable differences, Swinburne and Wilde joined in this crusade. Of the three, Morris surely was the deepest pragmatic political thinker; Wilde's strength was his aesthetics, although the political imagination of "Soul under Socialism" should not be underestimated; Swinburne had the most resonant ear for poetry, although his *Blake* is an important political and aesthetic tract.

The powerful antipositivist critique of these writers is still of urgent topicality: Swinburne's aestheticism and Wilde's artificiality, especially when considered in the light of Mallarmean "Symbolist" indefiniteness, prove a useful alternative both to Thomas Eliot's reassertion of an imperial Island English yardstick—the objective correlative as well as the "tradition"—and to the Imagist reductivism of Pound's "direct treatment of the 'thing'" and "use absolutely no word that does not contribute" (statements that dramatically contradict Pound's actual poetic practice and conceal his important debt to Swinburne).[16] On the one hand, much of the most touted and least interesting verse of our century follows even more reductivist High Antimodernist (also known as New Critical) precepts (following the most conservative doctrines, but not the more verbally adventurous practices of Pound, Eliot, or Williams). Compare Wilde's Nietzschean ambivalence to the staid and staged irony of neoconventionalist parasymbolism from Lowell to Larkin; compare Swinburne's sonorous paradise of excess to the linguistically anemic contemporary plain

15. Both this citation and the one immediately preceding are from the "Envoi" to *The Earthly Paradise* (1870).

16. Ezra Pound, "A Retrospect", in *The Poetics of the New American Poetry*, ed. Donald Allen and Warren Tallman (New York: Grove Press, 1973), p. 42.

style. On the other hand, much of the most formally adventurous, sonically sublime, and politically exemplary poetry of our century has rejected imperial measures and pursued the possibilities inherent in a non-Island-oriented English-language writing.

Writing within an Island context, Swinburne, a Northumbrian, used prosodically formal means to rupture his language from an imperial standard for clarity of message: "Only the great masters of style succeed in being obscure," as Wilde puts it.[17] When I say he brought English Island poetry to the end of the line, I mean that after Swinburne the realization of the wordness of language would be more radically achieved by abandoning the conventional use of meter. In its extreme self-containment through refraction of Island literature from Chaucer to the Rossettis and back further to the classical grounds of that literature, Swinburne's writing detonates the "shut-inness" and "complete quality of completeness" that Stein describes:

> English literature then had a need to be what it had become. Browning Swinburne Meredith were no longer able to go on, they had come where they had come, because although island daily living was still island daily living every one could know that this was not what it was to be and if it was not to be this with all the outside belonging to it what was it to be. They Swinburne Browning and Meredith were giving the last extension . . . And so, this is the thing to know, American literature was ready to go on, because where English literature had ceased to be because it had no further to go, American literature had always had it as the way to go.[18]

Now, as I've said, what Stein is calling American literature should, I think, be called English-language literature, because there is New Zealand and Canada and Australia and because there are many different Americas. The Island English verse tradition is only one of many streams feeding non-Island English poetry, and for many contemporary poets it has little or no importance, and need have none. But then even Island English is a misnomer since there is no one imperial standard for all the English-speaking people of England, with

17. *Critical Writings of Oscar Wilde*, p. 434.
18. Stein, *Look at Me Now Here I Am*, pp. 56–57.

its dozens of dialects, much less for all of Britain and Ireland. (By *imperial* I mean a single, imposed standard for correctness of speaking or writing or thinking or knowing; I mean a unitary cultural canon, an artifice denying its artificiality.) "I do not want art for a few, any more than education for a few, or freedom for a few", Morris said.[19] He believed that for art not to perish utterly it must cross over "a river of fire", making a decisive break with imperialist politics as well as with imperial language. And this was not, he said, something only for *other* countries, quoting Goethe's response to a man who said he was going to America to begin life again: "Here is America, or nowhere".[20] So even in the so-called British Isles the most imaginative poetries of this century, to my view, have staged a series of secessions from imperial English. Think of Bunting's Northumbrian or Mac-Diarmid's Scots; think of the escalating series of Irish secessions from Yeats's founding of the Irish Literary Society in 1891 and publishing *The Celtic Twilight* in 1893; think of Woolf's revealing of an inside of Island English's imaginary that previously had been mostly hidden. So that today the poetry of the most interesting English poets is Island poetry in the sense of being local and specific, decisively breaking from an English that is meant as an empire's Standard; and the variety and eccentricity and vitality in British poetry at this time is enormous—with the best of it almost completely excluded from the official organs of Island literary culture.

For the present, I value eccentricity in poetry for its ability to rekindle writing and thinking, for the possibility of sounding an alternative to the drab conformist fashion-minded thinking that blights our mental landscape full as much as the nineteenth-century mills poxed the English countryside. Not eccentricity as opposed to

19. "The Lesser Arts" (1877), in *Political Writings of William Morris,* p. 54. "No, rather than art should live this poor thin life among a few exceptional men, despising those beneath them for an ignorance for which they themselves are responsible, for a brutality that they will not struggle with—rather than this, I would that the world should sweep away all art for awhile . . . rather than the wheat should rot in the miser's granary, I would that the earth had it, that it might yet have a chance to quicken in the dark." Morris hopes that life might become simpler; but, as Raymond Williams has observed, the sort of social transformation imagined by Morris would in fact result in *greater* complexity: this suggests the limits of Morris' thinking. "That art will make our streets as beautiful as the weeds, as elevating as the mountain-sides: it will be a pleasure and a rest, and not a weight upon the spirits to come from the open country into a town; every man's house will be fair and decent, soothing to his mind and helpful to his work." (p. 55).

20. *Political Writings of William Morris,* pp. 131–132.

centrism—there is no center, only the hegemony of homogenizing processes—but particularity and peculiarity of place and time and person acknowledged as such. The alternative to "art for a few" is not one art for all, which tends to degrade and level as it comes under the sway of commercial incentives—but many arts, many poetries. The possibly good intentions of "one art for all"—and the related agendas of clarity, plainness, accessibility—unfortunately tend to merge with the oligarchic marketing imperatives of modern telecommunications, "Keep your message simple and repeat it many times"— a formula that dominates not only American commercial advertising but also political and aesthetic discourse. (The "simple message" is the visible effect of a series of hidden agendas—call them ideologies— that remain obscured.) The cultural segmentation, complexity, and communicative refractoriness of much contemporary poetry, which excludes it from major-media dissemination, are in fact the kernels of its intertwined political and aesthetic value.

English is now one of the few global languages, in itself a lingua franca: this means that many different grammars and vocabularies are merged into constantly newly forming English tongues. In the face of this plethora, one centrist response has been to disparage a "poetry glut", while another has been to lament poetry's lack of significant social impact. Both these views are based on imperial standards that fail to comprehend that different English-language poetries are valuable to different groups or individuals; that the inability to evaluate overall poetic activity because of its amount or its diversity is a positive development; that more people read and write English-language poetry than ever before, except that they don't read and write a common poetry. Morris' contribution, for example, is not as one of the Immortal English Poets but as a monumental model for this new situation. Indeed, he "never made great claims for his own poetry, treating it as 'a mere matter of craftmanship.' 'If a chap can't compose an epic poem while he is weaving a tapestry,' said Morris, 'he had better shut up; he'll never do any good at all.'"[21]

By emphasizing eccentricity, I want to acknowledge the significance of group-identified poetries (ethnic, racial, linguistic, social, class, sexual, regional) in shattering the neoconventionalist ideal of fashioning by *masterly* artifice a neutral standard English, a common voice

21. William Morris, *News from Nowhere and Selected Writings,* ed. Asa Briggs (New York: Penguin, 1984), p. 19.

for all to speak (or, getting in deeper, a common voice for all mankind). All poetry is geographical and ethnic and sexual as much as historical, period-bound: these limits are any poetry's horizons. *A period is a sentence.* But groups are composed of subgroups, which are composed of fractionate differences that can be recombined into other formations incommensurable with the first. In principle, fashioning the common voice of a region or group is as problematic as fashioning the common voice of a nation or language, which, in turn, is as precarious as fashioning the common voice of an individual. In practice, the poetic force of expressing what has been repressed or simply unexpressed—whether individual or collective—has been considerable. Yet there is also the necessity of going beyond the Romantic idea of self and the Romantic idea of the spirit of a nation or group (volksgeist) or of a period (zeitgeist), a necessity for a poetry that does not organize itself around a dominant subject, whether that be understood as a self or a collectivity or a theme—writing, that is, that pushes the limits of what can be identified, that not only reproduces difference but invents it, spawning nomadic syntaxes of desire and excess that defy genre (birth, race, class) in order to relocate it.[22]

All these multifoliate creations of language chime—some would say clang—at once; so that there *is* an acentric locus to English-language poetry: the negative totalization of many separate chords, the better heard the more distinct each strain. Difference is not isolating, but the material ground of exchange; though perhaps it is a dream to hope, in these times, that the pleasurable labor of producing and discerning difference can go beyond the double bind of group identification/individual expression and find idle respite in blooming contrariety—the sonic shift from *KA* to *BOOP* in which the infinite finitude of sound and sensation swells.

---

22. Such a poetry of immanence is not waiting to be validated by a future that is, at best, inscrutable and, at worst, terminal. The loss of certainty of the future quickens the moment, heightens the torsions and tensions, and firms the resolve that whatever is to be published needs to be published now, that today's readers, however few, are the only ones we can count on. But negative millennialism quickly falls into cliché, despite the fact that ours is the product of sober empirical deduction, not religious projection. On the contrary, the religious fanaticism of our time is belief in a future, the pervasive orderliness by which we continue, day by day, to cling to comforts and distractions, only occasionally peeking into voids.

Pounding Fascism
(Appropriating Ideologies—Mystification, Aestheticization, and Authority in Pound's Poetic Practice)

> *I don't know how humanity stands it*
> *with a painted paradise at the end of it*
> *without a painted paradise at the end of it*
> —Pound, canto 74

The virulent antisemitism and fascism that are not only at the core of Ezra Pound's political beliefs but also taint his poetry and poetics can be excused, moderated, or rationalized only at the cost of all such special pleading: willed ignorance allowing for a continuing reign of totalitarianism masking as authority, racism posing as knowledge, and elitism claiming the prerogatives of culture. The ingenuity of exceptions made for friends—aesthetic fellow travelers or political allies—leads readily to the global hypocrisy of, for instance, the official U.S. policy of distinguishing between the benign authoritarianism of Pinochet's Chile and the malignant totalitarianism of Jaruzelski's Poland.

But perhaps the greatest danger in an account of Pound's fascism is not that he will be given an unearned pardon by literary history but that his guilt is bracketed off from our own. For Pound's fascism is all too easily censured, as by slap on hand, while the fascist ideas that infect his poetry and poetics seep unnamed into the orthodox cultural theory and criticism of this society.

Pound's fascism, far from hindering the canonization of his poetry by American literary culture, has been a major factor in its acceptance. Stripped of its obnoxious overtness, Pound's fascism becomes the stern but fatherly voice of authority, measuring by the Pound standard the absolute worth of the cultural production of all the societies of earth, the ultimate Core Curriculum. Without its righteously Eurocentric and imperiously authoritative undercurrent, the formal innovations of Pound's poetry would have contributed to its marginalization. This is evident from the relative marginalization of much of the formally innovative poetry of, sic, "The Pound Era". Pound's status, far from being jeopardized by his political ideas, is enhanced by them.

I do not, however, equate Pound's politics with Pound's poetry. *The Cantos* is in many ways radically (radially) at odds with the tenets of his fascist ideals. In this sense, Pound has systematically misinterpreted the nature of his own literary production; refused, that is, to recognize in it the process he vilified as usury and Jewishness. This blindness to the meaning of his work, to how in significant ways it represented what he claimed to revile most, contributed not only to the rabidness of his dogmatism but also to the heights of magnificent self-deception and elegiac confusion that is *The Cantos* at its best.

There is a price to be paid for poetry; its practice can poison as fatally as sniffing glue or inhaling coal dust. Madame Curie did not know about the lethal aftereffects of invisible radiation when she conducted her experiments; we know from her experience that there are risks that cannot be prevented until after the first victims have made the effects visible. Is cultural megalomania a symptom of being overwhelmed by the incommensurable and intractable autonomy of fragments, that will not submit to a unitary measure, hierarchically predetermined, but which insist on making their own time and space, their own poem: never yielding to the totalizing of the autocratic arbitration of their place but allowing their own whole to come into being, not Coherence on the Pound standard, but a coherence of the displaced—disseminated and desecrated—making a home where it is to be found, where it occurs?

Pound, or part of him, wished to control the valuation of the materials he appropriated by arranging them in such a way that an immanent or "natural" order would be brought into being. As Pound seems to acknowledge in the final movements of the (for the moment) standard version of the poem, *The Cantos* never jells in this way. For Pound this was a measure, no matter how ambivalent he may have been about the evaluation, of the failure of *The Cantos*. In contrast, the success of *The Cantos* is that its coherence is of a kind totally different than Pound desired or could—in his more rigid moments—accept. For the coherence of the "hyperspace" of Pound's modernist collage is not a predetermined Truth of a pancultural

elitism but a product of a compositionally decentered multicultural-
ism.

Pound's great achievement was to create a work using ideological
swatches from many social and historical sectors of his own society
and an immense variety of other cultures. This complex, polyvocal
textuality was the result of his search—his unrequited desire for—
deeper truths than could be revealed by more monadically organized
poems operating with a single voice and a single perspective. But
Pound's ideas about what mediated these different materials are often
at odds with how these types of textual practices actually work in
The Cantos.

Pound's fascist ideology insists on the author's having an extralit-
erary point of "special knowledge" that creates a phallic order (these
are Pound's terms) over the female chaos of conflicting ideological
material. As Robert Casillo points out in his study of Pound's anti-
semitism, Pound contrasts the phallocentric/logocentric unswerving
pivot (citing Wang in canto 97: "man's phallic heart is from heaven /
a clear spring of rightness") with the castrated and nomadic Jew.[1]
Jews are the purveyors of fragmentation and therefore the dissolution
of fixed hierarchical cultural values (the Jews, says Pound on the
radio, want to "blot out the classics, blot out the record").[2] Again,
Jews, as usurers and in league with the Commies, represent "an
indistinct, rootless, destructive mass" eroding the agrarian ideal of
homestead, of nature and private property (values Pound equates with
order, clarity, *telos*).[3]

For Pound, Jews "as 'falsification incarnate' [aim] to distort, mis-
represent, and conceal language, to 'castrate' literature, origins, and
tradition [and] are largely responsible for introducing abstraction,
obscurity, verbiage, equivocation, ambiguity, and allegory into lan-
guage."[4] As Casillo goes on to note, Pound charges that the Kabbal-
istic Jews introduced allegorical interpretation into the West and so
distracted men—this is Pound speaking—"from the plain sense of the

---

1. Robert Casillo, "Anti-Semitism, Castration, and Usury in Ezra Pound", *Criti-
cism* 25:3 (1983), 239–265. Casillo quotes canto 97 on pp. 242 and 250.
2. Ibid., p. 254, quoting from *Ezra Pound Speaking: Radio Speeches of World
War II*, ed. Leonard W. Doob (Westport, Conn.: Greenwood Press, 1978), p. 283.
3. Ibid., p. 251; citing *Radio Speeches*, p. 184.
4. Ibid., p. 254.

word, of the sentence".[5] As Casillo concludes, "Pound turned to
Fascism because he shares not only its deep fear of indeterminacy"—
of the vague, inchoate, and incommensurable, of all that is mysterious
or ambiguous or unknown—"but also its central desire, which is to
banish the indeterminate from social life . . . And, as in Fascism, in
Pound's work the ultimate sign of such fearful [indefiniteness] is the
Jew."[6]

What grotesque views for someone whose work is filled with in-
determinacy, fragmentation, abstraction, obscurity, verbiage, equiv-
ocation, ambiguity, allegory; who has made the highest art of remov-
ing ideologies from their origins and creating for them a nomadic
economy whose roots are neither in the land nor in property but
rather in the abstraction of aestheticization and the irresolution of
the jarring harmonies of incommensurable sounds. As Richard Sie-
burth has noted, the ultimate irony of *The Cantos* is that all its
irreconcilable elements can be reconciled only in the abstract, by the
authority of the author, *on credit*.[7] Indeed, the real economy of *The
Cantos* is the one Pound constantly struggled to repress and to lay
bare: the economy of reader and writer and book; the economy of
language not as Logos but as exchange.[8] Overall, *The Cantos*, despite
Pound's ravings within it, represents less the crude economism of
Pound's fascism, "with a painted paradise at the end of it", than the
utopian chaos of a negative dialectic, "without a painted paradise at
the end of it".

The technology of Pound's textual practice created its own logic of
desire, which Pound could not derail without giving up an achieve-
ment beyond the comprehension of his small-minded, penurious po-

5. Ibid., p. 264n46; citing *Radio Speeches*, p. 284.
6. Robert Casillo, *The Geneology of Demons: Anti-Semitism, Fascism, and the
Myths of Ezra Pound* (Evanston: Northwestern University Press, 1988), p. 324.
Casillo's earlier article is included in this book.
7. Richard Sieburth, "In Pound We Trust: The Economy of Poetry / The Poetry of
Economy", in *Critical Inquiry* 14:1 (1987). Sieburth's cogent essay integrates
Pound's economic ideas with other motifs in *The Cantos*, making a convincing case
for the spillage among the different metaphoric systems of the poem. I am indebted
to his reading at several points in my account.
8. In "The Pound Error: The Limits of Authority in the Modern Epic", which is
chap. 3 of *To Write Paradise: Style and Authority in Pound's Cantos*, Christine
Froula documents Pound's inclusion of printer's errors, misattributions, mistransla-
tions, and the like into *The Cantos*. See my "Pound and the Poetry of Today" in
Yale Review 75:4 (1986) for a supplement to my arguments here.

litical accounting system. He was obviously unsatisfied with anything but a complexly polyphonic style and as a result did not allow his ideological predilections to completely compromise the scope of his formal innovations, especially since he was still able to inject his viewpoint into the poem ad nauseam. But the power of his method—his poetic ear above his spouting mouth—was such that his rantings are absorbed into *The Cantos* not as truth but as befouled rubble, not as privileged material but as debased material, framed and denounced by those readers able to pick and choose for themselves. The center could not hold because the formal innovations of openly juxtaposing radically different materials undercut this possibility. The autonomy of the appropriated materials could not be sufficiently compromised without destroying the poetic power of the text, something Pound was unwilling to do. The authority, then, is not in Pound's opinions but in *The Cantos* itself—a situation Pound responded to not with insight or acknowledgment but with hysteria, paranoia, and megalomania. Having created a text so rich with tones that it could not be controlled in terms of traditional criteria of coherence and unity, Pound redoubled his effort to master an authority his textual practice had made impossible. The result was the claustrophobic formation of Pound's worldview. In the struggle for control, Pound's methods and materials routed Pound's authority and preconceptions; poisoned by this discontinuity, the straws he grasped for were reductivist economism and fascist racism.

Confronted with a superabundance of competing cultural practices and claims of knowledge, exacerbated by the escalation of available information about the present and past, responses can range from the humble to the arrogant. Pound's views about the authority of tradition and the poet's role as arbiter of the hierarchical value of cultural artifacts are not remarkably incongruent with the dominant, if highly contested, ideologies of American universities (the great ideas), communications media (exclusion of all but those defined as mainstream), and government ("cops of the world")—despite Pound's own belief that Mussolini did it better. But while these institutions maintain their ideologies largely by avoiding direct confrontation of disparate material, Pound propounded a highly staged alternative approach. No doubt the poetic methods of *The Cantos,* by dint of the scope of appropriation and juxtaposition, were intended to go beyond any other in establishing the supremacy of the values in which Pound

believed. But only delusions of grandeur—an arrogance beyond pro-
portion—could have convinced the poet that he was capable of mak-
ing value judgments on all the material included, and excluded, from
The Cantos. Yet it is Pound's self-deceiving arrogance, and not *The
Cantos'* refusal to be subsumed by it, that has largely secured his
stature; that is, prevented the subversiveness of *The Cantos'* meth-
odology from undermining the false authority Pound and many of
his supporters claim for his criticism and poetry. When we read *The
Cantos* with the full incredulity it demands, as a text filled with
systematic self-delusions and fragmentary illuminations, with mag-
nificent gleanings and indulgent fraudulences, we will find not the
mastertext of modernism but the wreck of Enlightenment rationalism:
scarred remnants of a struggle among the divine, the satanic, and the
ordinary—a text made beautiful by its damages and ugly by its claims
of knowledge.

So I don't wish to back away from the methods of *The Cantos;*
fascism, even in the hands of a poet so consummately resourceful as
Pound, could not, finally, claim these methods for itself. But neither
do I wish to ignore the warning implicit in these considerations: that
aesthetic processes can be used for a variety of purposes; that to
understand a work requires interrogating its motivations and social
context. It is always revealing to ask of a work: what does it serve
and how? The answer to this question, however, is not identical to
what the worker's intentions may be. A response to this challenge is
that some work may usefully evade any single social or political claim
made for or against it because of the nature of its contradictions,
surpluses, and negations. Perhaps this is the most positive thing that
might be said of Pound's poetic works.

But perhaps fascism has won the day, anyway. When Pound the
great artist is excused for his politics, fascism has won. When Pound's
politics are used to categorically discredit the compositional methods
of his poetry, fascism has won. When Pound's poetry is exalted and
his politics dismissed as largely irrelevant to his achievement, fascism
has won. When Pound's politics are condemned, his poetry acknowl-
edged or ignored in passing, but sanitized forms of his ideas prevail—
the virtue of authority, property, and the homestead ("family values"),
the sanctity of the classics, the condemnation of the nonstandard in
favor of "the plain sense of the word" and the divine right of the
West (or East) to harness and bleed the rest of the world—fascism
has won.

Pound's inflammatory rhetoric would, perhaps, be better met by calmed reason. But it is the nightmare of this tale that an exorcism cannot be initiated until the teller also has been implicated in the tale. And then a waking moment brings the solace of explanation and rationalization, but not understanding; and then this wakefulness becomes more horrible than sleep. The outrage is not without, as if one could be shielded from contamination by the balm of historical contextualization, but within oneself. It is not that it is prudent to fight fire with fire, but that one burns.

Perhaps William Carlos Williams, writing in an early issue of *Furioso,* says it better: "We all like to believe we are master minds. But what men seldom learn is that the end of poetry is the poem; I don't know a thing about the value of a poem as such or a hunk of gold as such or of a man himself as such but I do know *that.*"[9]

The questions raised by these remarks dog us into the present. The use of preexisting or source or found materials in poetry and the other arts remains an occasion for political concern. Are these materials permitted to exist in and for themselves as inviolable artifacts—or are they appropriated into a frame that invests them with specified meaning determined by the author's ideological position? Or are they debauched and defused as mere codes, empty signifiers—trophies for a postmodernist library? The double bind of an impossible universal or historical truth versus a fraudulent narrative invention is no more than the shadow play of those who do not wish to live in any here or now. It is possible for poetry to make the consciousness-constituting activity of ideology audible, to respect the origins of words and to invent new worlds for them. This project persists.

9. "A Letter" in 1:2 (1940).

Play It Again, Pac-Man

Your quarter rolls into the slot and you are tossed, suddenly and as if without warning, into a world of controllable danger. Your "man" is under attack and you must simulate his defense, lest humanity perish and another quarter is required to renew the quest.

Drop in, turn on, tune out.

The theories of video games abound: poststructuralist, neomarxian, psychoanalytic, and puritanical interpretations are on hand to guide us on our journey through the conceptual mazes spawned by the phenomenon. Acting out male aggression. A return, for adolescent boys, to the site of mom's body. Technological utopia. As American as autoeroticism. The best introduction to computer programming. No more than an occasion for loitering in seedy arcades. A new mind-obliterating technodrug. Marvelous exercise of hand-eye coordination. Corrupter of youth. Capital entertainment for the whole family. Not since the advent of TV has an entertainment medium been subjected to such wildly ambivalent reactions or such skyrocketing sales.

If the Depression dream was a chicken in every pot, today's middle-class adolescent's dream is a video game in every TV.

More and faster: better graphics and faster action, so fast you transcend the barriers of gravity, so vivid it's realer than real.

A surprising amount of the literature on video games has concerned the social context of the games: arcade culture, troubled youth, vocational training for tomorrow's *Top Gun*. So much so that these scenarios seem to have become a part of video-game culture: Nerdy kid who can't get out a full sentence and whose social skills resemble Godzilla's is the star of the arcade; as taciturn as a Gary Cooper sheriff, he gets the job done without designer sweaters or the girl.

In the Saturday Night Fever of Computer Wizardry, achievement with your joy stick is the only thing that counts; success is solitary, objectively measured, undeniable.

Or, say, a 1980s Horatio Alger: A failure at school, marginal drug experimenter, hanging out on the wrong side of the tracks with a no-future bunch of kids, develops a $30-a-day video-game habit, can't unplug from the machine without the lights going out in his head.

Haunts the arcade till all hours, till the cops come in their beeping cruisers, bounding into the mall like the beeping spaceships on the video screen, and start to check IDs, seems some parents complained they don't know where Johnny is and it's pushing two. Cut to: young man in chalk-striped suit, vice-prez for software devel. of Data Futurians Inc. of Electronic Valley, California; pulling down fifty thou in his third year after dropping out of college. (Though the downside sequel has him, at thirty, working till two every morning, divorced, personal life not accessible at this time, waiting for new data to be loaded, trouble reading disk drive.)

Like the story boards of the games, the narratives that surround video games seem to promise a very American ending: redemption through the technology of perseverance and the perseverance of technology. Salvation from social degeneracy (alien menace) comes in the form of squeaky-clean high tech (no moving parts, no grease). Turns out, no big surprise, that the Alien who keeps coming at you in these games is none other than Ourselves, split off and on the war path.

The combination of low culture and high technology is one of the most fascinating social features of the video-game phenomenon. Computers were invented as superdrones to do tasks no human in her or his right mind (much less left brain) would have the patience, or the perseverance, to manage. Enter multitask electronic calculators that would work out obsessively repetitive calculations involving billions of individual operations, calculations that if you had to do by hand would take you centuries to finish, assuming you never stopped for a Coke or a quick game of Pac-Man. Now our robot drones, the ones designed to take all the boring jobs, become the instrument for libidinal extravaganzas devoid of any socially productive component. Video games are computers neutered of purpose, liberated from functionality. The idea is intoxicating; like playing with the help on their night off, except the leisure industry begins to outstrip the labors of the day as video games become the main interface between John Q. and Beth B. Public and the computer.

Instruments of labor removed from workaday tasks, set free to roam the unconscious, dark spaces of the Imaginary—dragons and assault asteroids, dreadful losses and miraculous reincarnations.

If a typewriter could talk, it probably would have very little to say; our automatic washers are probably not hiding secret dream machines deep inside their drums.

But these microchips really blow you away.

Uh, err, um, oh. TILT!

Okay, then, let's slow down and unpack these equations one by one, or else this will begin to resemble the assault on our ability to track that seems so much at the heart of the tease of the games themselves.

Spending Time or Killing It?

The arcade games are designed, in part, to convince players to part, and keep parting, with their quarters. This part of the action feels like slot-machine gambling, with the obvious difference that there is no cash payoff, only more time on line. Staying plugged in, more time to play, is the fix. The arcade games are all about buying time and the possibility of extending the nominal, intensely atomized, 30-second (or so) minimum play to a duration that feels, for all impractical purposes, unbounded. Clearly the dynamic of the ever-more popular home games is different enough that the two need to be considered as quite distinct social phenomena, even though they share the same medium.

Like sex, good play on an arcade video game not only earns extra plays but also extends the length of the current play, with the ultimate lure of an unlimited stretch of time in which the end bell never tolls: a freedom from the constraints of time that resembles the temporal plenitude of uninterrupted live TV (or close-circuit video monitoring) as well as the timeless, continuous present of the personal computer (PC). In contrast, a film ticket or video rental buys you just 90 or 120 minutes of "media", no extensions (as opposed to reruns) possible. Meanwhile, the home video game, by allowing longer play with greater skills, simulates the temporal economy of the arcade product while drastically blunting the threat of closure, since on the home version it costs nothing to replay.

Video games create an artificial economy of scarcity in a medium characterized by plenitude. In one of the most popular genres, you desperately fight to prolong your staying power, which is threatened by alien objects you must shoot down. There's no intrinsic reason that the threat of premature closure should drive so many of these games; for example, if your quarter always bought two minutes of play, the effect of artificial scarcity would largely disappear. Is this

desire to postpone closure a particular male drive, suggesting a pe-
culiarly male fear? It may be that the emphasis on the overt aggression
of a number of the games distracts from seeing other dynamics in-
herent in the formats.

Another dynamic of the arcade games is the ubiquitous emphasis
on scoring. These games are not open-ended; you try not only to
accumulate the most points in order to extend play and win bonus
games but also to compete with the machine's lifetime memory of
best-ever scores. If achievement-directed scoring suggests sex as op-
posed to love, games more than play, then it seems relevant to consider
this a central part of the appeal of video games.

An economy of scarcity suggests goal-oriented behavior: the desire
for accumulation; this is what Georges Bataille has dubbed a "re-
stricted" economy, in contrast to an unrestricted or "general" econ-
omy, which involves exchange or loss or waste or discharge. The drive
to accumulate capital and commodities is the classic sign of a re-
stricted economy. Potlatch (the festive exchange of gifts) or other
rituals or carnivals of waste ("A hellava wedding!", "Boy, what a bar
mitzvah!") suggest a general economy.

While the dominant formats and genres of video games seem to
involve a restricted economy, the social context of the games seems
to suggest features of an unrestricted economy. For while the games
often mime the purposive behavior of accumulation/acquisition, they
are played out in a context that stigmatizes them as wastes of time,
purposeless, idle, even degenerate.

These considerations link up video games with those other games,
in our own and other cultures, whose social function is to celebrate
waste, abandon, excess; though the carnival or orgiastic rite is clearly
something that is repressed in a society, like ours, where the puritan
ethic stills hold powerful sway. What redeems many sports from being
conceived as carnivals of waste is the emphasis on athletics (*improve-
ment* of the body) and the forging of team or group or community
spirit (*building* a community, learning *fair* play)—two compensatory
features conspicuously absent from solitary, suggestively antiphysical
video gaming.

In a society where the desire for general economy is routinely
sublimated into utilitarian behaviors, the lure of video games has to
be understood as, in part, related to their sheer unproductivity. Put
more simply, our unrestricted play is constantly being channeled into

goal-directed games; how appealing then to find a game whose essence seems to be totally useless play. Yet it would be a mistake to think of the erotic as wed to de-creative flows rather than to pro-creative formations: both are in play, at work. Thus the synthesis of play and games that characterizes most available video games addresses the conflictual nature of our responses to eros and labor, play and work.

So what's really being shot down or gobbled up in so many of the popular games? Maybe the death wish played out is not a simulation at all; maybe it's time that's being killed or absorbed—real-life productive time that could be better "spent" elsewhere.

If the Massage Is the Medium and the Genre Is the Message, Who's Minding the Store?

Like movies, especially in the early period, video games are primarily characterized by their genre. The earliest arcade video game, *Pong* from 1971, is an arcade version of ping-pong, and the progenitor of a series of more sophisticated games based on popular sports, including *Atari Football, Track and Field, 720°* (skateboarding), and *Pole Position* (car racing). (Perhaps driving-simulation games are a genre of their own; they certainly have the potential to be played in an open-ended way, outside any scoring: just to drive fast and take the curves.)

Quest or "fantasy" adventures, typically using a maze format, is another very popular genre, especially in the home version. Arcade versions include *Dragon's Lair, Gauntlet,* and *Thayer's Quest.* Dragons, wizards, and warriors are often featured players, and each new level of the game triggers more complex action, as the protagonist journeys toward an often magical destination at the end of a series of labyrinths. In the home versions, where there may be up to a dozen levels or scenes, the narrative can become increasingly elaborate. Still the basis of this genre is getting the protagonist through a series (or maze) of possibly fatal mishaps. In its simplest form, these games involve a single protagonist moving toward a destination, the quest being to complete the labyrinth, against all odds. So we have Pac-Man gobbling to avoid being gobbled, or *Donkey Kong*'s Mario trying to save his beloved from a family of gorillas who roll barrels at him, or, in *Berzerk,* humanoids who must destroy all the pursuing robots before reaching the end of the maze.

But the genre that most characterizes the arcade game is the war games in which successive waves of enemy projectiles must be shot down or blown up by counterprojectiles controlled by joystick, push button, or track ball. Some of the more famous of these games include *Star Wars* (a movie tie-in), *Space Invaders* (squadrons of alien craft swoop in from outer space while the player fights it out with one lone spacecraft locked in fixed position), *Asteroids* (weightless, drifting shooter, lost in space, tries to blast way through meteor showers and occasional scout ship), *Defender* (wild variety of space aliens to dodge/shoot down in spaceman rescue), *Galaxian* (invaders break ranks and take looping dives in attack), *Stratovox* (stranded astronauts on alien planet), *Centipede* (waves of insects), *Missile Command* (ICBM attack), *Robotron: 2084* (robots against humanity), *Seawolf* (naval action), *Zaxxon* (enemy-armed flying fortress), *Battlezone* (such accurately simulated tank warfare, so the press kit says, that the army used it for training), and finally the quite recent "total environment" sit-down, pilot's view war games—*Strike Avenger, Afterburner,* and *Star Fire.*

A related, newer genre is the martial arts fighting-man video games, such as *Double Dragon* and *Karate Champ,* where star wars have come home to earth in graphically violent street wars reminiscent of Bruce Lee's mystically alluring kung-fu action movies: another example of film and video-game versions of the same genre.

Discussions of video games rarely distinguish between medium and genre, probably because the limited number of genres so far developed dominates the popular conception of the phenomenon. But to imagine that video games are restricted to shoot-'em-ups, quest adventures, or sports transcriptions would be equivalent to imagining, seventy years ago, that the *Perils of Pauline* or slapstick revealed the essence of cinema.

A medium of art has traditionally been defined as the material or technical means of expression; thus paint on canvas, lithography, photography, film, and writing are different media; while detective stories, science fiction, rhymed verse, or penny dreadfuls are genres of writing. This is altogether too neat, however. Since we learn what a medium is through instances of its use in genres, the cart really comes before the horse, or anyway the medium is a sort of projected, or imaginary, constant that is actually much more socially and practically constituted than may at first be apparent.

When trying to understand the nature of different media, it's often useful to think about what characterizes one medium in a way that distinguishes it from all other media—what is its essence, what can it do that no other medium can do? Stanley Cavell has suggested that the essence of the two predominant moving-image media, TV and movies, are quite distinct. The experience of film is voyeuristic—I *view* a world ("a succession of automatic world projections") from a position of being unseen, indeed unseeable. TV, in contrast, involves not viewing but *monitoring* events as its basic mode of perception—live broadcast of news or sports events being the purest examples of this.

It's helpful to distinguish the video display monitor from TV-as-medium. Several media use the video monitor for non-TV purposes. One distinction is between *broadcast* TV and VCR technologies that, like PCs, use the television screen for non-event-monitoring functions. Video games, then, are a moving-image medium distinct from TV and film.

In distinguishing medium and genre, it becomes useful to introduce a middle term, *format*. Coin-op and home-cassette video games are one type of—hardware—format distinction I have in mind; but another—software—difference would be between, for example, scored and open-ended games, time-constrained and untimed play. Similar or different genres could then be imagined for these different formats.

The Computer Unconscious

The medium of video games is the CPU—the computer's central processing unit. Video games share this medium with PCs. Video games and PCs are different hardware formats of the same medium. Indeed, a video game is a computer that is set up (dedicated) to play only one program.

The experiential basis of the computer-as-medium is *prediction and control* of a limited set of variables. The fascination with all computer technology—gamesware or straightware—is figuring out all the permutations of a limited set of variables. This accounts for the obsessively repetitive behavior of both PC hackers and game players (which mimes the hyperrepetiveness of computer processing). As a computer-game designer remarked to me, working with computers is the only thing she can do for hours a day without noticing the time going by: a quintessentially absorbing activity.

Computers, because they are a new kind of medium, are likely to change the basic conception of what a medium is. This is not because computers are uniquely interactive—that claim, if pursued, becomes hollow quite quickly. Rather, computers provide a different definition of a medium: not a physical support but an operating environment. Perhaps it overstates the point to talk about computer consciousness, but the experiential dynamic in operating computers—whether playing games or otherwise—has yet to receive a full accounting. Yet the fascination of relating to this alien consciousness is at the heart of the experience of PCs as much as video games.

Video games are the purest manifestation of computer consciousness. Liberated from the restricted economy of purpose or function, they express the inner, nonverbal world of the computer.

What is this world like? Computers, including video games, are relatively invariant in their response to commands. This means that they will always respond in the same way to the same input but also that they demand the input to be precisely the same to produce the same results. For this reason, any interaction with computers is extremely circumscribed and affectless (which is to say, all the affect is a result of transference and projection). Computers don't respond or give forth, they process or calculate.

Computers are either on or off—you're plugged in or you're out of the loop. There is a kind of visceral click in your brain when the screen lights up with "System Ready," or your quarter triggers the switch and the game comes on line, which is unrelated to other media interactions such as watching TV, reading, or viewing a painting. Moreover—and this is crucial to the addictive attraction so many operators feel—the on-ness of the computer is alien to any sort of relation we have with people or things or nature, which are always and ever possibly present but can't be toggled on and off in anything like this peculiar way. The computer infantalizes our relation to the external, representing the structure of the infant's world as described by Piaget, where objects seem to disappear when you turn your back to them or close your eyes. For you know when you turn your PC on it will be just as you left it: nothing will have changed.

TV is for many people simulated company, freely flowing with an unlimited supply of stuff that 'fills up "real time". Computers, in contrast, seem inert and atemporal, vigilant and self-contained. It's as if all their data is simultaneously and immediately available to be called up. It's unnecessary to go through any linear or temporal sequence to find a particular bit of information. No searching on fastforward as in video, or waiting as in TV, or flipping pages as in a book: you specify and instantly access. When you are into it, time disappears, only to become visible again during "down time". Even those who can't conceive that they will care about speed become increasingly irritated at computer operations that take more than a few seconds to complete. For the nonoperator, it may seem that a ten-second wait to access data is inconsequential. But the computer junkie finds such waits an affront to the medium's utopian lure of timeless and immediate access, with no resistance, no gravitational pull—no sweat, no wait, no labor on the part of the computer: a dream of weightless instantaneousness, continuous presentness. The fix of speed for the computer or video-game player is not from the visceral thrill of fastness, as with racing cars, where the speed is physically felt. The computer ensnares with a siren's song of time stopping, ceasing to be experienced, transcended. Speed is not an end in itself, a roller-coaster ride, but a means to escape from the very sensation of speed or duration: an escape from history, waiting, embodied space.

The Anxiety of Control / The Control of Anxiety

Invariance, accuracy, and synchronicity are not qualities that generally characterize human information processing, although they are related to certain idealizations of our reasoning processes. Certainly, insofar as a person took on these characterizations, he or she would frighten: either lobotomized or paranoid. In this sense, the computer can again be seen as an alien form of consciousness; our interactions with it are unrelated to the forms of communication to which we otherwise are accustomed.

Many people using computers and video games experience a surprisingly high level of anxiety; controlled anxiety is one of the primary "hooks" into the medium.

Since so many of the video-game genres highlight paranoid fantasies, it's revealing to compare these to the paranoia and anxiety inscribed in PC operating systems. Consider the catastrophic nature of numerous PC error messages: invalid sector, allocation error, sector not found, attempted write–protect violation, disk error, divide overflow, disk not ready, invalid drive specification, data error, format failure, incompatible system size, insufficient memory, invalid parameter, general failure, bad sector, fatal error, bad data, sector not found, track bad, disk unusable, unrecoverable read error—or the ubiquitous screen prompts: "Are you sure?" and "Abort, Retry, Ignore?".

The experience of invoking and avoiding these sometimes "fatal" errors is not altogether unlike the action of a number of video games. Just consider how these standard PC operating terms suggest both scenarios and action of many video games and at the same time underscore some of the ontological features of the medium: *escape* and *exit* and *save* functions (you must escape from the dungeon, exit to the next level, and save the nuclear family), *path support* (knowing your way through the maze), data *loss*/data *recovery* (your man only disappears if he gets hit three times), *defaults* (are not in the stars but in ourselves), *erase* (liquidate, disappear, destroy, bombard, obliterate), *abandon* (ship!), *unerase* (see data recovery), delete (kill me but don't delete me), *searches* (I always think of John Ford's *The Searchers*, rather the opposite of perhaps the most offensive of video games, *Custer's Revenge*), and of course *backups* (the cavalry's on its way, or else: a new set of missiles is just a flick of the wrist away).

The pitch of computer paranoia is vividly demonstrated in the cover copy for a program designed to prevent your hard drive from *crashing*: "Why, your hard disk may be only seconds away from total failure! Be a real hero! Solve hard-disk torture and grief. You don't need to reformat. You don't need to clobber data. How much have these errors already cost you in *unrecoverable* data, time, torture, money, missing deadlines, schedule delays, poor performance, damage to business reputation, etc."

Loss preventable only by constant saving is one PC structural metaphor that seems played out in video games. Another one, though perhaps less metaphoric than phenomenological, revolves around *location*. Here it's not loss, in the sense of being blipped out, but rather being lost—dislocation—as in how to get from one place to another, or getting your bearings so that the move you make with the controls corresponds to what you see on the far-from-silver screen. Or else the intoxicating anxiety of disorientation: vertigo, slipping, falling, tumbling . . .

What's going on? The dark side of uniformity and control is an intense fear of failure, of crashing, disaster, down time. Of not getting it right, getting lost, losing control. Since the computer doesn't make mistakes, if something goes wrong it must be something in you. How many times does an operator get a new program and run it through just to see how it works, what it can do, what the glitches are, what the action is? Moving phrases around in multiple block operations may not be so different from shooting down asteroids. Deleting data on purpose or by mistake may be something like gobbling up little illuminated blips on the display screen of a game. And figuring out how a new piece of software works by making slight mistakes that the computer rejects—because there's only one optimal way to do something—may be like learning to get from a 30-second Game Over to bonus points.

If films offer voyeuristic pleasures, video games provide vicarious thrills. You're not peeking into a world in which you can't be seen, you're acting in a world by means of tokens, designated hitters, color-coded dummies, polymorphous standins. The much-admired inter-activeness of video games amounts to less than it might appear given the circumscribed control players have over their men. Joy sticks and buttons (like keyboards or mice) allow for a series of binary opera-tions; even the most complex games allow for only a highly limited amount of player control. Narrowing down the field of possible choices to a manageable few is one of the great attractions of the games, in just the way that a film's ability to narrow down the field of possible vision to a *view* is one of the main attractions of the movies.

Video games offer a narrowed range of choices in the context of a predictable field of action. Because the games are so mechanically predictable, and the context invariant, normal sorts of predictive judgments based on situational adjustments are unnecessary and in-deed a positive hindrance. The rationality of the system is what makes it so unlike everyday life and therefore such a pleasurable release from everyday experience. With a video game, if you do the same thing in the same way it will always produce the same results. Here is an arena where a person can have some real control, an illusion of power, as "things" respond to the snap of our fingers, the flick of our wrists. In a world where it is not just infantile or adolescent but all too human to feel powerless in the face of bombarding events, where the same action never seems to produce the same results because the contexts are always shifting, the uniformity of stimulus and response in video games can be exhilarating.

In the social world of our everyday lives, repetition is near impossible if often promised. You can never utter the same sentence twice not only technically, in the sense of slight acoustic variation, but semantically, in that it won't mean the same thing the second time around, won't always command the same effect. With video games, as with all computers, you can return to the site of the same problem, the same anxiety, the same blockage, and get exactly the same effect in response to the same set of actions.

In the timeless time of the video screen, where there is no future and no history, just a series of events that can be read in any sequence, we act out a tireless existential drama of "now" time. The risks are simulated, the mastery imaginary; only the compulsiveness is real.

Paranoia or Paramilitary?

Paranoia literally means being beside one's mind. Operating a computer or video game does give you the eerie sensation of being next to something like a mind, something like a mind that is doing something like responding to your control. Yet one is not in control of the computer. That's what's scary. Unlike your relation to your own body, being in it and of it, the computer only simulates a small window of operator control. The real controller of the game is hidden from us, the inaccessible system core that goes under the name of Read Only Memory (ROM), which is neither hardware that you can touch or software that you can change but "firmware." Like ideology, ROM is out of sight only to control more efficiently.

We live in a computer age in which the systems that control the formats that determine the genres of our everyday life are inaccessible to us. It's not that we can't "know" a computer's mind in some metaphysical sense; computers don't have minds. Rather, we are structurally excluded from having access to the command structure: very few know the language, and even fewer can (re)write it. And even if we could rewrite these deep structures, the systems are hardwired in such a way as to prevent tampering. In computer terms, to reformat risks losing all your data: it is something to avoid at all costs. Playing video games, like working with computers, we learn to

adapt ourselves to fixed systems of control. *All the adapting is ours.*
No wonder it's called good vocational training—but not just for Air
Force Mission Control or, more likely, the word-processing pool: the
real training is for the new regulatory environment we used to call
1984 until it came on line without an off switch. After that we didn't
call it anything.

In the machine age, a man or woman or girl or boy could fix an
engine, put in a new piston, clean a carburetor. A filmgoer could look
at a piece of film, or watch each frame being pulled by sprockets
across a beam of light at a speed that he or she could imagine
changing. A person operating a threshing machine may have known
all the basic principles, and all the parts, that made it work. But how
many of us have even the foggiest notion—beyond something about
binary coding and microchips and overpriced Japanese memory—
about how video games or computers work?

Yet isn't that so much romantic nonsense? Haven't societies always
run on secrets, hidden codes, inaccessible scriptures?

The origins of computers can be traced to several sources. But it
was military funding that allowed for the development of the first
computers. Moreover, the first video game is generally considered to
be *Spacewar,* which was developed on mainframes at MIT in the late
1950s, a byproduct of strategic research and development, and a
vastly popular "diversion" among the computer scientists working
with the new technology.

The secrecy of the controlling ROM cannot be divorced from the
Spacewar scenario that developed out of it and later inspired the
dominant arcade game genre. Computer systems, and the games that
are their product, reveal a military obsession with secrecy and control
and the related paranoia that secrets will be exposed or control lost.
Computers were designed not to solve problems per se, not to make
visually entertaining graphics, not to improve manuscript presentation
or production, not to do bookkeeping or facilitate searches through
the *Oxford English Dictionary.* Computers have their start in the
need to simulate attack/response scenarios. To predict trajectories of
rockets coming at target and the trajectory of rockets shot at these
rockets. The first computers were developed in the late 1940s to
compute bombing trajectories. When we get to the essence of the
computer consciousness, if that word can still be stomached for some-
thing so foreign to all we have known as consciousness, these origins
have an acidic sting.

Which is not to say other fantasies, or purposes, can't be spun on top of these beginnings. Programs and games may subvert the command and control nature of computers, but they can never fully transcend their disturbing, even ominous, origins.

So one more time around this maze. I've suggested that the Alien who keeps coming at us in so many of these games is ourselves, split off; that what we keep shooting down or gobbling up or obliterating is our temporality: which is to say that we have "erring" bodies, call them flesh, which is to say we live in time, even history. And that the cost of escaping history is paranoia: being beside oneself, split off (which brings us back to where we started).

But isn't the computer really the alien—the robot—that is bombarding us with its world picture (not *view*), its operating environment; that is always faster and more accurate than we can ever hope to be; and that we can only pretend to protect ourselves from, as in the Pyhrric victory, sweet but unconvincing, when we beat the machine, like so many John Henrys in dungarees and baseball hats, hunching over a pleasure machine designed to let us win once in a while?

The Luddites wanted to smash the machines of the Industrial Revolution—and who can fail to see the touching beauty in their impossible dream? But there can be no returns, no repetitions, only deposits, depositions. Perhaps the genius of these early video games—for the games, like computers, are not yet even toddlers—is that they give us a place to play out these neo-Luddite sentiments: slay the dragon, the ghost in the machine, the beserk robots. What we are fighting is the projection of our sense of inferiority before our own creation. I don't mean that the computer must always play us. Maybe, with just a few more quarters, we can turn the tables.

Professing Stein / Stein Professing

> *I never understood this sex symbol stuff. I thought cymbals were what they played in a marching band.*
> —Marilyn Monroe

"Sex", Michel Foucault is reported to have said in conversation with James Clifford, "is without doubt very interesting to do: but the discourse *about* sex is very boring. Then again, religion may not be very interesting to practice: but the discourse about religion—this is very interesting!"

By which I mean to say: Reading Stein is one of the great pleasures, but the discourse about Stein . . . well, it's not nearly as interesting. Not that there hasn't been a substantial amount of useful interpretation and, perhaps more important, vital textual scholarship about Stein. It's something I feel for myself: I've never managed to think what to say about Stein that was anywhere near as engaging as what she says about herself and of course what she does herself. Stein's own "Composition as Explanation" is a hard act to follow because it seems to rule out just the sort of explanations that we've grown used to making, because it shows that explanations of the usual sort won't work, have nothing to hold on to.

Stein criticism is haunted by the ghost of explanation. Too much of the commentary on her work starts with the premise that there is something wrong, something unintelligible, something troubling in its difficulty, something puzzling, something disturbing or deranged or missing or lacking or defective or absent or restricted or nonsensical or impossible or perverse, something enigmatic or something hidden: a puzzle that must be cracked, a code that must be deciphered, a problem that must be solved or dissolved, an inchoate phenomenon that must be theoretically psychoanalyzed; and, worst of all, a secret that must be detected.

Yet my own primary and continuing response to Stein's poetry is one of intense pleasure in the music of the language: of hearing a palpable, intense, I'm tempted to say absolute, sense-making: you can almost taste it; a great plenitude of meaning, of possibility for language, in language. Reading a Stein poem I feel an enormous satisfaction in the words coming to mean in their moment of enfolding outward and a correlative falling away of my need to explain, to figure out. I find the work satisfying, self-sufficient. It makes me want to savor its words more than account for them.

I think this is the meaning of Stein's great discovery—call it invention—of "wordness" in the last section of *The Making of Americans* and in *Tender Buttons:* satisfaction in language made present, contemporary; the pleasure/plenitude in the immersion in language, where language is not understood as a code for something else or a representation of somewhere else—a kind of eating or drinking or tasting, endowing an object status to language, if objects are realized not to be nouns; a revelation of the ordinary as sufficient unto itself, a revelation about the everyday things of life that make up a life, the activity of living, of speaking, and the fullness of every word, *of*s and *in*s and *as*s, in the communal partaking—call it meal—of language arts.

Stein spoke not of being avant-garde, not of futurity, but of being contemporary. In "Composition as Explanation" she writes that no one is ahead of her time—her specific rebuke to the idea of avant-garde, advanced guard—it's just that few are able to acknowledge their contemporaneity with their time. Yet you can't help being in your time even if you never register this fact, if you are not in it you are out of it and even then you are in it, despite yourself. The failure of contemporaneity—the failure of one's contemporaries to be contemporaries—does not make the "modern composition" the future, for this would be one more displacement of the poem's presence in a now that is actually happening, as Stein would say, as it is happening.

The failure, the refusal, to acknowledge the contemporaneity of the modern composition—that which is made by making it—results in the projection of this failure, or refusal, onto the text: the text becomes puzzling, enigmatic, ahead of is time, *avant la lettre;* or it becomes the independent private property of the author's own subjectivity.

Stein's writing is not postmodernism before its time but radical modernism in its time. If this basic fact—to insist with Stein that she is at least her own contemporary—is taken in its full force, it will wreak havoc with the maps of Anglo-American literary modernism, since much of what is called High Modernism will come to be called Antimodernist—indeed, the Counter Modernist Movement. It also will refute those theorists of postmodernism who claim that radical modernism has been completely assimilated *before they themselves have been able to assimilate it*. In this sense poststructuralism can be understood, but only in part, as a preliminary account of radical modernism, *après la lettre*.

Let me be specific, if grotesquely schematic, as to what I mean by a radical modernism that constitutes a paradigm shift in the "wording" of the world in North America and Europe. I mean the multiple contemporaneous discoveries (and twined inventions) of and in language of the first decades of the twentieth century: say the discovery of the plasticity of language in the visual art of the cubists and constructivists; the discovery of the language of the unconscious in Freud and the language of relativity in Einstein; the recognition of the use value of language in Wittgenstein and, why not?, the nonuse value of language in Stein.

What is it to be contemporary? What is it to be where we are, to be present *in* language, *to* language: and for language to be present for you?

If Stein has been less critically assimilable than her modernist contemporaries, it is not because she is more enigmatic but because she is more totally present. What you see is what you get or, better, what you get is what you hear. Stein's poems strike me dumb, are dumbfounding; not in the sense of being confusing but amazing: they are specifically designed not to send us *away from* the experience of the words happening in time, confirmable (coming again to constant confirmation) only by reading these same words again, rechecking our experience against the pulse of words as they are occurring. That is, what this is is *not* a hunt for literary allusions or historical references to assuage anxiety that the "new" is not a choice but a lived actuality from which none escape. Stein deploys no traditional prosodic markers or etymological regresses. She quotes neither from Chinese nor Greek. As if whether it's "Shift" or "Shrift" will help us to recover what we've lost, as if linguistic indeterminacy can be compensated for by scholarly thrift—as suggested in the almost pornographic display of the political unconscious of modernist, or at least Joycean, literary studies as obsessive-compulsive that has suffused the pages of the *New York Review of Books* during the past year. (Not that I'm not a bit obsessive-compulsive myself.)

Stein's works not only do not require but also positively hinder allegorical and metaphorical interpretations or paraphrases. Being what they are, they go further than almost any texts contemporary to them toward creating a literary writing that is not symbolic or allegorical: promoting anaphor and cataphor (forward and backward pointing in the text) over exophor (outward pointing), to borrow Peter Quartermain's useful observation. To note the opacity or materiality of this language is to note an ineffability that is a banquet of delight rather than a sign of lack. It's not that these poems don't refer but that they refuse to treat words as mere dummies for objects standing behind or under or, anyway, *away* from them. So yes it is presentation more than representation, if by that we hear how Stein collapses the Euclidian space of words and their displaced doubles— the objects they supposedly name ("One does not use nouns"). In Stein's modernist composition, the meaning is not something seated *behind* the words, but something revealing itself *in* the words, to formulate this in a way that echoes both Otto Weininger and Ludwig Wittgenstein.

Nor is Stein's poetry a return to the hidden—or is it private?— infant language ("preverbal"?) of the pre-symbolic of some versions of Lacanian and Kristevan theory: if anything, Stein's language is para-or post-symbolic, not regressing into babble or nonsense but *redefining by constituting* (rather than transgressing) the "law"—as any grammarian must ("I am a grammarian I do not hesitate I rearrange"). The Kristevan approach to Stein is to repeat, now as farce, B. F. Skinner's 1934 *Atlantic Monthly* attack, "Has Gertrude Stein a Secret?": which is that she was not in control of her words, that her writing was automatic in the sense of random, inchoate. (There is no such thing as automatic writing, although there are several writing procedures—not Stein's—that can be identified with the "spontaneous" production of text.)

Stein's poems return us constantly, constantly return us, turn us, constituting, to where we are. No wonder it's been hard for the industrious hermeneuticist. No wonder enigma and secrets have had to be projected, to make these texts *treatable*—that is to locate, establish, fix their meanings *outside* the poem's immediate words and self-created contexts, to rob them of their maturity as sense-making and meaning-constituting.

A purely formalist approach will never exhaust all there is to say about Stein. But acknowledging by recognizing the terms of this work is, at present, a prerequisite for informed sociohistorical or biblio-graphic interrogation.

This remark of Wittgenstein's might serve as a cautionary note for much Stein criticism: "[The] mistake is to look for an explanation where we ought to look at what happens as a 'proto-phenomenon'. That is where we ought to have said: *this language game is played* . . . The question is [one of] . . . noting a language-game" [*Philosophical Investigations,* tr. G. E. M. Anscombe (New York: Macmillan, 1958), §654, §655].

Faced with the sound, the materiality, or the presence (present) of language as music of sense in our ears, we project a secret: a hidden language. It's no coincidence that the projection of "the hidden language of the Jews" is the ghost that haunts the production and reception of Jewish literature, as Sander Gilman's crucial study *Jewish Self-Hatred* documents. No matter how richly a Jew may speak German or English, a hidden language underneath the English or German is projected as the Jew's "real" language, as if the Jew must always be translating from another language, even if she or he has no other language. (Gilman suggests that the common phenomenon of Jewish self-hatred may involve the Jew's internalization of the idea of a secret language.)

This idea of a secret language mimes the false picture of private language that Wittgenstein exorcises in the opening sections of *Philosophical Investigations,* where Augustine imagines that learning his native language was like translating a preexisting language into a new one.

Yet it is interesting to note that the American modernist poets who were among the most resourceful in creating a nonsymbological po-etry were, like Stein, second-language speakers of English, or children of second-language speakers: Williams and then two other Jewish poets—Reznikoff and Zukofsky. (In contrast, Joyce had to invent a language within English to be able to achieve all that he did.)

Why were these poets able to create a new world in English, a new word for what they called America? It's both what they heard in their own coming to English, learning to speak it, and also what they heard in the opacity of English *as foreign* and at the same time as a *fullness* of sound. Not something to be translated away but something to enter into, to inhabit without losing the wildness, the ineffable largesse and poetry, of hearing without mastering or commanding. Unmaster-ing language is not a position of inadequacy; on the contrary, mastery requires repression and is the mark of an almost unrecoverable lack. To be immersed in a language without the obsession to dominate it, conquer, take personal (even "subjective") possession of it, as if it were property: perhaps this is virtualizing space of the modernist composition.

It was in *Three Lives* (1909) that Stein instructed herself in the plenitude of a new English, an "American" English.

Three Lives is a focus of A. L. Nielsen's productively disturbing book, *Reading Race: White American Poets and the Racial Discourse in the Twentieth Century* (1989). In his study Nielsen confronts the implicit and explicit racism in twentieth-century American poetry. He finds Stein's "Melanctha" racist in its images of African-Americans as long-suffering but almost untroubled in their earthy spirituality, as say more "musical" than "rational". When Stein writes, on the second page of "Melanctha", of "the wide, abandoned laughter that makes for the warm broad glow of negro sunshine" you can see the justice of Nielsen's accusation. Then, too, white writers trying to depict what could be construed as "colorful" or, worse, culturally limited "black folks' talk" create a serious, perhaps not-to-be overcome problem that is not mitigated by an author's positive intentions or implicit psychological identification with the characters and their language.

Rather than dispel such concerns as those prompted by Nielsen, Jayne L. Walker, in her earlier *The Making of a Modernist: Gertrude Stein from Three Lives to Tender Buttons* (1984) lends credibility to Nielsen's charge: that is, if her troubling account of the politics of dialect is accepted. This is what Walker has to say about the use of black idiom in "Melanctha": "Recasting *Q.E.D.* in the 'negro' community of 'Bridgeport' posed the challenge of creating a character who . . . lacks the verbal and conceptual resources provided by their class and educational background" [p. 30]. Here Walker is comparing the black dialect of native English speakers to the "broken English" (my phrase) of German immigrants' first English—the linguistic material of the other two works in *Three Lives*. Walker labels this the "linguistic inadequacy" [p. 25] "of characters whose imperfect command of English makes self-expression an arduous labor" [p. 22]; she notes the "awkward syntax" [p. 23] of these Germans speaking English.

Walker understands that Stein is "materializing" the language in this way, but fails to note the richness in Stein's stylized dialect—a kind of (kindness in) language use that *surpasses* the standard language forms. "By dramatizing these linguistic struggles, the stories in *Three Lives* foreground the material reality of language as an arbitrary and problematic system, far from a transparent medium of communication" [p. 22]: Walker sees only loss where Stein has found the germinal sound of a new language, of a modernist composition. One might just as well say that language is *not* an arbitrary and problematic system, which would be more in the spirit of Stein.

Walker goes on to stigmatize black colloquial speech, along with immigrant English, as *impotent*—which, however, Walker does not present as a negative quality, comparing it favorably to the language of Samuel Beckett. In *Three Lives,* Walker says, Stein "used the verbal impotence of her characters, combined with a similarly restricted narrative idiom, to create a poetics of impotence, of antieloquence" [p. 27]. While Black English may technically be called a "restricted code", as in Basil Bernstein's terminology for context-dependent language in *Class, Code, and Language,* it is offensive to have it so characterized without further elaboration. Every language is as fully capable of expression, reason, and nuance—the *whole* world of its speakers—as every other language. Language, and dialects of languages, should not be hierarchically graded.

Walker goes on to write: "Although it makes use of some syntactical features common to nonstandard dialects, the language of 'Melanctha' is not a literal transcription of Black English but a stylization of the speech and thought patterns of characters whose language is inadequate to their experience" [p. 38]. The disturbing, possibly unwitting, implication here is that Black English is not a fully adequate, expressive language; that it is in some way less rational and complex than standard—or White—English. Walker is partially right when she notes, "In 'Melanctha,' deformations of syntax and repetitions of words and syntactical structures radically foreground the materiality of language as an unwieldy medium the characters must work with, and against, in their efforts to resolve complex moral and emotional issues" [p. 33]. But it is linguistic supremacism to suggest that one language practice is inferior to, or possibly a damaged form of, another—especially, but not exclusively, if we speak of blacks and whites. If this is what Stein is doing, then Nielsen is right to criticize her practice; but I think Walker's account misreads the significance of dialect in Stein's early work, just as Nielsen, in his unnuanced dismissal of "Melanctha", fails to acknowledge the counterracist currents that flow through the linguistic explorations of *Three*

Lives. This is not to say that Stein transcends the racism that per-
meated American culture in the first decade of this century (as fully
as it does the last decade).

For truly it is hard for any one of us to know just what we are
meaning by what we are saying. I mean it's hard since all we have is
our dialects, our ways with words and the rhythms of our saying;
sometimes when we think we don't know what we mean we find out
what we do mean, language is like that. The meaning is saying.

This is the difference between blues and despair.

Stein was creating a nonsymbological language for a poetry that
was "American"; that is, a literary writing not rooted in the literary
tradition of England, not using English words in a way that locked
them into their Island-bound associations and meanings, as words
had been used in the canonical English verse tradition since Chaucer.
In her own or possibly her parents' broken English and, more im-
portant, the spoken language of African-Americans, Stein found a
linguistic utopia—a domain not colonized by England, not Island
English's sovereign subject. This "new word" is surely anything but
impotent, I won't say seminal either, I'm running out of adjectives:
bounteous.

Who were Stein's contemporaries? Both Langston Hughes and Ster-
ling Brown share with Stein the project of rooting American poetry
in ordinary rather than literary language, in relying on spoken idioms
as sources for music rather than literary symbolism and traditional
English meter. (I don't mean that Hughes and Brown and Stein were
doing the same thing, but that "Melanctha" represents an *initial* point
of intersection between radially different poetries.)

Hughes's *Montage of a Dream Deferred* (1951) is, along with
Tender Buttons (1914), one of the great antiepics (not a "poem
including history" but a poem embodying the present) of the first half
of this century. Hughes's opening title in *Montage* is a methodological
principle that applies to both works: "Boogie segue to Bop." If we
take *boogie* as a verb, then Hughes is saying how we segue—move,
cut, jam, jump—from one textual moment (detail, particular, sen-
tence, word, frame) to another: you boogie from one to another and
you get to *bop*—bebop, sure, but just to swing in this textual space
is the new prosodic measure of this radical modernist collage/mon-
tage. "Boogie segue to Bop" is the contemporary enactment of mod-
ernist parataxis. Stein & Hughes open the door by building the
bridges.

Optimism and Critical Excess (Process)

This is not a transcription. More like a reenactment of the possibilities of performative poetics as improvisatory, open-ended.

As a way to engage the relation of poetics to poetry and by implication differentiate poetics from literary theory and philosophy, although not necessarily from poetry.

As a way to extend ideas about closure—the rejection of closure—into the discussion of essays and critical writing.

To eject, that is, the idea that there is something containable to say: completed saying.

So that poetics becomes an activity that is ongoing, that moves in different directions at the same time, and that tries to disrupt or problematicize any formulation that seems too final or preemptively restrictive.

Linda Reinfeld has pointed to the wedding that is being enacted (which is really always being enacted) between critical theory and poetry as a kind of subtext of this gathering.[1] Hearing Rosmarie Waldrop read from *Reproduction of Profiles* suggests something very much along these lines: Waldrop has created a literal wedding, in the sense of wedding together, or fusing, philosophy and poetry. In this work, she has taken phrases from Elizabeth Anscombe's translation of Wittgenstein's *Philosophical Investigations* and weaved in phrases of her own making. The structure of *Reproduction of Profiles* provokes a number of questions, including the status of Wittgenstein's original text, which may itself be taken as a poetic work, and also the status of the *Reproduction of Profiles*—what kind of a work is that?

My idea of a wedding may seem one-sided: I see it from the point of view of poetry. From this bias, poetry is the trump; that is to say, in my philosophy, poetry has the power to absorb these other forms of writing, but these other forms do not have that power over poetry.

---

1. Originally that gathering at the Buffalo conference at which these remarks were initially improvised and at which Rosmarie Waldrop read.

This is because I imagine poetry, impossibly—I know others won't share this view—as that which can't be contained by any set of formal qualities, while, in contrast, one might be able to read novels or letters or scientific treatises in terms of *their* poetic qualities, as sort of formally fixed genres of poetry. So when I think of the relation of poetry to philosophy, I'm always thinking of the poeticizing of philosophy, or making the poetic thinking that is involved in philosophy more explicit.

Or else I imagine poetics as an invasion of the poetic into other realms: overflowing the bounds of genres, spilling into talk, essays, politics, philosophy . . . Poetics as a sort of *applied poetic,* in the sense that engineering is a form of applied mathematics.

One of the discarded titles for the Buffalo conference was "Approaching Radical Poetries". I was thinking of the idea of approaching radical poetries much in the way that various space exhibitions allow you to imagine approaching, say, Saturn from a spaceship.

After several weeks at light-speed, we sight our destination. A small expeditionary force is sent down in the module to explore the imposing, cratered surface. After several days of experiments and sample collecting, the crew returns to the mother ship, leaving a small force to colonize the new terrain.

—You're approaching radical poetries, and then you're arriving at them, and then you're departing . . . Approaching suggesting movement. And maybe you make a rapprochement with them, or not.

It's the kinetics of criticism I want to address. While the spatial and temporal dynamics of poetics are not new topics, they are nonetheless all too rarely accessed (activated), at least when we enter the realm of academic criticism or, more generally, "public" discourse or "nonfiction".

Let me hasten to note that I think of public discourse as a form of fiction. I always appreciated the fact that the Dewey decimal system classifies poetry as nonfiction. Still, when *Content's Dream* was published I wanted that to be classified as "essays/fiction". People sometimes ask me if I'm interested in writing a novel. I say, well, I did, that's it.

Maybe this begins, in talking about the poetics of criticism, to suggest what I mean by excess, enthusiasm, or, as Marjorie Perloff has it in a review of Steve McCaffery's essays, passion. These terms are absolutely crucial for understanding not only the motivation but also the quality of the writing in the poetics that I'm talking about. It is also an important consideration in evaluating these works' status, if any, as theory.

I planned to expand on this last point later on, but let me switch to that, if only to emphasize the combinatorial nature of the composition I'm developing. Anything can be moved. Rearrangement is not only possible but desirable.

By combinatorial, I'm referring to Waldrop's discussion of the modular style of Lyn Hejinian's *My Life* and other works, where various units—sentences, phrases, words—are permuted or, more important, permutable; the sort of disjunctive collage or serial ordering that characterizes much recent poetry.[2]

Essays can also be combinatorial, marking a sharp break from essays that are developmentally narrative. We are trained by expository writing models not to think of essays as combinatorial; that is, that you could, and might well, reorder all the sentences. You have an outline and there's supposed to be some sort of quasi-logical development.

This is specifically not what I am interested in doing.

Except that I do wish to employ such rhetorical modes insofar as they appear to be invested with greater social power—not only to expose or explode the relation between style and status but also to access the power in these high-status forms. Certain writing styles have more status than others—a status that shifts with time and place and audience, status applying not only to intrageneric styles but also to genres themselves—the status of theory versus the status of poetics, the status of criticism versus the status of poetry. This social dynamic is something I consider when determining what writing style to deploy in a given circumstance.

To put the worst possible light on this, I'm interested not in what theory can do in an abstract way, but in what theory can do in a political way, in a pragmatic way. Some people will listen just to poetry and poetics, anything else they think of as highly problematic; for them poetry's got the real, if necessarily marginalized, status.

---

2. Rosmarie Waldrop, "Chinese Windmills Turn Horizontally", presented at the Buffalo conference, in *Temblor* 10 (1989), pp. 219–22.

But for a whole realm of other people, maybe some of you here have met them—*maybe you, sir, in the second row*—authoritative theoretical discourse has much more impact and much more social status.

(Theory without authoritativeness—which is not the same as theory without authority—begins to resemble what I've been calling poetics.)

I don't mean to exclude myself. The less I know about something, the more susceptible I am to "authoritative" discourse about it—authoritative discourses that are continually being disseminated by both the mass communications systems and by the specialized knowledge producers of the social and natural and human sciences: that is to say, by the dominant players in setting the rules for official public discourse—what I call *acceptable communication behavior*. And what are these rules? Alvin Gouldner defines two of them: using terms that are relatively independent of context and making intellectual claims whose validity is justified without reference to the author(ity)'s (speaker's) social role (and, I would add, choice of discursive and aesthetic presentational style).

Coming out of the political culture of the late 1960s, I sometimes imagined that one should seize these means of power rather than simply refuse them or try to operate without them. But this is a very questionable tactic, I hesitate to call it a strategy, because insofar as you seize these authoritative modes, you become them. There's no way to use them without reproducing them. So it's always an ambivalent thing, and I don't think it's possible not to err when you do this. You err on the side of power.

Yet this approach enabled me, empowered me I think is the term often used now . . . I mean what would it be like to empower white male heterosexuals? It's a curiously warped notion . . . This empowered me to resume the activity that was happily bracketed off. But resume it in a different way, from a different direction.

Not that anyone naturally produces these various authoritative styles; it's always an effort of self-fashioning, of forging, whether more or less consciously. I think of Edmond Jabès's comment that a Jew, in his remarkable sense that Jewishness is the condition of writing, is always in exile, even in her own words.

I want to raise the implicit error in these lines of reasoning because one of the main things I want to suggest is that poetics must necessarily involve error. Error in the sense of wandering, errantry, but also error in the sense of mistake, misperception, incorrectness, contradiction. Error as projection (expression of desire unmediated by rationalized explanation): as slips, slides . . .

Then again the issue of error is transformed for me into a question of humor.

I am interested, insofar as possible, to try to put into talks like this, essays, certain kinds of pratfalls, the equivalent of slipping on a banana, or throwing a pie in my own face. So that that error is made explicit as part of the process.

And then the humor itself begins to make dialectical or trilectical or quadralectical some of the power dynamics I am talking about.

It can be like juggling four or five or six different things.

But alas I can only juggle one thing at a time, so as I am juggling all these different things hopefully three or four of them will fall to the ground.

Hopefully some of them will be rotten tomatoes.

And you'll say what happened to that one.

And you'll begin to get it.

Here's the thing.

I want to suggest that there is a mismatch between poetics and poems. The poetics of a poet will often seem at odds with the poems; there's an incommensurability between the two.

This mismatch strikes people in different ways. For example they may say, "Your poetry doesn't seem to conform to your theory." For me this is as if to say, "That poem you read last night doesn't seem like the same kind of poem you read just now." But it's not as likely that someone will think that one poem is an attempt to explain, or mirror, another poem. One doesn't have the sense, at least not as strongly, that different poems by the same writer will match.

Poetics needn't be understood as explanations of some prior body of work. Even theoretical pronouncements, or manifestoes, that say "Poetry should be . . ." or "Poetry could do . . ." or "My poetry stands for . . ." For rhetorical reasons, these *my*s or *we*s seem to suggest that you are talking about yourself or your own work. But it ain't necessarily so. For example, I'm very apt, if someone asks me for an explanation of one of my poems, to give a wrong explanation. I'm not interested in giving accurate explanations. I'm very often interested in giving misleading explanations because I want to use the occasion to say what I want to say *at that time*. Not to explain what it was I meant some other time. I'm not a scholar of my work trying to give a legitimating account or justification. I think to mislead is one of the great pleasures of being a poet and a poet who writes essays.

I know many poets aspire to be leading poets. I've already achieved my aim of being a misleading poet.

Not that I would ever mislead you.

Bruce Comens makes a useful distinction, talking of Zukofsky, between "a" and "the" or, even more radically, "an" and "the": a discourse, a theory, or an discourse, an theory, versus *the*.[3]

I would also emphasize the *a* rather than the *the,* although I would always want to use the *the* in situations where I needed to convince somebody of something.

See, if you say "a" people say "eh!"; if you say "the" they say "THE!". So you sometimes have to use "the".

I have a lot of background in doing that.

The distinction between "a" and "the" is *the* distinction I want to make here about critical theory.

Charles Altieri, writing recently on the politics of contemporary poetry, seems appalled by the claims made by, and in behalf of, various formally innovative poetries of the present moment. The claims, he says, get in the way of the poetry's capacity to explore individual "imaginative investments"; to make bald, even grandiose political claims for what appear to be a poem's formal qualities is a disservice to what poetry can actually do.[4]

Altieri specifically contrasts specious political claims with "elabo-*rations* of the specific writerly intensities and reflexive qualities that can *justify* some of the difficulties in the poetry" [emphasis added]. Thus criticism has its proper role not in promulgating unfounded claims, confabulating difficulties, and proceeding to incite poetical

---

3. Bruce Comens, "From A to An: The Postmodern Twist in Louis Zukofsky", presented at the Buffalo conference.

4. Charles Altieri, "Without Consequences Is No Politics: A Response to Jerome McGann", in *Politics and Poetic Value*, ed. Robert von Hallberg (Chicago: University of Chicago Press, 1987), pp. 301–307, as subsequently cited.

riotousness, but in explaining (away?) difficulties, adjudicating tones, and deflating the rhetoric of poetics, if any is found.

Yet claims for poetry, even of the most theoretical or untenable or theatrical kinds, have the same status as any other type of poetic utterance. Claims have a *kind of* beauty, and certainly *kind in* tropicality, whether they are modest or exaggerated or overly enthusiastic or erroneous. I hear claims as engaging, moving sometimes, disturbing. To separate claims from poetry, even claims made "outside" the poem, and say "well that to me seems peripheral", is foreign to my conception of poetry, though certainly not foreign to other conceptions of poetry about which Altieri has written persuasively.

Making claims is an aspect of a poet's work that has vast potential—staking out ground to inhabit—especially insofar as these claims preempt or *needlessly* complicate subsequent, ostensibly more accurate, critical approaches. (They often have the opposite effect.) This means speaking for yourself in different tongues, even if other people might speak for you more accurately: for it is just this accuracy that you might wish to contest.

That is to say, you might wish to make claims for your work and the work you support that are inaccurate and need to be put out in order to misrepresent that work properly.

Now is that remark ironic or is it humorous or is it comic?

What I'm emphasizing is a provisional quality of the enterprise of poetics.

In other words, I think that activities such as this one have to be understood as situational. For one thing, you're responding to factors that exist historically, at the most concrete level. The poetic positions taken have to be understood within the context of other poetic positions that are articulated by other poets, or nonpoets, at the moment but also in the past. It's not just a question of differentiating your position. You have to take account of the claims of your poetic predecessors which were made partly in response to situations no longer immediately apparent. These are less claims about poetry in the abstract or their own work as such than attempts to redress or respond to other contemporaneous and historical claims. Nonetheless, if their claims have become generalized or decontextualized—*romanticized*—then these claims may also require re*dress,* in order to tip the balance the other way. The positions you may be disputing may have arisen because it was, at one time, necessary to emphasize a term or process or mode to combat a prevalent, but poetically disenfranchising, view. Poetics is all about changing the current poetic course. Putting on a dress, not strapping yourself into a uniform.

It's almost like sailing . . . I've never been on a sailing boat . . . but I like metaphors where I know nothing about . . . where somehow you're tacking one way, you're moving back and forth, based on which way the wind is blowing.

If spirit is taken to mean religiosity, then one might well emphasize materiality. But if materiality withers as an active poetic term, then it may require critique as, say, overly desiccated or deanimated. Strictly speaking, it's absurd to be for or against subjectivity; yet the subject may be an area of poetic contest that forces philosophically odd, but poetically comprehensible, polarizations. Key categories like these, or ones such as form, process, tradition, communication, subject matter, abstraction, representation, concreteness, expression, emotion, intellectuality, plainness, voice, meaning, clarity, difficulty, content, history, elegance, beauty, craft, simplicity, complexity, prosody, theme, sincerity, objectification, style, imagination, language, and realism have no unitary or definitive sense within poetics; they are, like the personal pronouns, *shifters,* dependent for their meaning on the particular context in which they are used.

Equally at play in the context of poetics is the political and social situation, including the social configuration of poetry in terms of distribution, publishing, capitalization, jobs, awards, reviews. I am motivated to speak as persuasively or eloquently as I can for any number of poets and poetic perspectives left out of that loop. In contrast, there are various prominent poets and poetic commonplaces that I sometimes have negative things to say about which I might wish to support, or call attention to, if they were unknown. Resisting the institutionalization of interpretation is a motivation for both poetics and poetry.

Maybe this is why the sort of official nonpartisanship of the post-*Self-Portrait* John Ashbery is—not "the great disaster" but a great disappointment for our letters (to appropriate Williams' comment on Eliot).—Yes, I know, some poets may recoil from playing Quixote or weave the windmills into their poems and leave the charging to Sanchos of more desperate circumstance. Ashbery, of any period, could never be a disappointment for "our" poetry, quite the opposite; the very sweep of his poetic achievement may accelerate his recoil from the burden of poetics.

These are factors that should not be overlooked—it's what I mean by "optimism," what motivates me to write about various individuals or make certain poetic claims. I'm motivated to write about someone or something partly because I have something to advocate that is not otherwise advocated, not just because I have some abstract idea to express. For one thing, an abstract idea could be expressed in terms of different subject matter or references. It's a social optimism expressed by worldly partiality rather than intellectual disinterestedness. These references are not there to invoke closure, though they may seem so in retrospect, but rather to open up ground, to contribute toward the works' continuing: a sort of critical plowing and fertilizing in the meadows of my enthusiasms.

I'm advocating a poetics that is not adjudicating, not authoritative for all other poetry, not legislating rules for composition. But rather a poetics that is both tropical and socially invested: in short, poetic rather than normative. A view that is related to those critical theorists who in the past few years have insisted that all criticism, like all historiography or anthropology, indeed all nonfiction genres, are tropical because of the inevitable literary biases of all modes of writing. This means that positivist, value-free, claims made for any mode of writing are more a matter of social positioning for authority than of unequivocal knowledgeability. This is not to deny the passionate belief that prompts such blindness to epistemic underdeterminacy, or that there is real social value, in particular circumstances, of unchastened belief—what has been called, after all, the operating principle of normal science.

Given the status accorded to scientific reasoning, it is imperative to leaven claims of technorational disinterestedness with a recognition of the heightened social power enabled by such claims to authority. The use of such authoritativeness can be justified, in the sense that using violence can be justified in certain situations, such as self-defense; but it's a precarious road. And authoritative language, while hardly equatable with physical violence, is nonetheless a form of manipulation and coercion.

Still, at times, it may be necessary to resort to authoritative discourse.

For instance, if you're being billed improperly and are trying to get your bill adjusted.

Surely it's apparent that operating within a paradigm is technologically very productive, even at times poetically productive. Yet we may want to set aside some domain in the arts and sciences for radical questioning of assumptions: not to insist that this must be the preoccupation of all cultural or scientific work but that it should be the preoccupation of *some*. I would argue that poetry has assumed this role, not exclusively, but with a great deal of resourcefulness at its disposal: kind of the unappointed philosophy (epistemology without portfolio) of, if not the age, at least sectors of it.

In *The Future of Intellectuals,* Alvin Gouldner argues that "the culture of careful and critical discourse (CCD)" is the social glue of a New Class of intellectuals and technical intelligentsia that is becoming dominant worldwide. CCD is a grammar of discourse shared by a speech community and centered on modes of *justification* based on "explicit and articulate rules, rather than diffuse precedents or tacit features of the speech context". CCD "values expressly legislated meanings and devalues . . . context-limited meanings. Its ideal is: 'one word, one meaning,' for everyone and forever . . . [CCD] requires that the validity of claims be justified without reference to the speaker's *societal position or authority*". This delegitimation of context-sensitivity and context-variability is part of CCD's own privileged claim to "theoreticity" as a universal and incontestable standard of "*all* serious speech. From now on, persons and their social positions must not be visible in their speech. Speech becomes impersonal. Speakers hide behind their speech. Speech seems to be disembodied, de-contextualized, and self-grounded." Thus CCD is a descendant of both Romanticism (in its revolt against imposed rules and traditions) and positivism (in its adoption of mathematical models of reasoning).[5]

5. Alvin W. Gouldner, *The Future of Intellectuals and the Rise of the New Class* (New York: Seabury Press, 1979), pp. 27–29, 34; p. 7 is cited in the next paragraph. See especially "Thesis Six: The New Class as a Speech Community". Jeffrey Escoffier usefully discusses this work in his excellent critique of Allan Bloom and Russell Jacoby, "Pessimism of the Mind: Intellectuals, Universities and the Left", *Socialist Review* 18:1 (1988), 118–135. It's worth emphasizing the positive features of CCD as much as its limitations. CCD encourages freedom of critical thought, in the best sense of rationality, as opposed to ethnocentrism and knowledge by uncritical accep-

The most important point of Gouldner's discussion of the culture of critical discourse is that it is politically motivated. "The New Class is elitist and self-seeking and uses its special knowledge [CCD] to advance its own interests and power, and to control its own work situation." The culture of critical discourse is a tool in its users' historically successful contests for power, control, and dominance.

Poetics don't explain; they redress and address.

Poetics are not supplemental but rather complementary (in the sense of giving compliments and in the sense of being additional, spilling over).

They are not directed to the unspecified world at large but rather intervene in specific contexts and are addressed to specific audiences or communities of readers.

Poetics is the continuation of poetry by other means. Just as poetry is the continuation of politics by other means.

Some tactics of poetics include hyperbole (though personally I would never exaggerate), understatement, metonymy, evasion, paranoia, aphorism, assonance, cacophony, caesura, rime, mosaic, blurring . . .

Poetics makes explicit what is otherwise unexplicit and, perhaps more important, makes unexplicit what is otherwise explicit.

Yet, without the expectation of correctness or the assurances of closure, what ground do we have for going on, for taking positions, for speaking with assurance or conviction? What recourse is there from the inhibition of only being able to speak when you are sure about the appropriateness and propriety of what you are going to say?

Optimism is my Emersonian answer, at least today, as my mood allows (or else, more blackly disposed, I fall silent): a willingness to try, to speak up for, to propose, to make claims; enthusiasm versus the cautiousness and passivity of never advancing what is not already known; judgment versus instrumental analysis; reason not ratio.

---

tance of authority. As such, CCD makes its connection to a social totality, rejecting at least on principle the epistemologic tyranny of vested interests.

In "The American Scholar" Emerson talks about a boy standing before water not realizing that he can swim. It's an image I find very useful in responding to questions about how people can understand poetry that hasn't already been written, that they've not learned about previously. Moreover, how can it be written?

People often ask how it's possible to make distinctions among poems that depart from certain conventional restraints. What happens is that you become aware of all kinds of other conventions. But when you don't see that second part—the new conventions—you just can't get how distinctions are to be made, how you can judge what you like from what you don't. Such a reader is like the boy in Emerson's essay, who can't imagine that the water will buoy him up. But when you jump in, you discover that you can swim, if you don't sink in a panic of disbelief.

Trust your private thoughts, Emerson urges his young scholars, because they will speak the most publicly. Trust the associations that make sense to you, even if they appear out of tune or inarticulate or inconsistent: allow them to speak. "Self-reliance is the aversion of conformity."[6]

(Why do I mention Emerson here? Is it purely a rhetorical gesture to try to pull someone with that kind of legitimating authority into an otherwise . . .)

One of the pleasures of poetics is to try on a paradigm—a series of related terms that characterize various poetic enterprises—and see where *it* leads you; not to lay down the line as *the* way to read poems, or even the poems considered, but a way . . . For there is great pleasure in compartmentalizing, in considering various works under a single stylistic sign, in generalizing about the common features in a varied assortment of work you like and don't like.

Yet, no matter how provisionally I cast my net, the work that results seems to develop an authority of its own that belies the investigatory premise. (Or so response to various of my essays has suggested.) Here's the dark side, the ghost that haunts my optimism and

---

6. Ralph Waldo Emerson, *Essays and Lectures,* ed. Joel Porte (New York: Library of America, 1983). The citation from "Self-Reliance" is quoted in Stanley Cavell's *This New Yet Unapproachable America: Lectures after Emerson after Wittgenstein* (Albuquerque: Living Batch Press, 1989), p. 69. Cavell discusses Emerson's "aversion of conformity" as both disobedience and conversion: contradiction as a countering of diction (p. 81).

turns it into a pale rider on the plains of compromise and misgiving. What started as playful considerations of possibility becomes, after the fact, an edifice of molten lead; the nimble clay dries into a stone figure removed from the process that gave birth to it.

If poetry is beyond compare (desire for what is objectively perfect, in Zukofsky's terms; a form of truthtelling, in Laura [Riding] Jackson's words) then any comparison, no matter how bracketed, risks being reductive or encapsulating or dismissive. For any mapping of poetic terrain is at the same time a mismapping, just as any positive statement (enthusiasm) can lead to a sclerotic authority that is based on the exclusionary force of the terms of engagement. This is because proposing any set of terms through which to read poems necessarily excludes other terms, other enthusiasms ("binding with briars / my joys and desires"). And no account of a poem can do justice to its many contradictory dimensions, even if the idea of contradiction is itself invoked. Criticism is necessarily insulting to the poetic work; it gives injury by its intrinsic belittling. [Riding] Jackson's relentless epistolary interventions are just the most extreme form of a commonly held view among poets.)

The idealization of the poetic as being without compare is worth contesting. I want to taint poetry if only so that you can see it better— *taint* in the sense of *staining*, giving *tint;* poetry not as transcendent but as colored: *of* the world.

I think the answer is neither to make more correct maps nor to abandon cartography altogether.

In the end, you don't have to choose between enthusiasm (desire unbounded by argument) and systematization (reasoning by principles).

But that doesn't mean I don't have to.

Bruce Comens has pointed to Zukofsky's distinction between tactics and strategy. In the Zukofskian sense of the local and the particular, as opposed to the general and universal, I would also advocate a pragmatics of tactics. But this would be a strategy of tactics, a method of tactics. And therefore can be criticized as a self-canceling strategy. Except if canceling yourself is a value.

In *The Practice of Everyday Life (Arts de faire)*, Michel de Certeau distinguishes between the strategy of power and the tactics of the dispossessed. Strategy represents a panoptic "triumph of place over time". One instance of the power of strategic knowledge is manifested by the historical ascent of rationality and the prerogatives of the culture of critical discourse documented by Gouldner. "A *tactic* is a calculated action determined by the absence of a proper locus [*un lieu propre:* a place of its own]. No delimitation of an exteriority . . . provides it with the condition necessary for autonomy . . . Thus it must play on and with the terrain imposed on it and organized by the law of a foreign power. It does not have the means to *keep to itself,* at a distance, in a position of withdrawal, foresight, and self-collection: it is a maneuver 'within the enemy's field of vision' . . . and within enemy territory. It does not, therefore, have the options of planning general strategy and viewing the adversary as a whole within a . . . visible and objectifiable space. It operates in isolated actions, blow by blow. It takes advantage of 'opportunities' and depends on them, being without any base where it could stockpile its winnings, build up its own position, and plan raids. What it wins it cannot keep."[7]

De Certeau, citing Clausewitz's theory of war, calls tactics the art of the weak. Poetics, as tactics, is also the art of the weak, or rather *poetics is "minor" philosophy,* in Gilles Deleuze's and Felix Guattari's sense of "minor literature". The tactician, Clausewitz's weak strategist, uses cunning, deception, and wit. Unable to operate from entrenched positions of power, she becomes a trickster or schtick artist who turns situations around by taking advantage of opportunities, using comedy to subvert occasions, employing the know-how and make-do of "cross-cuts, fragments, cracks and lucky hits".

Sophism, says de Certeau, is the dialectics of tactics. "As the author of a great 'strategic' system, Aristotle was already very interested in the procedures of this enemy which perverted, as he saw it, the order of the truth [by] 'making the worse argument seem the better' [in the words of Corax] . . . this formula . . . is the starting point for an intellectual creativity as persistent as it is subtle, tireless . . . scattered

7. Michel de Certeau, tr. Steven F. Rendell, *The Practice of Everyday Life* (Berkeley: University of California Press, 1984), pp. 36–37; also cited in the next two paragraphs, pp. 37–38.

over the terrain of the dominant order and foreign to the rules laid down and imposed by a rationality founded on established rights and property."

But isn't this just another trick of the tactician—to feign dispossession in the face of a stagnant assurance of ground? For the strategist and his "strong" philosophy, deception is not a matter of tactics but a form of self-blindness: defending territory that belongs to no one, accumulating knowledge that would have value only in use. This is as if to say that syntax makes grammar, but grammar is only a reflection of a syntax that once was. The strategist-as-grammarian is the nomad, for he possesses his home in name only: his insistence on occupation and territorial defense precludes inhabitation. The syntactician makes her home where she finds herself, where she *attends*—and that is the only possession that's worth anything, a soil in which things can grow.

But here, as in some lunatic game of Dr. Tarr and Prof. Fether, everything's gone topsyturvy. After all, it must be admitted in evidence that a theory of poetics—even a poetics of poetics—would no longer be poetics, would, that is, relinquish its tactical advantages as underdog and assume its proper place as strategy.

A strategy of tactics would be a way to hint at the totalizing counterhegemonic project that Bruce Andrews has advanced.[8] A way to think through, via parataxis, the relation among formal, antiaccommodationist, group-identified, cultural, regional, and gender-based poetic tactics so that they form a complementarity of critiques, projected onto an imaginary social whole in the manner of negative dialectics. That is, a social whole that can never be pictured since it is a "potentializing" formation, a "forming blank" in Arakawa and Madeline Gins's sense.

On a similar tack, I'm suggesting a syntax of motives (a sin tax on criticism) rather than a grammar of criticism, where grammar is the normative term. The motive being to provoke response and evoke company. To acknowledge. To recognize. Though surely to recognize is also to misrecognize.

---

8. Bruce Andrews, "Poetry as Explanation, Poetry as Praxis" in *The Politics of Poetic Form: Poetry and Public Policy,* ed. Charles Bernstein (New York: Roof Books, 1990), pp. 23–44.

You see someone's face coming out of the fog and you are propelled to make out who it is—maybe they're looking for you—and you shout out some words of recognition.

Recognition and acknowledgment are much more important motivations for me than any sort of theoretical or explanatory paradigms.

Yet to provoke is wildly different than to evoke.

Provocation is very useful, though obviously overused in many situations . . . or used by the wrong people. —If only the people who are now provoking, by and large, would stop, and the ones who are being provoked would start, it wouldn't be so bad.

Belligerence in the pursuit of justice may not be a virtue. Yet even the articulation of a variant view in a nonprovocative way is seen, by many, as provocation. There may be no way not to be provocative when you're articulating positions that go against the grain. But you can also heighten the provocation. Sometimes you may wish to do just that for explicit reasons, while other times it's just a disagreeable "personal trip", an echo of the worst traits of what you ostensibly oppose.

Belligerence produces belligerent responses. It's instructive to remember how radically Stein's poetics refused this particular vicious circle.

The defense of belligerent provocation is that you are not mediating, or smoothing over, what you say. At the same time, there are overwhelming problems with this form of communication behavior, especially as it seems to be stereotypically male behavior. The spectrum of response from evocation to provocation is perhaps not controllable but it can be monitored. Sometimes you may want an angry response, but continually provoking angry responses stops being useful. At least in the context of poetry: in other spheres, such as foreign policy or civil rights, the dynamics are different.

Reading Michael Davidson's study of the poetry communities comprising the San Francisco Renaissance has given me the chance to reconsider my assumptions about what seems to be a—to some degree continuing—valorization of confrontation and initiation as the surest signs of poetic authenticity. Davidson points to the use-value of behavior that might otherwise seem cliquish and intolerant; indeed, he contextualizes these troubling communication "behaviors" so that they are transformed into a significant collective practice of cultural

opposition and poetic integrity, given a specific sociocultural environ-
ment in which such behavior sustained the ability to make indepen-
dent critiques at the margins (sexually, geographically, stylistically) of
U.S. culture. Davidson argues that the "bonding" that may seem
exclusivist and narrow to outsiders was essential for the self-fashion-
ing and survival of these poetry communities and their poetry.

"For [Jack] Spicer", Davidson writes, "it was essential to use such
[intergroup] conflicts to create a disturbance, however unpleasant,
and thereby challenge complacency and tolerance. Such disturbances
were a way of verifying the loyalty of community members at the
same time excluding those who would enter from without. To some
extent Spicer's sectarian and oppositional spirit can be found in all
bohemian enclaves, based as they [are] on elaborate pecking orders
and cult loyalties."[9]

Since Spicer and others intentionally violated the rules of "official
communication behavior", to understand their poetics one has to
reverse Gouldner's rules of critical discourse: it is necessary to ac-
knowledge who is speaking and to recognize their terms as interested
and context-dependent. Thus what appears to be dogmatic and her-
metic by official standards must simultaneously be understood as an
effective oppositional strategy that allows the needed social space for
the poetry to be created. Yet a high price is paid for the blurring of
the lines between aesthetic issues and personal/community power
struggles. And the *legacy* of such power struggles as "poetic" behavior
is no more fruitful than any of the other received ideas of Romantic
ideology.

The test of a poetics is the poetry and poetic thinking that results.

In the case of the San Francisco Renaissance, and Spicer in partic-
ular, one has to start with the considerable, indeed stunning, successes
achieved.

Maps—these schema so many of us love to create—have their
primary value as imaginary constructions. Since art is not a fixed
subject, it does not have a fixed group or series of objects, such as

---

9. Michael Davidson, *The San Francisco Renaissance* (New York: Cambridge Uni-
versity Press, 1990), pp. 173–174.

land masses, to chart. Our critical maps make various possible con-
figurations seem real; it's almost as if the dynamic, shifting field of
the works is frozen by our icy projections onto them. Potentiality is
taken for actuality.

Radical poetics thus shares with quantum physics or string theory
a similar approach to the status of the objects of its scrutiny. In
contrast, official critical discourse is rooted in a Darwinian method-
ology of classification and advancement.

The Darwinian model requires a relatively fixed idea of categories.
Yet as George Lakoff argues in *Women, Fire, and Dangerous Things,*
all categories—material or aesthetic—arise from "actual" human ex-
periences shaped by biological and ideological and imaginative and
mythopoetic predispositions and interactions.[10] Categories are not
logically consistent, a priori abstractions; rather, like languages, they
are social and historical constructions.

I'm not suggesting that poetics, or poetry, is a chaotic system;
though if I did, who among you would launch the first inflated
balloon? We've flown about as high as we can and the air is thinning
out. I feel descent is in the works, if you count your cards right.

Chaotic phenomena are not susceptible to rational analysis: they
are unpredictable because they are nonlinear. This instability is the
result of their "sensitivity to initial conditions".

I want to suggest that poetry, insofar as it charts the turbulent
phenomenon known as human being, must reflect this in the *nonper-
iodic flow* of its "chaotic" prosody: clock time (regularized metrics)
will not do, nor will structures that aspire to formal or structural
(rationalized) stability or geometric conceptions of shape. As the stress
of the world impinges on form, the uniformity of the flow rate is
disrupted by interference patterns caused by bifurcation and oscilla-
tion.

Chaos in the heart can be dangerous—yet the stressed heart beat,
in which fibrillation makes rhythm unpredictable, is an image of the
poetic line. Studies show that a chaotic electroencephalograph is a

---

10. George Lakoff, *Woman, Fire, and Dangerous Things* (Chicago: University of
Chicago Press, 1987).

sign of healthy brain functioning, while a regular EEG reflects the pathological order of an epileptic fit.

Poetry in its most ecstatic manifestation is a nonlinear dynamic system. The vortex that poetics spins is a bubbling desynchronization chamber.

But poetic chaos, like the chaotic phenomena mapped by recent physics, is not absolute but constrained. It is controllable not in its flowering but in the progression toward chaos and the regression from it. We can study this progression into chaos or move backward out of it: perhaps this is the narrative of a poem that poetics can address.

Here's my theory of surplus explanation:

Multiple incompatible hypotheses are needed to provide an adequate account of any phenomenon—aesthetic, material, or psychological.

Which of course means no explanation at all.

I want to say that aesthetic objects are partly constituted by our maps of them so that this idea can be collapsed onto the way that a poem constructs a world by stringing together a series of particulars: the syntax or prosody being the means by which we get from one place to another. That's what poems map: how you get from one detail to another—one morpheme or moment or element to the next. *A poem,* to appropriate Duchamp's phrase, *is a network of details or stoppages.*

Or else maps define and prefix—scleroticize—the domain of poetic activity.

We don't know what "art" is or does but we are forever finding out.

Sclerotic is a word I like very much. It means hardening, as for instance *arteriosclerosis.* —A word like "scleroticize" could have been just as big as "reified". It just didn't happen.

While sclerotic is a biological metaphor, referring to an organic process, reify is more conceptual—to make into a thing. With sclerosis you are still alive, just stiff, swollen, pained. The human is evoked by that—are the joints moving? What did the Tin Man want?—not to be rust-proof aluminum (a better machine) but to have a heart. Stiffness may run roughshod over the malleability of flesh, but the real sadness is to not have the heart to care.

Samuel Weber gives a lucid account of the sclerosis—he usefully calls it the *institutionalization*—of interpretative systems in an essay on Charles Sanders Peirce: "despite the tendency of semiotic processes to be open-ended and relatively indeterminate, determination takes place all the time, has always taken place, and will always take place, over and above the efforts of individual thinkers . . . This is why Peirce develops a notion of the 'real,' 'the actual' or 'experience' not as a given state of affairs, but as a violent shock, involving conflict, struggle, and resistance. Reality and resistance recover their etymological kinship in Peirce. The problem then becomes that of defining the conditions under which such a violent arrestation—in other words: institution—takes place."[11]

Now here's Luce Irigaray: "In other words, the issue is not one of elaborating a new theory of which woman would be the *subject* or the *object,* but of jamming the theoretical machinery itself, of suspending its pretension to the production of a truth and of a meaning that are excessively univocal . . . This 'style' does not privilege sight; instead, it takes each figure back to its source, which is among other things *tactile* . . . Its 'style' resists and explodes every firmly established form, figure, idea or concept. Which does not mean that it lacks style, as we might be led to believe by a discursivity that cannot conceive of it. But its 'style' cannot be upheld as a thesis, cannot be the object of a position."[12]

"In other words": which always points to these words and no where else.

I fly off the handle at right angles to my last thought and return to it only after much mileage and a lot of burned, smelly rubber.

In other words . . .

I have argued, here I go again, that the acceptance (reification) of formalist and New Critical master maps of modernism—by modern-

11. Samuel Weber, *Institution and Interpretation* (Minneapolis: University of Minneapolis, 1987), pp. 20–21.

12. Luce Irigaray, tr. Catherine Porter with Carolyn Burke, *This Sex Which Is Not One* (Ithaca: Cornell University Press, 1985), pp. 78–79.

ism's supporters and detractors alike—has, in some ways tragically, streamlined (in other words, institutionalized) an otherwise messy, *poly*dictory arena of activity and precipitated an often farcical series of spinoff maps under the rubric of postmodernism.

Formalist criticism provides some of the most detailed, and illuminating, readings we have of modernist visual art. But it is a map, not the map; one possible narrative not the master narrative.

Arthur Danto's essay on the "end of art" that concludes his thoughtful collection of essays, *The State of the Art,* provides an interesting case study of some of these issues. Danto starts with the Hegelian premise that art "in its highest vocation" will come to an end as it reaches maximum self-reflectiveness or self-consciousness as art, when, in effect, it turns into "its own" philosophy and thus comes to its "natural end" as art. He then notes that when he first saw Andy Warhol's Brillo cartons in 1964, he realized that art *had* effectively come to an end: the art object had become totally conscious of itself and could not be distinguished from commonplace nonart objects in the world. No further formal advance was possible; and while art might go on, art in the sense of formal advance could not—everything after Warhol would just be a footnote.[13]

Even accepting this argument, it's hard to understand why art would not have come to end with Duchamp's readymades, thereby shortcircuiting the very series of formal advances of the '40s, '50s, and '60s that gave rise to Greenbergian formalism. Then again, Warhol made art identical not to any old objects but to commodities, which is not the same thing at all.

Danto's is not an argument for postmodernism but for the end of art; still it clearly parallels some postmodernist maps. For Danto, a hundreds-year-old Hegelian narrative of western art comes to an end with Warhol. But as he says, though a narrative may end, it doesn't mean the story doesn't continue (a narrative ends with "they all lived happily ever after" but the characters continue into that future). The activity continues but it doesn't have the same narrative necessity; closure has already occurred. This, then, for Danto, will explain the relatively bland pluralism of the '80s where no new movement usurps the formal stage every two years, just more or less interesting recyclings of the already known.

---

13. Arthur Danto, "Approaching the End of Art", *The State of the Art* (New York: Prentice Hall, 1987), pp. 202–218, as subsequently cited.

Still this argument is based not on Western art's master narrative but on a story Danto is attached to; not History unfolding but a story being told. The idea that art as an activity is completely absorbed into the Hegelian narrative precludes the possibility that there are other, incommensurable, "Western" stories based on different socio-cultural and aesthetic assumptions. What Danto documents in his essay is a certain cultural moment of acute awareness about art that changed his and no doubt many other viewers' way of seeing all subsequent art. But this story can never be *the* narrative of art because art, even of the West, has no single story with beginning, middle, and end; new stories are being told every day. I'm telling one now.

These arguments suggest more a change of dominant critical para-digms for art than an end to art. Word has gotten out, and from different quarters with different agendas, that the critical narratives of art's history and contemporaneity are multiple and incommensur-able (don't jibe). Yet this view reflects less an end to superexplanatory (master) narratives than a new superexplanatory (anti-"master") nar-rative.

When Warhol's "Brillo box asked, in effect, why it was art when something else just like it was not," Danto says, "the history of art attained that point where it had to turn into its own philosophy. It had gone, as art, as far as it could go. In turning into philosophy, art had come to its end. From now on progress could only be enacted on a level of abstract self-consciousness of the kind which philosophy alone must consist in. If artists wished to participate in this progress, they would have to undertake a study very different from what the art schools could prepare them for. They would have to become philosophers."

One can only imagine a professional philosopher or critic—Danto is both—making such an argument, and one might wonder if this isn't Danto's own "modest proposal", a subtly satiric critique of hegemonizing tendencies of recent critical theory. But Danto seems the most generously reasonable and least ironic of writers. So it will apparently have to be seen more as an instance of theoretical usur-pation of not only the interpretation but also the grounds (the estate?) of art.

Yet it would seem, from Danto's argument, that it is neo-Hegelian philosophy that has come to an end, or anyway impasse, insofar as it can't account for the contemporaneity of art given its always-already defined conception of what art is. "Progress" is the loaded term (turn), but it may not be contemporary art's most important product. The messiness of the current art scene is at least a progressive critique of the narrowcasting of neoformalist and "postmodernist" criticism; but it's not messy enough. If Warhol brings us to a dead end it's not because art, in its highest vocation, has ended but that we need new maps, new kinds of maps, of the past hundreds-of-years that don't lead to the inevitability of this sort of reductivist closure or conclusion.

If your map tells you you've reached the edge of the world and better turn back, it may not be that the world has ended but that your map has failed you. Even the idea of globes is not enough.

I take Danto's argument more seriously than many of the more fashionable ideas about the postmodern break because he has focused in on many of the assumptions—the lenses—through which I was first taught to view the Western art tradition. Strangely, though, this argument makes me see the Hegelian conception of art's history not as the end but as a beginning. Duchamp's, or Warhol's (the names seem dictated by the discourse in a blinding ferocity of repetition) (or Martin's, or Malevich's, or Manet's, or Resnick's, or Twombly's . . .) [or Stein's, or Benjamin's, or Celan's . . .] self-reflexivity *marks* not the end of art but a *preface* to what is now possible.

Emerging from the long tunnel of totemized historicity, we come face to face with the materiality of language and the identification of—or, better, transference between—art and its others. These are, so to say, foundational projects for art. Though we may find that these foundations are being built directly under the castles-in-the-air that we have learned to call the history of our arts—that have soared, so to say, without benefit of our finishing touches (torches), to borrow an image of Thoreau's.

Yet with these foundations in view, we can begin to see the art of the present and the past in less categorical ways; begin to acknowledge art that includes fourth-world (nonwestern, nonoriental, nondeveloping) cultures and third-world politics along with ethnicities and sexualities often excluded from our "own" world; the arts of the East and of the West, North, and South (Canada and Mexico for two). It means that we can stop thinking of art in narrowly "progressivist" lines, as if advances were something to occur at yearly intervals rather than being constantly discovered/revealed both at every moment and in every geographical region of the world, every time in human history: a deepening conception of art that takes its time as in some ways synchronous in respect to achievement, although completely bound to its historical and material moment.

Art's perpetually new beginning means that anything is possible and that there is an inexhaustible amount for artists to do. "[Our] capacities have never been measured," Thoreau writes in *Walden,* "nor are we to judge of what [one] can do by any precedents, so little has been tried . . . It matters not what the clocks say or the attitudes and labors of men. Morning is when I am awake and there is a dawn in me."[14]

So little has been tried.

We control the horizontal, we control the vertical.

Philosophy, or criticism, participates in this adventure in culture reciprocally, equally; but insofar as its procedures remain rationalistic, tied to a clock's (or computer's) sense of sequence, its race is not with art but with its own discursive conventions.

"Criticism takes more risks than art", Donald Kuspit writes in the preface to his recent collection of art criticism, "for it subsumes art's imagination in its own deconstructive imagination, which moves even more deliberately towards an uncertain infinity. Paradoxically, this gives criticism more impact and import than art, for it indicates that criticism generates a more dynamic sense of relevance than art— extends imagination into realms of relevance unimaginable to the art it addresses."[15]

Surely this, finally, must be parody: of Nietzschean resentment of the train by the conductor. Or is it rather a critical endgame of desperation turned to hysteria, where to interact you must condescend, to take note you must take possession?

The man who drives the car is on top of the world, thinks he invented speed.

One imagines that a critic who feels this way will seek out works he feels superior to, whether or not he is. Surely he will have difficulty confronting that which questions his cryptoauthority (his authority as decoder). He will miss the one lesson he might learn from art,

---

14. Henry David Thoreau, *Walden:* "Economy", para. 12; "Where I Lived and What I Lived For", para. 14.

15. Donald Kuspit, *The Critic Is Artist* (Ann Arbor: UMI Research Press, 1984), p. xviii.

which is never dreamt of in his philosophy: that no method, much less professionalization of method, has the answers. Art is still our greatest teacher of methodologies, and we risk losing our ground when we forget what art teaches, that art teaches.

What do we talk about when we talk about art?
Art, man, he could blow!
No thesis advanced, many declined.
What remains is a series of related remarks.
—"I've had just about enough of your remarks!"
A good joke never wears out its welcome, its preternatural inapplicability.

Another interesting case study is the "Primitivism" show at the Museum of Modern Art a few years ago. One thing the curators seemed to be suggesting, by putting tribal works next to Picassos, was that these tribal works were as aesthetically beautiful as the juxtaposed "masterpieces" of modern art. But what might be more interesting than how tribal works can be understood aesthetically, or how "magical" qualities can be seen in Picasso, is how the very concept of art can be exploded in terms of function, ideology, and culture.

Imagine tribal societies making use of *our* art as culturally functioning.

This "other way around" is what interests me: how we can understand our art as *not* being merely aesthetic.

Tribal work—I take this from James Clifford—is *not* artifact, not evidence, not document, not aesthetic object.[16]

Then what is it?

The answer to that question might help us to understand what our art work is. Which we don't know. Because we don't know what the objects are, or quite what to make of them.

Not that we should.

16. James Clifford, *The Predicament of Culture* (Cambridge: Harvard University Press, 1988).

Or we know sometimes and then lose it, need to find out again, only differently.

Let me come at this from a different angle, introduce a new tangle.

Benjamin Friedlander, talking about Charles Olson in a letter, makes a useful distinction between discovered and received traditions. While Olson went about finding his sources in a particular, idiosyncratic way, the danger is that the results of this process can be turned into a core curriculum of poetics, assigned readings and all, along the lines of what Pound actually advocated.

Recently a scholarly poet friend was telling me that he thought he would have to undertake two years of background reading in philosophy and literary theory and linguistics to find out what $L=A=N=G=U=A=G=E$ was all about. In which case he would have read far more comprehensively in this area than most of the poets published in $L=A=N=G=U=A=G=E$.

The point is not to retrace the steps but to respond to the process of discovery. The idea that you've got to read what I read, or what he or she reads or read: awful nightmare of sameness.

"If you can't sleep at night it's not the coffee it's the bunk." You'll remember (or maybe not) that this line (virtually) wins Dick Powell the coffee company's contest for best slogan in Preston Sturges' film *Christmas in July*.

It could be that the distress generated by ideas of underdeterminacy, relativism, closureless poetics (double button-down flaps or open pocket), antiabsorptive poetry . . . is not the reason we're not sleeping, or getting our accounts straight. It's not the coffee (in the sense of these alternative modes of communication). It's the *bunk*.

So you either get a new bed or get rid of the bunk, in the other sense . . .

. . . and start talking sense to the *American* people . . . (shooting sense into the *body politic*).

Or maybe it's a way of trying to address the bunk, and yet the hostility is directed against the coffee.

To chart your way out of a cave you might want to use consistent syllogistic thought. But that's not the only problem we have. And it's not the only pleasure we can have. Sometimes judgment is at odds with analysis.

It is the continued fate of the contemporary to be misunderstood by some in exact proportion to the intensified comprehensibility it provides to others.

When someone says that they can't understand something, you can reasonably assume that someone else is going to absolutely be able to click with that, split infinitive and all. Making certain choices intensifies the communication for some while leaving others higher and drier than ever. This isn't elitist. Elitism suggests that there's one best way to say something, which conveniently segues either into the argument for mass communication: say it so that the most people will think they understand it; or for the sole legitimacy of the culture of critical discourse—only we can say it right. Our mutual incomprehensibility to each other is not a matter that can be legislated, or schooled, away: it is an active site of a democratic political process requiring negotiation not repression, translation not transubstantiation into a single common language above the fray of conflicting interests.

Over and against the claims of a radical poetry to resist or disrupt official critical and cultural discourse is the totalizing frame of the period, whereby even the most refractory cultural production may be interpreted as expressive of the contemporary cultural logic.

Reading poems under the frame of periodization is as reasonable as reading them in terms of the politics of their form. Such approaches tend to neutralize aspects of the work that may otherwise be claimed as critique or attacked as random or nihilistic.

Fast cutting, fragmentation, polyphony, polyglot, neologism may all be features of late twentieth-century life, in some areas, as much as aesthetic "inventions". My linguistic environment might include, within the space of an hour, bites of Donahue on incest, street fights in several languages, a Beethoven quartet with commentary, calls to the phone company followed by intimate discussions of personal affairs followed by a computer-voiced marketing survey—with a Weill song interpreted by John Zorn in the background, segueing into close readings of Spinoza followed by a recitation of the Brothers Grimm.

When a poem includes some of these varieties of language use, it's not as if this is a totally synthesized experiment: you're listening to what you're hearing, charting the verbal environment of the moment. Of course, there are many choices you make . . .

Because periodization is a compelling interpretive horizon for poetry, poets who do not wish to acquiesce to this reading will find it necessary to speak up and make political claims for the work that otherwise might not be apparent. It's these claims that may make the poetry political insofar as they provide an interpretive wedge against the poem's newly apparent transparent absorption in its period.

The political frame provides a way of reading that might otherwise not be accessible, or not as accessible. The words, and their configurations, do not necessarily tell this story. The value of poetics is just that they can provide such an excess, or, better, a complementarity of explanation.

Making the contemporary aware of itself, conscious of its own thought processes, is a necessary ground for the political. For this reason, a poetry's historical (structural) expressivity is a necessary but not sufficient measure of its values: it locates but does not determine, or exhaust, its political dynamic. An acute awareness of contemporaneity can produce (or abet) resistance: can provide information, in the sense of formal imagination, to readers. You have to understand what you're confronted with, have maps, identify the bunk—the virus coming into your system—know *what it is,* where that *what* is, as much as anything else, formal or ideological, and so *not visible.*

The new historicism and the "death" of the author are both useful responses to New Criticism and its many fiduciary and moral beneficiaries. Yet they are, largely, positionally and situationally reactive, providing for critiques that make possible a revitalized reconsideration of poetry as a complex sociohistorical *event,* recalling literature from its long critical banishment to the nether world of free-floating texts. But I would argue not for the death of the author as much as for the exploding of a stable presentation of the author's identity, perhaps to reveal the multiple vectors (*including* intention and individuality) that constitute the author and the field in which she operates. That is, I am on guard against too literal an acceptance of these polemical arguments lest they become as reductive as what they sought to redress: poems and authors disappearing as agents into the reified mist of historical determination.

Poets can operate as agents of resistance, poems can be sites of social struggle, in ways explicitly at odds with Romantic ideology or related New Critical doxa. Insofar as these new critiques erase all authorial agency in the name of structural causation, they extend the worst features of the New Criticism's depoliticizing of poetry. It's the one-two punch all over again: first the poem "itself" is shorn of its biographical and bibliographical and sociocultural wings; then unable to fly, it's assumed to be a half-dead thing, slapping around in the historical winds like so many Joe Palookas, read not for its substance but as barometric measure by the supercritics swooping overhead, looking for prey.

Whoa, Nellybell! Just a minute there. Not so fast.

I wonder if humor isn't getting lost in the shuffle, getting the short end of the rib, so to speak, playing backseat driver to anecdote on a slow trip on the backroads late at night in the dense, unforgiving fog.

Against seriousness as such: Humor breaks the "high poetic" frame, showcases conflict.

—"But you're such a serious guy!"

Yet while irony and sarcasm can suggest an authoritative/controlling discourse, comedy can end up as so many minstrel shows of critical excess, where care, passion, and commitment become a kind of charade and real issues are turned into schtick: evading the kind of responsibility we expect from critical works.

—Humor, insofar as it destabilizes any unitary message, seems to undermine truth and authority. But that doesn't mean this approach to critical discourse eliminates the possibility of truthfulness or good faith or communication.

. . . any more than avoiding the most heavily traveled freeways of communication behavior means you don't want to communicate. Maybe you can get there faster going through the streets. Maybe you get out to walk. Maybe you have another destination in mind.

Maybe all the visible veins are already spent with hourly injections and all you're doing is looking for a new vein to shoot into.

Is that comic or is that ironic?

Ten-second pause.

Blackout.

Censers of the Unknown—

Margins, Dissent, and the Poetic Horizon

TOM BECKETT: Charles, back in 1981 we ended our interview for *The Difficulties* with your comment about the authorial *I* as social construction. Since then, it seems to me, you have become more of a public figure within the world of poetry writing. I don't want to overstate the situation: you're not Michael Jackson or even, sorry, Pee-Wee Herman. Nonetheless, I think that the eyes of your colleagues and your "reading public" are focused on you differently than in the past. What I'm straining towards is a question appertaining to a poetics of reading—to issues of *reception*. What are your thoughts about the ways in which your work is currently being bracketed or received?

CHARLES BERNSTEIN: I'm not all that interested in focusing on the reception of my work except insofar as this can become material for me to absorb into the work. The companionship that poetry can provide, as if "I hear what you're saying" were not just a hollow formula registering that the sound waves had hit the tympanic apparatus, as if to hear meant to act more than react, has been for me a fundamental resource and motivation, and one that occupies me constantly, even when I should like to break off from it for a spell. And, seemingly inevitably, to be heard in this way is to cause disruption, as if to use the channels of communication is to offend some who choose not to, or to use different ones, because the waves are felt, rightly, as conflict. I think I could go on, no doubt differently, in the face of silence too; although I wouldn't want to imagine a situation in which I would be content with such silence; but then being content has an uneasy relation to my engagement with poetry.

Perhaps I'd better start by saying that I have been surprised and encouraged by the degree of attention focused on the context for writing proposed by such projects as $L=A=N=G=U=A=G=E$. But both positive and negative reactions suggest as much the neglect or repression of a range of acoustic, syntactic, structural, and political

dynamics in the reception of twentieth-century English-language po-
etry as any specific response to the works of an individual poet or
poem.

Insofar as the climate of response to the sort of poetry and poetic
thinking I've been involved with has opened up, or deepened, this can
be attributed to the efforts of a number of individuals pursuing dis-
tinctly different—and, significantly, conflicting—courses who have
nonetheless created *communities of response* as an alternative to the
deadening isolation that has often been the fate of iconoclastic North
American artists and intellectuals. That is, the conscious social artic-
ulation of a way out of "me-too" Romantic individualism—so often
misinterpreted as collectivization and group formation—amounts not
to the creation of a school of thought but to a poetic of response: a
conversation not a thesis. Ironically, this process attests to the crucial
role that individuals must play in resisting the "collective imperative",
in Roland Barthes's phrase, of gregariousness, whether the collectivity
is a national or local culture (society) or uniformitarian (including
uniformitarian oppositional) aesthetic principles. Dissent and subver-
sion remain operations that cannot be collectivized without losing
their most powerful psychic effect; but only response—*in the form of
exchange*—allows such acts to enter into a social space where they
can begin to lead a life of their own.

Such rehearsings of who or where or what we or I or you are or
may be or may be doing is part of the process of poetic thinking that
makes me want to "bracket" however my work is being bracketed,
to turn your question on itself.

If I say that my writing can be understood as research, I mean this
literally as searching for new—in the sense of uncharted or undiscov-
ered *(unarticulated)*—worlds within language. For New Worlds can
be discovered within language just as surely as on the face of a globe
or inside an atom. This is called invention from the creative side; but
how can you invent what was a potential all along? (You don't have
to know it's there to find it, said the man who fell over his own
place.) At a certain point people stop saying the world is flat because
they look at the horizon differently; they still may walk flat streets
and write flat poems. Yet the investigation—in the sense of procrea-
tion and composition, in-vestment and instigation—takes its own
course, what makes it possible to go on. What I mean is that these
inhabitations so created are there to be heard and seen. It's more that

the complete breakdown of response can make you feel—and so *go*—crazy; to have some acknowledgment confirms that the compass you've made of foolscap and twine has gotten you through—rough trades, after all.

TB: Within the communities of response you have mentioned, within the chorus of gestures of mastery those communities support, the issue (as in all communities?) of censorship (and at many levels) arises. I'm thinking now particularly of Marcuse's notion of "repressive tolerance", the idea that to tolerate what you oppose is to condone it. What roles do you see for censorship in your own work? What roles do you see within the communities of response you have described?

CB: I see a number of thornily intertwined issues here and I'm not sure whether you want them untangled or fused. On one end of the spectrum is police-enforced censorship; on the other end is a poet's—or a poetry community's collective—myopia or arrogance or intolerance; and in between the more elusive, but surely pertinent, specter of self-regulated "sense-orship", in Bernard Noel's term ("the police are in our mouths") and "repressive tolerance", which perhaps is today better understood as marginalization (free to publish in the sense of free to have a warehouse of undistributed books).

There is a thickening line between commitment and intolerance, between conviction and arrogance, between opposition and competition. Many artists, literary and otherwise, become productively fixed (fixated?) on their particular methods of practice and criteria of evaluation. This can lead to partisanship but does not have to produce dogmatism or sectarianism. (I would define "sectarianism" as when one party to a participatory community of response declares its own narratives of origin and value to be authoritative despite—or really *because of*—competing claims.) While "avant-garde" artists have traditionally been associated with a sometimes strident partisanship, the experience of twentieth-century modernisms suggests the relative modesty of such partisanship compared to the militant intolerance of those who define themselves against the "new" ("neoconservatism" is, after all, a byproduct [wasteproduct] of an avant-garde).

Naturally, when you are provocative people will be provoked—and it is an interesting spectacle to see such a panoply of fulsome anti-intellectualism and New Critical pieties provoked by recent poetic developments. And while it's unpleasant to be attacked, especially when an attack willfully misrepresents the positions it claims to be attacking, it is crucial to resist the paranoia (us/them) that such attacks induce—because paranoia destabilizes the ability to differentiate those who are sympathetic or neutral (part of the conversation) from those who are dismissively rejecting in their antipathy (trying to shut the conversation up). A result may be that divergent, but not repudiating, views come to seem unacceptable, wrong-headed, and, finally, malicious: "Either you are with us or you're in the way." (Although this *us* has by now become hard to distinguish from the individual ambitions of the combatant.) Bullying under the guise of "confronting the terms" of those with whom you are conversing is seldom innocent.

However (always *however*), one person's sectarianism is another person's dissidence. In this sense, sectarianism is the opposite of censorship.

Surely, repressive tolerance is better than repressive *intolerance*. (The contradictions don't need more heightening.) It's instructive to keep in mind that the structure of repressive tolerance allows for a wedge to be driven between its two terms: a wedge that makes possible a movement toward "progressive" tolerance. That is, the *potential* power of the margins is enormous but the effect of *repressive tolerance* is to neutralize (I wanted to say depotentiate) this power. The very conceptualizing of repressive tolerance can have this effect, for it can reinforce an already pervasive sense of despair if it's understood as a catch-22: you can't win. "Pessimism of the intellect, optimism of the will": except that it is precisely the intellect that needs to be activated, and the "idea" of repressive tolerance can be sufficiently dispiriting to fan the self-immolating flames of passivity. Indeed, repressive tolerance counts on a *self-regulating* passivity and insularity: the "margins" accepting that they are, and can only be, marginal; although all there are are (all there be be) margins [the ruling class is a margin with a nuclear strikeforce].

I'm always amazed at just how much any action can accomplish—doing what you've been told, or told yourself, can't be done. Acting in the face of disinterest or rejection and at the risk of incomprehensibility. Speaking out rather than *censuring* yourself out of the conviction that no one, or not enough people, are listening, or the occasion's not right.

One thing that poetry can do is challenge such self-censoring (& censuring) mechanisms: that is, articulate that which is repressed not only by the individual psyche but also by the socius (collectively), a censoring that is encoded into the grammar of all our signification systems.

Out of fear of being opaque to one another, we play the charade of comprehensibility—for if you say nothing you void the risk of not being found empty. We censure the unknown because it has not always/already been understood, and we call this communication, clarity, expression, content. But only when the taboos against incomprehensibility are transgressed does it become apparent that there is an excess of meaning in the cracks we have spent our days sanding down and sealing over. The theory of relativity is well known: what is incomprehensible to one is, to another, the exact words of her or his particular condition-in-the-world. To be comprehensible to all— the telos of the language of what is called science—is to censor (a collective repression) all that is antagonistic, anarchic, odd, antipathetic, anachronistic, other. (Marginal.) *(Outside.)* So poetry can be the *censer* of these spirits from the unknown, untried, unconsidered— really just unacknowledged—that now, as if they always had, bloom in vividness.

Fear of contamination by the "other" is a foundational taboo of U.S. society, and a prerequisite to repressive tolerance. If I stop defining myself/my group against stigmatized others, I will lose my identity. —I'm constantly struck by the fact that hostile/contentious/competitive remarks made about other individuals, other groups, or other ideas are considered more honest (uncensored) than conciliatory/supportive/ameliorative attitudes. Certainly bad faith comes in all shapes: sycophantic compromising behavior is as endemic as competition in a hierarchic, corporatized society like ours. But the censoring mechanisms involved in competition are not adequately appreciated. For competition perverts the identification of difference ("opposition") from a source of pleasure-in-exchange to a source of invalidation, contempt, and exclusion.

A great aesthetic pleasure comes from the transgression of the already known in an exchange with the incomprehensible, the marginal, the outside (which in the instant cease to be any of these things). Exclusion is self-regulating: it requires something like a leap of faith— not arguments—to bridge this particular gap: *a conversion into a conversation.* This is the pleasure that verse promises—and why one reader speaks of hearing cascades from the worlds within this one, while another sees only inert black marks on a blank page.

TB: Ambliopia is the medical term for reduction or dimming of vision in the absence of apparent pathology. It is also the title of one of your recent poems (in *The Sophist*)—and an interesting ethico-cultural metaphor. Could you extend your discussion of censorship into the mythos of this work?

CB: A task of poetry is to make audible (*tangible* but not necessarily *graspable*) those dimensions of the real that cannot be heard as much as to imagine new reals that have never before existed. Perhaps this amounts to the same thing.

The body-with-only-organs may still be intact (there's still some time but the planet and those on it are in danger); then this dimming of vision (what I've called "sight") is something like hysterical, imaginary, but there remains the material organic possibility of ambi-opia, multilevel seeing, which is to say, vision repossessed.

This hints at the distinction between the earth and the world. As long as the earth lives, there can be hope that the world can be transformed; but the world can destroy, though perhaps not kill, the earth (which has not yet happened) or it can occlude its communion with it (which happened long ago, perhaps when history began).

Could it be that language is as much a part of the earth as of the world? And that this is what is censored? That the tools we use to construct our worlds belong to the earth and so continuously (re)inscribe our material and spiritual communion with it?

TB: Are you saying there may be a "natural language" we are somehow prevented from hearing?

CB: No, only that the distinction between nature and culture may obscure the bodily rootedness of language, which is impossible not to hear but difficult to recognize and to articulate. Perhaps beauty, or anyway aesthetic pleasure, needs to be understood along these lines rather than in terms of idealizations designed to erase just this earthbound fact. And if we leave the earth, will we not still be creatures of it?

TB: "Think of dead ideas as deposited in language and writing, as the compost heap in which present language and writing grows. Suppose dead ideas as comprising an historical unconscious lived out as perception, as smell and taste, as speech. Imagine consciousness resounding with an inexhaustible repository of ideas, as a cave to be mined. And consider poetry as that mining, so the incorporation of dead ideas (call them prior texts) into a work is not simply collage or a familiar, almost comforting, defamiliarization technique, but the spiritual domain of poetry, its *subject* (subjectness) percolating through." So you began a recent article, "Living Tissue/Dead Ideas" (*Social Text* 16, collected in *Content's Dream*). Talk about an organic, earth-bound poetics! How *does* beauty or aesthetic pleasure figure within the network of relations described above?

CB: I'm on call in Gibraltar but you can still use the number in Saskatoon. I'm out of sorts in Dominica but you can tune me in on Q frequency. Where there's air I breathe; otherwise you'll only see gas masks. *"But what the Devil is the **nonhuman**: or is all the universe consumed by your projections?"* "Let me out!" said the owl, but the fly just buzzed.

Yet "beauty is set apart". Or it's not beauty that we seek but someone on the other end of the line, a letter in the box, a song in the wind. Not the juridico-rational voice of authority, which has never made a place for any poetry that claims to *matter*. (Charley Altieri saying, all these *claims* get in the way! Give me a poetry that knows its place, that allays my suspicions that poetry's a disease for which criticism will find the cure.) The man in the silk jacket pales before the work and insists you dream in white and black.

For there's beauty in the *claims* of poetry; to think there are only texts—disembodied strokes—is to imagine that a plant has no roots; but a person can get only what she has staked out. There's beauty enough in that, a person standing by her word, finding the world in them. A journey to a star would be exactly half as far. After that, pleasure takes care of itself.

As if clouds needed to make room for sky. Not proportion but rage and regret; not the loss even of loss but *fabrication*. Spelling out what is on tip of tongue, words that break a spell in order to cast a new one, the effects of sound breaking into words (tangible as when a tractor hits square in legs).

Of course, we must bracket history and truth and reason else be deceived by the simulacrum; weave webs of veils. But Derrida is wrong to say that play and games are of a different order ("Play is always lost when it seeks salvation in games"—"Plato's Pharmacy"); for all play instantiates and games are just what we've learned to call it when we stare over our shoulders into the fog. This is what it means to be born free but everywhere enchained: just that even when we're tripping out we're buying in, and the most elaborate edifice is a mark of evasion. Or say that play is for the earth and games for the world. Then perhaps beauty reminds us of this fact or reminds us to take pleasure in it. And the chains, which don't so much shackle as weigh down ("the only chains I know are these chains of love"), hold us to earth's gravity and give us something to fight with.

The jury is sequestered after all plea bargains are refused. I'm so hungry I could eat a truck.

TB: Can you tell me, while the jury is out, before sentence is passed, how what is "other" figures in your work?

CB: I'm alone on the beach & the tide is racing toward me until the spot I had picked out for its distance from the shoreline has become completely submerged. My pad, pencil, & book float helplessly on the water's surface before being pulled, precipitously, toward the horizon, having met their destination.

For after all it is only when a work is completed—a journey that begins at the point a *text* becomes a *work*—that others may enter into it, trace its figures, ride its trails along tracks that are called lines. The other defines the work, completes the process and makes it definite. No matter how heterogeneous I try to make a poem, no matter what incommensurabilities I attempt to rend my writing with, it becomes absorbed in that self-same project stipulated by the limits of my name: my origins & residencies, my time & language, what I can hear & see enough to contain by force of form. Yet it is precisely what I have contained but cannot identify that the other, being other, makes palpable, lets figure, & (hopefully) flower. It is only an other that, *in the final instance,* constitutes the work, makes it more than a text (test), resurrects it from the purgatory of its production, which is to say its production of self-sameness.

Bakhtin puts this very eloquently in a 1970 interview in *Novy mir* (tr. V. McGee): "In order to understand, it is immensely important for the person who understands to be *located outside* the object of his or her creative understanding—in time, in space, in culture. For one cannot even really see one's own exterior and comprehend it as a whole, and no mirrors or photographs can help; our real exterior can be seen and understood only by other people, because they are

located outside us in space and because they are *others* . . . A meaning
only reveals its depths once it has encountered and come into contact
with another, foreign meaning: they engage in a kind of dialogue,
which surmounts the closedness and one-sidedness of these particular
meanings, these cultures."

To *conceive* of the relationship of the writer and reader (which
gives birth to the poem) as dialogue is more fruitful than to speak of
the reader (or writer) as originator of the meaning of the text—and
it would help frame (as in "I've been . . .") the systematic misconcep-
tion (as in barrenness) of this perspective as the *non*determinacy of
the text, open to the reader's sole discretion as if without constraint:
as if to avoid nonintentionality you have to write commands, not
allow for conversation. (To have a conversation is not to stare mutely,
or to utter minimally directive words & be consumed by the other—
but to allow room for response while responding in turn.)

Part of the arrogance of what is sometimes miscalled modernism,
as if the modernists didn't know the Heavenly had passed into an
other world but we, "after" this fact, have learned the lesson (which
would be better to unlearn), is that one could incorporate the other
within oneself (one's work), contain "all". For instance that one could
be *representative* of "man" or of a cultural moment or of a people.
But every particular is such precisely because of what it necessarily
excludes. So what is to be proclaimed is this not-all, this insistence
that there are only margins no universals; only partialities that are
constituted by their exclusions even more than inclusions; that any
claim to incorporate the other is, in effect, an attempt to discorporate
or dispossess it—call it heterocide or ektocide. This points again to
the arrogance of an art (or critical theory or cultural dominant) that
claims to speak *for* all (whether high art/high theory or mass media)
rather than an art that speaks for one among many to others among
even more, literally and figurally, *unimaginable* others; for to imagine
is to contain & to imagine all there is is contained in our unforgivable
blasphemy (which we compartmentalize as technorationality & ra-
cism, sexism & standardization). For "one" lives not to proclaim only
but to listen for that which is not conceivable in one's "own" self-
same world—that which violates its premises & perimeters, shaking
them with the life forever *beyond* and *outside*.

Yet circling back with the dyspepsia of hindsight, it can also be
said that language is *other*, which we make ours without it belonging

to us; that self-sameness is a stylistic illusion in which individuation allows recognition of the social body that we are each a part of/apart from.

TB: In a recent interview, Larry Price remarks to Beverly Dahlen and Ted Pearson apropos their discussion of the writer's marginality: "the idea of a periphery, i.e., points in relation to a so-called center. I thought of two analogies: one would be the standing wave, and the other would be the relation between phenomena and noumena. The standing wave is not generated by a motion in the center, but from multiple points on the boundary, so that the President is in fact one sense of an illusion, as we might likewise hold the subject as an illusion, a fiction, created *by* the boundary, only one of whose points is, say, the young Lyndon, or the actor Ronald. The other analogy, noumenon/phenomenon, is really more complicated because it doesn't assume a duplicity." Comments?

CB: The theory of relativity of the center: the center is a projection from the periphery. Or rather, there is no center, only peripheries that agglomerate in various ways—like blood clots at the sites of trauma. Or again, things are central only in specific contexts—for many people, the local paper (or maybe the folded sheets of a distant poetry magazine) is what is first read and one man's national media is another woman's regional effluvium. Or do I confute centrality and priority?

But there is power, and dominance, and these, anyway, need to be differentiated from centrality. Power and dominance are a function of violence. And this violence is not so much a "hidden" truth but a very explicit—and necessarily contested—dynamic. "Fashion" might be a useful middle term between power and dominance, on the one side, and centrality as its legitimizing facticity on the other. Fashion seeks hegemony but produces *resistance*—not just to "fashion itself" but also as the motor of fashion, Paris versus Milano, last year's shoes versus this year's socks. Fashion and dominance logically entail contestation and contra-diction, along with a sliding scale of consequences if you are "wrong"—from losing a sale to losing your mind. That is, you don't need to "agree with" power, just acknowledge it: centrality is the power of the dominant margin. For while power appears factional, centrality has the epistemological clout of the given or normative, conventional or standard: power we've grown accustomed to.

In *The Genealogy of Morals* Nietzsche disdains attempts of the weak or oppressed to turn their marginality into a moral asset—that "slave's revolt" or "sublime sleight of hand which gives weakness the appearance of free choice and one's natural disposition the distinction of merit". "It was the Jew . . . with the furious hatred of the under-privileged and impotent [who first maintained] that 'only the poor, the powerless, are good; only the suffering, sick and ugly, truly blessed. But you noble and mighty ones of the earth will be, to all eternity, the evil, cruel, the avaricious, the godless, and thus the cursed and damned!'" (tr. F. Golffing). Yet *all* power involves a self-recog-nition of marginality and finding some way to cash in on it: the powerful are not more noble in turning their violence into a virtue than the powerless are vile for turning their powerlessness into a kind of moral authority (phantom centrality). No doubt what Nietzsche is attacking is not powerlessness itself but the poison of self-delusion about one's marginality, the arrogance of self-righteousness based on one's marginal status, the devastating effect of a consuming and blinding hatred of the "center" in the absence of any self- or social understanding or definition. Yet what's repugnant about his analysis is that he excludes the dominant from censure since such dominance is raw (naked?) rather than self-delusory. Perhaps a deeper implication of Nietzsche's polemic is that mass culture has become dominant by means of stigmatizing nonmass cultural values: thus any form of divergence—regional, ethnic, formal—is rejected as elitist or special-ized or separatist, as *not us*. In this sense, what Nietzsche is charting is a mechanism of dominance based on centrality, at the epistemolog-ical level, or its moral equivalent—common voice/accessibility.

The fiction of centrality that I'm hinting at here is related to those other fictions that have been undermined in much recent poetry—voice and identity. In emphasizing the legitimacy of marginal voices, there may be a tendency to essentialize difference; so that from a promotion of decentralized dialects we can too easily arrive at ato-mized centralities (nationalisms)—that is, a reductively unified iden-tity/voice of a "marginal" people or country or region. The contes-tatory nature of identity exists at *all* levels; balkanization of identity is not necessarily a solution to multinational homogenization (or deterritorialization) of voice.

Essentializing the marginality of poetry into a transcendental hu-man experience beyond the divisive fray of history and ideology is just what Romantic ideology is all about. David Lloyd expresses this nicely in an article on the evasions of Seamus Heaney's Irish nationalism (*boundary* 2 8:2/3, 1985): "The discourse of culture itself originates in the moment that the division of intellectual and physical labor has become such that 'culture' as a specialization is privileged yet entirely marginalized in relation to productive forces, and seeks to disguise, or convert, both privilege and marginalization in a sublimation which places it beyond division and into a position whence it can appear to form the work of unification . . . The discourse of culture consistently seeks, by representing itself as withdrawn from implication in social divisions, as indifferent, to forge a domain in which divisions are overcome or made whole. The realization of human freedom is deferred into this transcendental domain, with the consequence that an ethical invocation is superadded to the exhortations of culture."

Is it, then, possible to have marginality as a value that is not perfused by resentment or Romantic evasion? Insofar as marginality is taken as a positive moral value, this dilemma holds. But it can begin to be dissolved when marginality is recognized, in contradistinction, as a t(r)opological prerequisite of all utterance.

TB: Linda Reinfeld's attentive review of *Content's Dream* appeared in a recent *Temblor.* Allow me to ask a question she asks: "Why, then, given the care and writerly consciousness of these essays, given their thoughtful articulation of theory, are they presented now as *Dream?*"

CB: *Dream* in the sense of *aspiration,* as to breathe in, to pronounce with a full breathing: "the legitimate aspirations of the heart". I have a dream . . . "I have an exposition of sleep come upon me." (Say a condition of unsureness: "God's my life! Stolen hence, and left me asleep?") Or what is dream, a reverie that displaces the real or a hum that supersedes the repressed, whose logic is of desire not deduction, wherein we wake *to* dream not *from* it? Or, say, the dream of Content: what content would dream, if allo(u)wed, to sate its discontent, anticipate its aspirations.

"I have had a dream, past the wit of man to say what dream it was. Man is but an ass if he go about to expound this dream. Methought I was—there is no man can tell what. Methought I was, and methought I had—But man is but a patched fool if he will offer to say what methought I had. The eye of man hath not heard, the ear of man hath not seen, man's hand is not able to taste, his tongue to conceive, nor his heart to report what my dream was. I will get Peter Quince to write a ballet of this dream. It shall be called 'Bottom's Dream,' because it has no bottom."

"*When my cue comes, call me, and I will answer.*"

TB: With a cast of Liubov Popova, Jenny Lind, and John Milton, your poem "Entitlement" (in *The Sophist*) is in the form of a play. Popova, Lind, Milton—why these historical personages? What or whom is entitled?

CB: Maybe nobody. Maybe it's a dream to think anyone is. I was thinking of calling this dialogue (even more than play) "The Souls of White Folks" as in, do we have them? To say that white skin is a badge of some dishonor as long as there is apartheid, but yet we have some heroes too: heroes in the sense of those who made a habitation out of a mar(k)gin—how these artists to exist had to become, one way or another, "dented tokens": Milton in his failed attempt at public career; Lind whose voice could be heard only as sideshow act; Popova, dying of the scarlet fever contracted in the birth of her child (stark symbol of the revolution that the futurians gave birth to, putting so many of them to death—one way or another). So, yes, the margins again ("the soap in heaven's day–long wash"?), as a place to speak from, albeit a fictitious place with real-life scars. Thus, as comedy.

But: entitled to *what?* ("Bent is the promise.") Written as Reagan ascended to office on the premise of slashing entitlement programs (social security, unemployment insurance, public assistance grants), I wanted to picture these artists side*lined,* waiting on the bench—which is poetry's table, after all—and speaking against the end of time, *for time, in time, to time* (one and . . .), with the tools at hand—a piece of chalk perhaps to start, maybe loneliness ("like a sealed dove in the rain"), or the (re)vision of some other space ("patina breaks and under more patina").

Maybe to be entitled to speak—to articulate—without that effort being shot down as lacking content; yet none of these could hope that their sense would fall on much but deaf ears—and deaf ears still surround. Maybe everyone is entitled to be heard on their own terms, with a presumption of sense; but here we live a Napoleonic code: inarticulate until proven coherent; as if innocence has to be learned or that you need study diction to say you have hunger. (Yet no *one* is innocent just as no one is without hunger.) "You've got to learn to speak our language"—the carrot that hides the stick (so that's what is meant by a phallocratic grammar). As if learning a language was translating some primitive set of grunts into a mannered code, the primitive method cast as some hidden or private system to overcome yet which each of us knows, or fears, can never be overcome, always "holds us back". As if we are always translating our thoughts and feelings into foreign tongues, the most sure-"footed" still a bit shaky, and no one on solid ground. "Surely verges all obtain"—that might be this poem's dream; that we be content to allow for difference ("content as stubble at the eventide"), to accept that we cannot always or immediately understand what other people say and that those gaps speak as resonantly as—more resonantly than—any message extracted: so not make thought step to martial plan. So played as comedy.

The Second War and
Postmodern Memory

> *Now light your pipe; look, what a steady hand,*
> *Draw a deep breath; stop thinking, count fifteen,*
> *And you're as right as rain . . .*
> *Books; what a jolly company they are,*
> *Standing so quiet and patient on their*
> *shelves . . .*
> *they're so wise . . .*
> —Siegfried Sassoon, "Repression of War
> Experience" (1918)

We never discussed the Second World War much when I was growing up.

I don't feel much like discussing it now.

It seems presumptuous to interpret, much less give literary interpretations of, the Systematic Extermination Process or the dropping of the H Bomb, the two poles of the Second War.

When asked to speak on "Poetry after the Holocaust" my first reaction was to wonder what qualifications I had to speak—as if the topic of the war made me question my standing, made me wonder what I might say that could bear the weight of this subject matter. Stanley Diamond reassured me that the audience would be small: "For many the Holocaust is too far in the past to matter; for most of the rest, it's too painful to bring to mind."

My father-in-law, who left Berlin as a teenager on a youth aliyah and spent the war in Palestine, had a different reaction: all these Holocaust conferences are a fad. This reaction is as disturbing as it is right. The Holocaust has come to stand for a kind of Secular Satanism—everyone's against it, anyone can work up a feverish moral fervor denouncing the Nazi Monster.

Yet I've been struck by just the opposite: that the psychological effects of the Second War are still largely repressed and that we are just beginning to come out of the shock enough to try to make sense of the experience.

We stormed the citadel under the banner of amnesia,
Winning absolute victory over the Germans in 1943.
Fantasy that could leave nothing out but the pain . . .
  —Barrett Watten, *Under Erasure*[1]

Crysiles of cristle, piled
ankle high,   .
as wide as sound carries. Am I—
hearing it—algebras worth?

There is a wind
erases marks. I felt it on my cheek
Summers long
you can cross it

& still not approach time, de-
solidified, approaching mothish mists

felled, the way a price knocked down

puts purchase on its feet. Stammering

painful clamor   by coincidents
      appraised.   Refuse

   is a spilled constant.
   Let it loose.
—Benjamin Friedlander, "Kristallnacht"[2]

I don't remember when I first heard about the war, but I do remember
thinking of it as an historical event, something past and gone. It's
inconceivable to me now that I was born just five years after its end;
each year, the Extermination Process seems nearer, more recent. Yet
if the systematic extermination of the European Jews seemed to define,
implicitly, the horizon of the past for me, the bomb defined the
foreshortened horizon of the future.

1. Excerpted in "Postmodern Poetries", ed. Jerome McGann, in *Verse* 7:1 (1990),
33.
  2. *Kristallnacht: November 9–10, 1938* (privately printed, 1988), unpaginated.

hear
hear, where the dry blood talks
        where the old appetite walks . . .
where it hides, look
in the eye how it runs
in the flesh / chalk

        but under these petals
        in the emptiness
        regard the light, contemplate
        the flower

whence it arose

        with what violence benevolence is bought
        what cost in gesture justice brings
        what wrongs domestic rights involve
        what stalks
        this silence
        what pudor or perjorocracy affronts
        how awe, night-rest and neighborhood can rot
        what breeds where dirtiness is law
        what crawls
        below . . .
        —Charles Olson, "The Kingfishers" (1949)[3]

Fifty years is not a long time to absorb such a catastrophe for Western
Civilization. It seems to me that the current controversies surrounding
Paul de Man and, more significantly, Martin Heidegger reflect the
psychic economy of reason in face of enormous loss. In all our journals
of intellectual opinion, we are asked to consider, as if it were a divine
mystery, how such men of learning, who have shown such a profound
and subtle appreciation for the art and philosophy of the West, could
have countenanced, indeed be complicit in, an evil that seems to erode
any possible explanation, justification, or contextualization, despite
the attempt of well-meaning commentators to evade this issue by just
such explanations, justifications, and contextualizations.

3. *Collected Poems*, ed. George F. Butterick (Berkeley: University of California
Press, 1987), pp. 86–93.

The Heidegger question merely personalizes the basic situation of
the war: that European learning, the Enlightenment tradition (as
indeed devastatingly critiqued by Heidegger), and the ideals of reason
as embodied in the nation state, were as much a cause of the war as
a break from it. For to understand how Heidegger could be complicit
in the Second War is to understand how the Second War is not an
aberration but an extension of the Logos of Western Civilization. Jack
Spicer's dying words—"My vocabulary did this to me"—could be the
epitaph of the Second War as well: Our vocabulary did this to us.

Walter Benjamin, Primo Levi, and Paul Celan committed suicide;
de Man and Heidegger went on to prosper. What did the former
know that the latter never absorbed? To acknowledge the Second
War means to risk suicide and in the process to politicize philosophy;
and if we desire to avoid death and evade politics, repression is
inevitable. Which is to say that the death an acknowledgment of this
war brings on is not only the death of individuals but also of an
ideal—of reason unbounded to politics, of, that is, rationality as such.

fear smashes into
my double
out of nowhere
would shrink
flesh back in itself
before it vomits
a wet night from neck or forehead
passes
into the vague air
swallows
the liquid stays inside
my corneas extend
along the axis of
the flow
dries
    —Rosmarie Waldrop[4]

4. *The Road Is Everywhere Or Stop This Body* (Columbia, Missouri: Open Places,
1978), p. 26; p. 7 subsequently cited.

I'd be reluctant to say that any of my own poems was about the war or should be read within that frame—none would hold up to the scrutiny such a reading would promote. But I do want to make a broad, very provisional, claim that much of the innovative poetry of these soon-to-be fifty years following the war register the twined events of Extermination in the West and Holocaust in the East in ways that have not been accounted for.

> From the stately violence of the State
> a classic war, World War Two, punctuated by Hiroshima
> all the action classically taking place on one day
> visible to one group in invisible terms
> beside a fountain of imagefree water
> "trees" with brown "trunks" and "leafy" green crowns
> 50s chipmunks sitting beneath, buck teeth representing
> mental tranquility, they sit in rows
> and read their book and the fountain gushes forth
> all the letters at once, permanently
> a playful excrescence, an erotic war against nature . . .
> —Bob Perelman, "The Broken Mirror"[5]

Every cultural development I ascribe to the Second War can be just as readily traced to some other cause and can also be said to preexist the war. My argument is not deterministic; rather I want to suggest that the frame of the Second War, Auschwitz and Hiroshima, transforms the social meaning of these cultural developments.

Racism and cultural supremacism do not begin or end with the Second War, but they are the precise ideological instruments that mark the most unrecuperable aspects of the war—the Lagers and the mutilated survivors of the bomb. The war did not make racism and cultural supremacism intolerable, they always were, but it demonstrated, as if demonstration was necessary, their absolute corrosiveness.

The war made it apparent, if it wasn't already, that racism and cultural supremacism are not correctable flaws of Western logocen-

---

5. *The First World* (Great Barrington, Mass.: The Figures, 1986), p. 45.

trism but its nonbiodegradable byproduct. I don't mean this as a thesis to be systematically argued. Rather I am suggesting that the war undermined, subliminally more than consciously, the belief in virtually every basic value of the Enlightenment, insofar as these values are in any way Eurosupremacist or hierarchic.

> Not one death but many,
> not accumulation but change, the feed-back proves, the feed-
> back is
> the law
>
> > Into the same river no man steps twice
> > When the fire dies air dies
> > No one remains, nor is, one . . .
>
> To be in different states without a change
> is not a possibility . . .
> —Olson, "The Kingfishers"

Racism and cultural supremacism contaminate everything that is associated with them; if this guilt by association is necessarily too farreaching, that is because it sets loose a radical skepticism that knows no immediate place to stop.

The Second War undermines authority in all its prescriptive forms and voices: the rights of the Father, of Law, of the Nation and National Spirit, of Technorationality, of Scientific Certainty, of Axiomatic Judgment, of Hierarchy, of Progress, of Tradition. It's a chain reaction. No truths are self-evident, certainly not the prerogatives of patriarchy, authority, rationality, order, control.

"But it's not reason but unreason that caused the war! It's just a parody of the Enlightenment to associate it with Nazi dementia, or to see the telos of science in a mushroom cloud! The Enlightenment was a force for *toleration* and consideration as opposed to mysticism, irrationality, and theological or state authority. Didn't the Allies represent these Western values against the Nazis?"

But the matter is altogether more complicated, and my account risks swerving into something too grandiose: for this is not a matter of principle but of shock and grief. If the values associated with the Enlightenment are undermined, this is not to remove the Romantic legacy from its undoing. For if the Second War casts doubt on systematicity, it is no less destructive to the vatic, the occult, the charismatic, the emotional solidarity of communion.

There are new difficulties. It's difficult to see order in the same way after the war, hard to accept control as a neutral value or domination by one group of another as justifiable, hard not to associate systematic operations with the systematicity of the extermination process or preemptory authority with fascism. These associations overgeneralize: but the pairs are subliminally linked, the one stigmatized by the other. Benjamin said it best and the Second War made it ineradicable (roughly): Every act of Civilization is at the same time an act of Barbarism.

> When the attentions change / the jungle
> leaps in
>   even the stones are split
>   they rive . . .
> —Olson, "The Kingfishers"

The vehemence of the civil rights movement and the anti-Vietnam War movement can be seen in this context: the shadow of the Second War, growing darker as the immediate compensatory shock of the first postwar decades wore off, spurred the pace of demands for change and contributed to a sometimes millenarian we-can't-go-on-the-old-way-anymore zeal. In the U.S., the war on the war in Vietnam inaugurates the externalization of the response to the Second War— the beginning of the end of the repression of the experience of the war.

The realization that white heterosexual Christian men of the west have no exclusive franchise for articulating the "highest" values of humankind was certainly around prior to the Second War, but the war added a nauseating repulsiveness to such canonical views; as if they were not just something to dispute but could no longer be stomached at all. The depth and breadth of the challenge to the Western canon may be a measure of the effect of the war, though few of the parties to the controversy choose to frame it this way.

It's now a commonplace to read the poetry that followed the Great War in the context of the bitter disillusionment brought about by that cataclysm; just as we better understand the Romantics when we keep in the mind the context of the French Revolution. The effects of the Second War are greater than those of the first, but less frequently cited.

I don't mean "war poetry" in the sense of poems about the war; they are notoriously scarce and beside the point I want to make here. Of course there are many accounts of the war—documentary, personal, theoretical—and many visualizations of the war in film, photography, painting. But the scope or core of the Second War cannot be represented only by the conventional techniques developed to depict events, scenes, battles, political infamies. Only the surface of the war can be pictured.

To be sure, the crisis of representation, which is to say the recognition that the Real is not representable, is associated with the great radical modernist poems of the period immediately before and after the First World War. In the wake of the Second War, however, the meaning and urgency of unrepresentability took on explosive new force as a political necessity, as the absolute need to reground polis. That is, such work which had started as a heady, even giddy, aesthetic investigation had become primarily an act of human reconstruction and reimagining.

Radical modernism can be characterized by the discovery of the entity status of language—not just verbal language but signification systems/processes; thus the working hypothesis about the autonomy of the medium, of the compositional space; the flattening of the Euclidian space of representing and its implicit metaphysics of displacement and reification of objects. I think all of these fundamental ontological and aesthetic discoveries and inventions are carried forward into the radical late twentieth-century work but with a different critical understanding of the implications of this new textual space.

> as if we could ignore
> the consequences of
> explosions fracture the present
> warm exhaust
> in our lungs would turn us
> inside out of
> gloves avoid words like
> "war" needs subtler
> poisons as if

conscious of ends and means
scream in every
nerve every breath every
grain of dust
to dust cancers over
the bloodstream
the bloodstream
the bloodstream
the bloodstream
the bloodstream
        —Waldrop, *The Road Is Everywhere*

After the Second War, there is a more conscious rejection of lingering positivist and romantic orientations toward, respectively, master systems and the poetic Spirit or Imagination as transcendent. The meaning of the modernist textual practice has been interpreted in ways that contrast with some of its original interpretations: *toward* the incommensurability of different discourse systems, *against* the idea of poetry as an imperializing or world-synthesizing agency (of the zeitgeist), not only because these ideas tend to impart to the poet a superhistorical or superhuman perspective but also because they diminish the partiality, and therefore particularity, of any poetic practice. Thus the emphasis in the New American Poetry and after on particularity, the detail rather than the overview, form understood as eccentric rather than systematic, process more than system, or if system then system that undermines any hegemonic role for itself.

In the center of movement, a debate.
Before beginning, a pause . . .

Pianissimo.

Curious symptom, this, that the man appears
mildly self-satisfied, as if, in spite of his
obvious confusion and . . . so ill at ease
        —Nick Piombino[6]

6. *Poems* (Los Angeles: Sun & Moon Press, 1988), p. 7.

After the war, there is also greater attention to the ideological function of language: taking the word/world-materializing techniques of radical modernism and applying them to show how "everyday" language practices manipulate and dominate; that is, the investigation of the social dimension of language as reality-producing through the use of radical modernist procedures.

> how we read it
>   line after line
>
>
>   given
>   one look
>
>
>   refresh the eyes
>   against the abyss
>
> —Larry Eigner[7]

Poetry after the war has its psychic imperatives: to dismantle the grammar of control and the syntax of command. This is one way to understand the political content of its form.

> We are
> in a sandheap
>
> We are
> discovered
> not solid
>   the floor
>   based
> on misunderstanding.
>
>   —Susan Howe, "The Liberties"[8]

7. *another time in fragments* (London: Fulcrum, 1967), frontispiece poem.
8. *The Europe of Trusts* (Los Angeles: Sun & Moon Press, 1990), pp. 210–211.

If racism and cultural supremacism are no longer tolerable, then literary history has to be rewritten. This has its primary expression in the proliferation of poetry that rejects a monoculturally centric point of view.

Jerome Rothenberg's anthologies epitomize one aspect of this development. *Technicians of the Sacred* insisted on the immediate (rather than simply historical or anthropological) relevance of the "tribal" poetries of Native Americans (on both American continents), Africans, peoples of Oceania. This was a concerted assault on the primacy of Western high culture and an active attempt to find in other, nonwestern/nonoriental cultures, what seemed missing from our own. Moreover, the "recovery" of Native American culture by a Jewish Brooklyn-born first-generation poet-as-anthologist whose aesthetic roots were in the European avant-garde implicitly acknowledges our *domestic* genocide. This gesture cannot be fully appreciated without recognizing that it functions as a way of recovering from the Second War by refusing to cover over the genocide that has allowed a false unity to the idea of American literature. Rothenberg's anthologies present a multicultural America of many voices in a way that explicitly rejects Eurosupremacism from *within* a European perspective—that is, dispensing with the demagogic rejection of Europe as such in favor of idealized "America".

The effect of the Second War is audible not only in the subject matter of the New American Poetry of the 1950s but also in its form, in its insistence on form (as never more than the extension of content, in Creeley's phrase, echoed by Olson).

> He had been stuttering, by the edge
> of the street, one foot still
> on the sidewalk, and the other
> in the gutter . . .
>
> like a bird, say, wired to flight, the
> wings, pinned to their motion, stuffed.
>
> The words, several, and for each, several
> senses.

> "It is very difficult to sum up
> briefly . . ."
> > It always was.
> > —Robert Creeley, "Hart Crane"[9]

"I saw the best minds of my generation destroyed by madness, starving hysterical naked" does not refer to the war, but it can't help doing so despite itself.[10] *Howl* makes it apparent that something has gone wrong with America by the early 1950s: the whole "calm" of this period can be read as a repression that Ginsberg, and others, reacted—powerfully, resonantly—against. Not like Sassoon—"I'm going crazy; I'm going stark, staring mad because of the guns". That's the difference between the two wars: the malaise is not locatable as the official event of the war, the battles; the whole of everyday life has lost its foundations. And the poetry—or some of it—either registered this loss of foundation in the everyday, or invented ways of articulating new foundations, strikingly without the grandiosity or optimism of some of its modernist sources.

> On the street I am met with constant hostility
> and I would have finally nothing else around me,
> except my children who are trained to love
> and whom I intend to leave as relics of my intentions.
> > —Creeley, "A Fragment"[11]

> These lacustrine cities grew out of loathing
> Into something forgetful, although angry with history.
> They are the product of an idea: that man is horrible,
> > for instance.
> Though this is only one example . . .
> > —John Ashbery, "These Lacustrine Cities"[12]

The New American Poetry, by and large, rejected the grandiosity of scheme, of world-spirit, of progress, of avant-garde advance: the

9. Opening poem in *For Love,* in *Collected Poems* (Berkeley: University of California Press, 1982), p. 109.

10. Allen Ginsberg, *Howl* (San Francisco: City Lights, 1956), p. 9.

11. "A Fragment" in *The Charm* (early poems), *Collected Poems,* p. 101.

12. Opening lines of *Rivers and Mountains* (New York: Ecco Press, 1966), p. 1.

positivist, quasi-authoritarian assumptions of Futurism, Vorticism, or the tradition of Eliot. It rejected the heroic universalizing of poetic genius in favor of particularization, process, detail; extending the innovations of the 1910–1917 period, but giving them an entirely different psychic registration. Think of the role of the ungeneralizable particular in Creeley or Eigner as opposed to the controlling allegories of Pound or Eliot, think of Ashbery's or Spicer's or Mac Low's self-cancelation compared to Williams' relaxed prerogatives of self or Stein's exuberant hubris.

This ocean, humiliating in its disguises
Tougher than anything.
No one listens to poetry. The ocean
Does not mean to be listened to. A drop
Or crash of water. It means
Nothing.
It
Is bread and butter
Pepper and salt. The death
That young men hope for. Aimlessly
It pounds the shore. White and aimless signals. No
One listens to poetry.
  —Jack Spicer, "Thing Language"[13]

Or think of Olson suggesting that his project as a poet is to find a way out of the "Western Box", or Duncan's *Before the War*, or Rothenberg, in his essay on the war, writing of discontent with "regularity and clarity as a reflection of the nature of God"[14]. (In his essay, Rothenberg quotes Creeley's recent poem from *Windows:* "Ever since Hitler / or well before that / fact of human appetite / addressed with brutal / indifference others / killed or tortured . . . / . . . no possible way / out of it smiled or cried / or tore at it and died."[15])

To link the New American poetry with the Second War in this way suggests that the systematic extermination process had a profound

---

13. *Language* (1964) in *The Collected Books of Jack Spicer,* ed. Robin Blaser (Los Angeles: Black Sparrow, 1975), p. 217; p. 223 cited subsequently.
14. Rothenberg's comments are from the manuscript of his essay forthcoming in *Dialectical Anthropology.*
15. Creeley, *Windows* (New York: New Directions, 1990), p. 123.

effect on American attitudes in the 1950s. No doubt this projects
more than is evident. While the effect of the Second War on the
United States has been farreaching, and not only for those who fought
in the war and their families, the Lagers may well have been a distant
issue for most Americans. In contrast, the cold war and the U.S.'s
new hegemonic global role would be a more obvious context for a
sociohistorical reading of the New American Poets. But something
else lurks in these poems of the "other" tradition that suggests a
discomfort with American complacency that the cold war does not
quite account for.

> 1st SF Home Rainout Since. Bounce Tabby-Cat Giants.
>   Newspapers
> Left in my house.
> My house is Aquarius. I don't believe
> The water-bearer
> Has equal weight on his shoulders.
> The lines never do.
> We give equal
> Space to everything in our lives. Eich-
> Mann proved that false in killing like you raise wildflowers.
>   Witlessly
> I
> Can-
> not
> accord
> sympathy
> to
> those
> who
> do
> not
> recognize
> The human crisis.
>   —Spicer, *Language*

The human crisis seems to have wounded a different, slightly younger
cluster of American poets that keeps forming and reforming in my
mind, and I find it difficult to ignore the fact they were born during

the Second War. Susan Howe gives an explicit account of what I take here to be significant:

> For me there was no silence before armies.
>
> I was born in Boston Massachusetts on June 10th, 1937, to an Irish mother and American father . . . By 1937 the Nazi dictatorship was well established in Germany. All dissenting political parties had been liquidated and Concentration Camps had already been set up . . . In the summer of 1938 my mother and I were staying . . . in Ireland and I had just learned to walk, when Czechoslovakia was dismembered . . . That October we sailed home on a ship crowded with refugees. When I was two the German army invaded Poland and World War II began in the West . . . American fathers march off into the hot Chronicles of global struggle but mothers were left . . . From 1939 until 1946 in news photographs, day after day I saw signs of culture exploding into murder . . . I became part of the ruin. In the blank skies over Europe I was Strife represented . . . Those black and white picture shots—moving or fixed—were a subversive generation.[16]

I wouldn't want to give an inclusive list of this extraordinary part-generation of *Newer* American Poets born between 1937 and 1944, but a partial list would include Clark Coolidge, Michael Palmer, Lyn Hejinian, David Melnick, Tom Mandel, Michael Lally, Ted Greenwald, Ray DiPalma, Nick Piombino, Ann Lauterbach, Peter Seaton, Jim Brodey, Charles North, Fanny Howe, George Quasha, Charles Stein, Robert Grenier, Ron Padgett, Stephen Rodefer, John Taggart, Maureen Owen, Lorenzo Thomas, Lewis Warsh, Michael Davidson, Tony Towle, Bill Berkson, Geoff Young, Kathleen Fraser, John Perlman—all contemporaries of John Lennon, Bob Dylan, and Richard Foreman. (I recognize how arbitrary it is to leave off the years just before and after, or not to mention Tom Raworth, born in England in 1938.)

16. Howe, "There Are Not Leaves Enough to Crown / To Cover to Crown to Cover", in *The Europe of Trusts*, pp. 9–12.

```
o – u –
u – u – ni –
form – ity – o –
u – u – u – ni –
formity – o –
u – unit – de –
formity – u –
unit deformity
```
    —Robert Grenier,
        "Song"[17]

While I don't want to stereotype individuals who, if anything, stand radically and determinately against stereotyping, generalizing, sweeping claims, ideological pronouncements, and the like, I've been struck by how much these individual artists have *that* in common: as if they share, without ever so stating, a rejection of anything extrinsic to the poetic process and to the poem—an insistence on the particularity of that process, the nonreducible nature of the choices made, the obscenity or absurdity of paraphrase or extrapoetic explanation, and a suspicion or rejection of conventional literary, and equally nonliterary, career patterns. In short, they share a radical rejection of conventional American values of conformism, fitting in, getting along/going along—of accessibility to the point of self-betrayal.

```
An evening . . .
Spent thinking
About what my life would be . . .
If I'd've been accepted to and gone
Where I applied . . .
Where I'd learned
Different social graces
Than the ones I have
Where some of the material
Values of the American dream
Had rubbed off . . .
If I'd settled down
```

17. *Phantom Anthems* (Oakland: O Books, 1986), unpaginated [p. 27].

And settled
For the foundation
On a house
For future generations
Instead of assuming
Immediately past generations
My foundation to mine
If I'd been
A little quicker to learn
What was expected of me . . .
I've probably been saved
By a streak of stubbornness
By a slow mind
And a tendency to drift
That requires
My personal understanding
Before happening . . .
   —Ted Greenwald, "Whiff "[18]

Uncompromising integrity is one way I'd put it, emphasizing that the social cost of such uncompromising integrity—inaudibility or marginality, difficult immediate personal and economic circumstance, isolation, feisty impatience with less exacting choices—are not unknown to some of these individuals.

it's embarrassing to feel
my self body image etc (often)
defined by people around me (my reaction to their reactions)
that embarrasses me a lot
zeal embarrasses me, your zeal for instance
always lining up poets and their poems
one up one down
in relation to you and your poems . . .
most of all . . . I'm embarrassed by death
death is really the only embarrassing thing

18. *Common Sense* (Kensington, Calif.: L Publications, 1978), pp. 11–12; "For Ted, On Election Day", cited next, p. 25.

and sometimes (unexpectedly these days more often)
it scares the shit out of me
—Greenwald, "For Ted, On Election Day"

Or put it this way: I find in many of the works of these poets an intense distrust of large-scale claims of any kind, an extreme questioning of public forms, a tireless tearing down or tearing away at authoritative/authoritarian language structures. I hear in their works an explosion of self-reflectiveness and a refusal of the systematic combined with a pervasive engagement with dislocation up to the point of personal terror: an insistence on the human scale of poetry—on the "human crisis"—in a culture going bonkers with mass markets, high technology, and faith in science as savior.

the lost family of scatter cabal
thought under disorder and music
filling the crumpled space owned
by another taught under disorder
to make a path through judgement . . .
—Ray DiPalma[19]

Although I would point to the remarkable amount of what is now reductively called "theory" implicit in the work of most of these poets, many of them have eloquently refused the mantle of poetics and theory, as if to engage in such secondary projects would implicate them in a grandiosity or even megalomania that the work itself abjures.

What we know is the way we fall
when we fall off the little we ride
when we ride away from the things we're given
to make us forget the things we gave up
—Michael Lally, "In the Distance"[20]

19. *RAIK* (New York: Roof Books, 1989), p. 80.
20. *Rocky Dies Yellow* (Berkeley: Blue Wind, 1975), p. 22.

While the formal invention and innovations among these poets is enormous, few of them have chosen to promote them in an impersonal or art-historical way; invention is not seen in avant-garde or canonical terms but rather as a necessary extension of a personally eccentric investigation, crucial because of the "internal" needs of the articulation and not justified or justifiable by external criteria.

> We're strange features, ignoring things. Our hero
> Separates from a problem in pink, the thought
> To be able to thing in the world . . .
>
> So this is the perfect plan. And here's a creative code.
> For all its on or off old self, immersion, power and
>
> Command. When the world was wars and wars, according
> To cause breaking out from the conditions for events
> And their obsessed leaders. Brute editing, the way
>
> The frame's the response to survival aids to lust
> Contains the round rations on an actual summit.
> One teaches sense to a child saying you sense
> How we've always talked . . .
>
> A deeper shelter, a deeper skin leaving
> Tracks the brain blew away . . .
> Predatory signs which whiz by and stop,
> The lid and the soul, there are reasons for this.
> —Peter Seaton, "Need from a Wound Would Do It"[21]

So the absence of a substantial amount of poetics or commentary (the exceptions are striking but not contradictory), more, the refusal of commentary as explanation, mark a complete engagement with the poetic act as *necessarily* self-sufficient. Thus: a reluctance to link up formal innovation—which is understood as eccentric and self-defined—with larger political, social or aesthetic activities, as in groups or movements, while at the same time refusing to romanticize

21. "Language Sampler", ed. Bernstein, in *Paris Review* 86 (1982), unpaginated [pp. 79–81].

or sentimentalize "individuality" in place of the values of poetic work itself.

> Not by
> 'today' but
> by
> recurrent light
> its course
> of blossoming
> is not effected
> by the sun at all?
> 'powers of
> darkness' at large?
> it 'unfolds'
> 'unfolding'
> *flowering*
> *of powers of*
> *darkness at large?*
> I 'see' at 'dawn'?
>   —Grenier, "Rose"[22]

This formulation suggests a relatively sharp demarcation with the generation born after 1945—the so-called baby boomers who came of age during a time when personal discomfort with, or distaste for, dominant American values could be linked up to national and international cultural and political movements that seemed to share these values. In 1958 cultural and political dissidence would have taken place against a totally different ground than ten years later. The situation of the fifties may have induced a sense of isolation or self-reliance in contrast to the sixties version of sometimes giddy group solidarity.

> Damage frightens sometimes—reminder
> of present danger—loss, deprivation . . .
> One didn't want to view the wreckage constantly

---

22. *Phantom Anthems,* [p. 78].

but sought the consolation of lovely sights and
subtle sounds. One could accept a single scratch
but in the midst of the thicket, the brambles burn
and the delay in walking at last annoys and one
loses patience.
  —Piombino[23]

The poetry of murder helped instigate the murder of poetry.

Looking for the root, I forgot the sun.
  —Piombino, "9/20/88"

Perhaps this can be described as a process of internalization, looking
downward or inward ("the root") rather than outward ("the sun")—
not upward as in idealism but falling down with the gravity of the
earth, the grace of the body, even the body—the materiality—of
language. There is, in many of the poems of these poets, a persistence
of dislocation, of going on in the face of all the terms being changed
while refusing to return to normalcy or a new equilibrium grounded
on repressing the old damage. This can be as much a cause for comedy
as solemnity.

weracki
dciece
hajf   wet pboru
eitusic at foerual bif
thorus
t'inalie thodo
to ~~tala~~
ienstable
ate sophoabl
  —David Melnick[24]

Poets are seismographs of the psychic realities that are not seen or
heard in less sensitive media; poems chart realities that otherwise go

---

23. *Poems*, p. 63; next citation from *Verse*, ed. McGann, p. 30.
24. *Pcoet* (San Francisco: G.A.W.K., 1975), poem no. 16.

unregistered. And they do this more in the minute particulars of registration than any idea of subject matter would otherwise suggest.

> What is said
> long before
> the chronicle
> is told   Smokey
> Stuff in damp rooms
> Carved out
> Blocked out
> Piled with slits
> And windows . . .
> 　—Ray DiPalma[25]

The psychic dislocation of the Second War occurred when these poets were toddlers; their first experience of language, of truth and repression, of fear and future, are inextricably tied to the Second War. Perhaps poetry presented a possible field for articulation for those who atypically stayed in touch with—perhaps could not successfully repress—these darker realities.

> A great block of wedge wood stint
> stays at the star of its corner which.
> A divider in pierces depends, wans.
> For is what I have made be only salvage?
> Sat in my robes, folds. Decomposed, fled.
> The world a height now brine, estuaries drained to the very pole.
> Geometric, a lingual dent? Drainage, albany. Where at the last
> stand all this sphere that herded me? My cell a corner on the
> filtering world, all out herein my belts. Things in trim they
> belt me, beg me, array my coined veils . . . The world in anger
> is an angled hole? . . .
> The light that leaks from composition alone.

25. "Five Poems from *Chan*" in "43 Poets (1984)", ed. Bernstein, *boundary 2* 14:1–2 (1986), 58.

Scalded by a tentative. Expels the tiny expounds thing huge,
things made be. Any and it's large. A universe is not of use.
    —Clark Coolidge[26]

These tentative angles into the unknown are a far cry from Rothenberg's explosive, disturbing, graphic struggle with the memories of the war in *Khurbn:*

"practice your scream" I said
(why did I say it?)
because it was his scream & wasn't my own
it hovered between us   bright
to our senses always bright it held
the center place
then somebody else came up & stared
deep in his eyes there found a memory
of horses galloping faster the wheels dyed red
behind them   the poles had resolved
a feast day but the jew
locked in his closet screamed
into his vest a scream
that had no sound therefore
spiralled around the world
so wild that it shattered stones . . .
    —"Dos Geshray (The Scream)"[27]

Khurbn risks the pornographic or voyeuristic out of a need to exorcise the images that hold us captive if not spoken or revisualized, marking an end to Rothenberg's own past refusal to depict the extermination process.

In contrast, Charles Reznikoff's last book, *Holocaust* (1975), which is based on documentary evidence about the Lagers gathered from the records of the Eichmann and Nuremberg trials, presents a series of details, fragments cut away from the horror. Reznikoff offers no explanation of the depicted events, and he provides neither explicit

---

26. *Melencolia* (Great Barrington, Mass.: The Figures, 1987), unpaginated [sec. 1].
27. Rothenberg, *Khurbn & Other Poems* (New York: New Directions, 1989), p. 11.

emotional nor moral response to them: he leaves us alone with our reactions, making us find our own screams or articulate our own silences. Seemingly flat, documentary, particularized, *Holocaust*—like all of Reznikoff's work since his first book in 1917—is a mosaic of salient incidents:

> A visitor once stopped one of the children
> a boy of seven or eight, handsome, alert and gay.
> He had only one shoe and the other foot was bare,
> and his coat of good quality had no buttons.
> The visitor asked him for his name
> and then what his parents were doing;
> and he said, "Father is working in the office
> and Mother is playing the piano."
> Then he asked the visitor if he would be joining his parents
> soon—
> they always told the children they would be leaving soon to rejoin
> their parents—
> and the visitor answered, "Certainly. In a day or two."
> At that the child took out of his pocket
> half an army biscuit he had been given in the camp
> and said, "I am keeping this half for Mother;"
> and then the child who had been so gay
> burst into tears.[28]

This detail from Reznikoff brings forward, in an ineffably shattering way, the atmosphere of willed forgetting of the 1950s, or now. We blithely go about our business—busy, gay, distracted; until that blistering moment of consciousness that shatters all hopes when we recognize that we are orphaned, have lost our parents—in the sense of our foundations, our bearing in the world; until, that is, a detail jolts the memory, when we feel, as in the fragments in our pocket, what we have held back out of denial.

Denial marks the refusal to mourn: to understand what we have lost and its absolute irreparability. Reznikoff and Rothenberg initiate

28. Reznikoff, "Children", *Holocaust* (Los Angeles: Black Sparrow, 1975), p. 69.

this process, but no more than other poets, ranges of poetry, that register this denial in the process of seeking forms that find ways out of the Western Box.

In contrast to—or is it an extension of ?—Adorno's famous remarks about the impossibility of (lyric?) poetry after Auschwitz, I would say poetry is a necessary way to register the unrepresentable loss of the Second War.

Comedy and the Poetics
of Political Form

> For if a swan could sing we would not know
> what she was insisting.
> But we are not, or few of us, swans, and have
> no excuse.
> —Flo Amber

> The Crooked shall be made Straight and the
> Straight sundered into a thousand Shards.
> —Ezekial Horn

No swan song will serenade these poetics to their close, only further complications to abet what has preceded, add some chiaroscuro to the dozing points of light; plug up some holes and drill some more, calling the leaks poetry, the clogs excess.

My theses have taken me some strange places, beyond Moorish interiors to an inlet inside a dome. An insistence whose luster is so much scotch-guard against spoilage, whose dethronements dissolve into valedictory reprise.

There's another way of saying it, of putting the cork back on the boat, the wheel around the spin: I mean to see the formal dynamics of a poem as communicative exchanges, as socially addressed, and as ideologically explicit. And, squinting to bring that into view, focus on the sometimes competing, sometimes reinforcing realms of convention and authority, persuasion and rhetoric, sincerity and conviction. For many a person has been convicted thanks to too much sincerity and not enough rhetoric, too much persuasion and not enough authority.

Conventions are made to be broken in that they are provisional rather than absolute, temporal rather than eternal. Differing conventions mark not only different times but also different classes and ethnicities. As we consider the conventions of writing, we are entering into the politics of language.

Writing conventions play a fundamental role in the legitimation of communicative acts. They determine what is allowed into a particular specific discourse: what is accepted as sensible or appropriate or within the bounds of morality.

Yet dominant conventions are hardly the only conventions with authority, and refusing the authority of particular conventions does not, in any sense, put one outside conventionality. Conventions are not identical to social norms or standards, although this distinction is purposely blurred in the legitimation process. Inflexible standardization is the arteriosclerosis of language. The shared counterconventions that may develop—whether among small constituencies of poets or political groupings or scientists or regional communities—are often a means of enhancing communication and articulation, in many cases because certain details (palpable material or social facts) are not articulable through prevailing linguistic conventions. Indeed, in its counterconventional investigations, poetry engages *public* language at its roots, in that it tests the limits of conventionality while forging alternate conventions (which, however, need not seek to replace other conventions in quest of becoming the new standard). Moreover, the contained scale of such poetic engagements allows for a more comprehensive understanding of the formation of public space: of polis.

Problems of authority emerge from counterestablishment conventions as much as from established conventions. The poetic authority to challenge dominant societal values, including conventional manners of communication, is a model for the individual political participation of each citizen. The peculiar act of exercising this authority has implications for the public sphere insofar as such independent exercise of authority is not legitimated within a political context that fosters passivity. What seems to be discouraged in American politics is any active participation in the designation and description of public policy issues—a ceding of authority that politicians, journalists, and the public are forced to accept if they are to play the political roles to which they seem to have been assigned. The poll remains the most conspicuous example of this disenfranchising process, for polls elicit binary reactions to always-already articulated policies—a stark contrast to proactive political participation that entails involvement in formulating these policies—*including formulating the way they are represented.*

This, in turn, suggests that authority must not be conflated into a single ambivalent figure; we must constantly be on guard to differentiate realms and degrees of authority, specifically in terms of the type of control exerted: the power of persuasion versus the coercion of physical force; vatic, perhaps even fatuous, poetic authority versus the psychological and behavioral manipulation of advertising or behavioral engineering; the authority of a school system versus that of an army, the authority of money versus aesthetic innovation.

Convention is a central means by which authority is made credible. As a result, convention can neutralize substantive conflicts: Tweedledum and Tweedledee may say the opposite things but this becomes a technicality within the context of their identical form.

> "If you think we're wax-works," [Tweedledee] said, "you ought to pay, you know. Wax-works weren't made to be looked at for nothing" . . .
> "I know what you're thinking about," said Tweedledum; "but it isn't so, nohow."
> "Contrawise," continued Tweedledee, "if it was so, it might be; and if it were so, it would be; but as it isn't, it ain't. That's logic."[1]

This is the logic of standardized form, the axiomatizing of difference, so that our opposition is so much waxwork, for which we are to be paid a penny a word. "They've got a laser printer, we'd better get a laser printer—lest our message will lack credibility."

I am not suggesting switching from an uptight business suit into sincere jeans, as if to reenact the fallacy of Romantic authenticity; but rather acting out, in dialectical play, the insincerity of form as much as content. Such poetic play does not open into a neat opposition of dry high irony and wet lyric expressiveness but, in contrast, collapses into a more destabilizing field of pathos, the ludicrous, schtick, sarcasm; a multidimensional textual field that is congenitally unable to maintain an evenness of surface tension or a flatness of affect, where linguistic shards of histrionic inappropriateness pierce the momentary calm of an obscure twist of phrase, before cantoring into the next available trope; less a shield than a probe.

The nonsincere, antiauthentic use of form is both antiformalist and, insofar as New Critical and Greenbergian formalism provides a con-

---

1. Lewis Carroll, "Tweedledum and Tweedledee", chap. 4, *Through the Looking Glass*, in *The Annotated Alice* (Cleveland: World Publishing, 1963), pp. 229–231.

ventional, highly partial reading of modernism, un-"Modern": though very much part of the radical modernist traditions. Both the formalist and New Critical maps of modernism tend to treat stylistic developments as a series of autonomous technical advances within an art medium and without recourse to sociohistorical explanation: a canonical strategy that underwrites the teaching of literature in most university settings.

The project of particularizing, historicizing, and ideologizing the interpretation of poetry must especially, even primarily, address itself to the stylistic features of the work. That means refusing to interpret formal dynamics as divorced from the historical and theatrical arena in which they are situated. In this context, Jerome McGann provides a useful model for reading Byron's formal strategies, specifically proposing Byron's direct confrontation with his audience, his inclusion of ungeneralizable and often savage personal details, and his blatant use of dissimulation as a refusal of the Romantic poetics of sincerity.[2] By Romantic sincerity, I mean the poet's lyric address to the human-eternal, to the Imagination, which seems to allow the poem to transcend the partiality of its origin. Thus the poet is able to speak for the "human" by refusing markers that would pull against the universality of "his" address—a strategy that enables us to misread Wordsworth as speaking as directly to us now as to his contemporaries. Indeed, Romantic sincerity engenders the idea of autonomy in New Critical and formalist approaches to twentieth-century art.

Historicizing a poem's deployment of artifice specifically brackets the canonical, teleological approach to stylistic innovation, which graphs particular innovations onto a master narrative of the medium's history. For one thing, these master narratives need to be partialized as specific historical projections for particular ideological purposes. Innovation "itself" may be thought of in social and not just structural terms (*equally* structural and social). That is, the rupturing of patriarchal discourse may be read in terms of sexual and racial politics as well as in terms of structural innovation in the abstract. At the same time, normative discursive practices need to be read in terms of the political meaning of their formal strategies.

On the one hand, this means considering how conventional writing—with and without oppositional content—participates in a legi-

---

2. See McGann's contribution to Charles Bernstein, ed., *The Politics of Poetic Form: Poetry and Public Policy* (New York: Roof Books, 1990).

timating process. On the other hand, this suggests the sort of pene-
trating analysis provided by Nathaniel Mackey on the social meaning
of stuttering/limping in Jean Toomer, Ralph Ellison, and William
Carlos Williams (a device that might also be interpreted, for example,
in terms of cubist fracturing);[3] or Nicole Brossard's framing of her
poetry in terms of the attempt to write without recourse to phallo-
cratic grammar (a project that might also be understood in terms of
its relation, for one example, to the new narrative strategies of writers
such as Alain Robbe-Grillet). Likewise, the innovations of white,
male, heterosexual artists are not "purely" stylistic—and perhaps the
harshness or bumpiness of the anticonventionality of Bruce Andrews
or myself needs to be read in terms of male sexual poetics as much
as we read Brossard or Mackey, at least in part, in terms of ethnic or
sexual identity.[4]

I do not think that all conventions are pernicious or that all au-
thority is corrupt. But I do think it is essential to trace how some uses
of convention and authority can hide the fact that both are historical

3. Nathaniel Mackey, "Sound and Sentiment, Sound and Symbol", ibid., pp. 91–
92: "the phantom limb is a felt recovery, a felt advance beyond severance and limita-
tion which contends with and questions conventional reality, that it's a feeling for
what's not there which reaches beyond as it calls into question what is . . . The
phantom limb haunts or critiques a condition in which feeling, consciousness itself,
would seem to have been cut off. It's this condition, the non-objective character of
reality, to which Michael Taussig applies the expression 'phantom objectivity,' by
which he means the veil by way of which a social order renders its role in the
construction of reality invisible."
   The stutter is a striking example of what I call an antiabsorptive or disruptive
device in "Artifice of Absorption". In an article on the video work of Jean-Luc
Godard, David Lévi-Strauss cites an interview with Gilles Deleuze in which he "char-
acterizes Godard's method of 'turning aside,' of diversion and interruption as a 'crea-
tive stutter'": "In a way, it's all about stuttering: not the literal speech impediment,
but that halting use of language itself. Generally speaking, you can only be a for-
eigner in a language other than your own. Here's it's a case of being a foreigner in
one's own language.'" Lévi-Strauss, "Oh Socrates: Visible Crisis in the Video &
Television Work of Jean-Luc Godard and Anne-Marie Mièville", Artscribe 74
(1989); Deleuze is quoted from an interview in Afterimage 7 (1978). —But, as I
argue in "Time Out of Motion", above, much of the most radical American poetry is
the writing of nonnative speakers: a nonnativeness that can range from a social given
to a cultural invention. The poet, like the Jew in Edmond Jabès's sense, is in exile,
even in her own words.
   4. Rosmarie Waldrop, in her contribution to Politics of Poetic Form, suggests that
the conception of poetry as quasi-legislative—certainly an aspect of my investiga-
tion—may be a particularly male aspiration. Bruce Andrews and Nicole Brossard
also contributed to the collection.

constructions rather than sovereign principles. For convention and authority can, and ought, serve at the will of the polis and not by the divine right of kings or the economic might of Capital. In this sense, _ I would speak of a phallocratic voice of truth and sincerity as one that hides its partiality by insisting on its centrality, objectivity, or neutrality—its claim to mainstream values; a voice that opts for expedience at the expense of depth, narrative continuity at the expense of detail, persuasion at the expense of conviction. This is a constantly self-proclaimed public voice, implicitly if not explicitly deriding the inarticulations, stutterings, inaudibilities, eccentricities, and linguistic deviance of specifically marked special-interest groups. The legitimating markers of persuasion and conviction in our society are intimately tied in to what can usefully be stigmatized as a male heterosexual form of discourse, one that I think "men" writers, given their specific vantage of being identified with this discourse, can also rupture, cut up, break apart in order to expose and defuse and reform.

In *The Politics of Poetic Form* Erica Hunt writes, specifically as a black woman, of feeling constrained by the private, fragmented, or subjective (subjugated) voices authorized for her and of her desire for, yet suspicion about, a "public voice", understood as one that carries the power and legitimacy of more conventional discursive practices. In contrast, I felt my initiation into such a public voice was the product of a profound humiliation and degradation that I had to undergo: a private-school hazing into Grammar, which once mastered I cannot unlearn but which, like many men, I am perennially suspicious of even as it continues to inform the expression of my (most well-founded) beliefs and convictions: the artifice of my authenticity.

So, again, I do not propose some private voice, some vatic image of sincerity or the absolute value of innovation, as an alternative to the limitations of the voices of authority I can never completely shake off. For I am a ventriloquist, happy as a raven to preach with blinding fervor of the corruptions of public life in a voice of pained honesty that is as much a conceit as the most formal legal brief for which my early education would seem to have prepared me. If my loops and short circuits, my love of elision, my Groucho Marxian refusal of irony, are an effort to explode the authority of those conventions I wish to discredit (disinherit), this constantly offers the consoling self-justification of being Art, as if I could escape the partiality of my condition by my investigation of it. But my art is just empty words on a page if it does not, indeed, persuade, if it enters into the world as self-justification or self-flagellation or aesthetic ornamentation rather than as interaction, conversation, provocation (for myself and others).

My sense of evacuating or undermining the public voice does not mean that I am giving anything up, except if gain is conceived purely in terms of the accumulation of tokens that can be used to buy things exclusively at the company store. It is a sort of aspect blindness that measures communication in numbers of "contact hours" rather than in depth of exchange, in terms of exposure rather than in the *company* that communicative exchange—human contact—can provide ("which [people] die miserably every day / for lack of / what is found there"[5]). The inarticulate, the stutter or limp that Mackey sees in black writing and music, the stammering fragmentation that Susan Howe hears in the earliest recorded voices of North American women, the ludicrous or awkward or damaged or crooked or humiliated, all open up into the "syncopated, the polyrhythmical, the heterogeneous",[6] the off-beat. In contrast, the dominant public language of our society, to use a male metaphor, has been so emptied of specific, socially refractory content that it can be easily and widely disseminated; but this is a dissemination without seed. It is not communicative action but communication behavior: one speaks less to particular individuals than to those aspects of their consciousness that have been programmed to receive the already digested scenes or commentaries provided.

The bent appears so only by dint of the refraction of the social medium that we see it through: so many straight sticks broken by an effect of light through water. And the straight is no less an auditory illusion (contrived elocution), unmasked in its collusions as a tortuously circuitous distance between two points, the result of a kind of grammatical red-lining or gerrymandering, yet stoically insistent on its own rectitude and irreducible economy.

Politics as opposed to what? For this begins to sketch the politics of a poetic form in the negative sense: what keeps the lid on; not only the straight but also the smug, the self-righteous, the certain, the sanctimonious, the arrogant, the correct, the paternalistic, the patri-

---

5. "Asphodel, That Greeny Flower", *Collected Poems of William Carlos Williams, vol. II: 1939–1962* , ed. Christopher MacGowan (New York: New Directions, 1988), p. 318.
6. Mackey, p. 100. See also Howe's essay in *Politics of Poetic Form*.

cian, the policing, the colonizing, the standardizing, and those structures, styles, tropes, methods of transition, that connote or mime or project (rather than confront or expose or redress) these approaches to the world.

Don't get me wrong: I know it's almost a joke to speak of poetry and national affairs. Yet in *The Social Contract* Rousseau writes that since our conventions are provisional, the public may choose to reconvene in order to withdraw authority from those conventions that no longer serve our purposes. Poetry is one of the few areas where this right of reconvening is exercised.

But what if the social body has spoken and one finds oneself outside the mainstream values it ratifies. For majority rule can mean forcing inhospitable conventions on unwilling subjects. An ominous example of this problem is the recent election, by a majority of voters, of an ACLU-baiting candidate for U.S. president. Equally disturbing is the success of the English First movement. Democracy, without individual and sectarian liberty, is a mockery of justice. So it is necessary to insist that any social contract has independent clauses that not only protect but also foster dissident forms of life, manners of speaking, ways of thinking.

Poetry and Public Policy. The two have rarely seemed, surely long have seemed, so far apart. As distant perhaps as conventions are from the authority that once gave them life and now have deserted them like so many ancient tumuli, monuments to what was a merciless Sovereignty but now is a vestigial software system that we call the Standard English of the living dead. One of the more remarkable insights of the sociologist Erving Goffman is that every interpersonal interaction should be read as an institutional and ideological event; indeed, that conventions, which are enacted at every level, can best be understood institutionally. This microcosmic view of public space suggests an arena for poetry that shortcircuits those near-moronic voices who each month, it seems, moan about the loss of celebrity status or mass audience for the "serious" writer. This repeated misapprehension, both of the history of the reception of poetry in the United States or Britain and of the meaning of "public", is a clinically precise instance of a particular picture holding one captive, in Wittgenstein's phrase, and so forcing the same conclusion again and again.

What is to be regretted is not the lack of mass audience for any particular poet but the lack of poetic thinking as an activated potential for all people. In a time of ecological catastrophe like ours, we say that wilderness areas must not only be preserved but also expanded regardless of how many people park their cars within two miles of the site. The effect these wilderness areas have is not measurable by audience but in terms of the regeneration of the earth that benefits all of us who live on it—and for the good of our collective unconscious as much as our collective consciousness. I've never been to Alaska but it makes a difference to me that it's *there*. Poets don't have to be read, any more than trees have to be sat under, to transform poisonous societal emissions into something that can be breathed. As a poet, you affect the public sphere with each reader, with the fact of the poem, and by exercising your prerogative to choose what collective forms you will legitimate. The political power of poetry is not measured in numbers; it instructs us to count differently.

Adorno writes in his *Aesthetic Theory* that "truth is the antithesis of existing society".[7] This suggests that the authority of our conventions is bogus, that only by negating the positive values that legitimate existing societies can we find truth. Yet the statement is a logical paradox that, like the paradigmatic example "This sentence is false", appears to contradict itself. If truth is the antithesis of existing society, then falsity is the thesis of existing society, including Adorno's statement; or perhaps truth pertains only to nonexisting societies, and once a socius actually exists only false-consciousness is possible (including mistaken views about the inevitability, or nature, of the Dark). I might wish to revise Adorno's remark by saying that truth is the synthesis of existing societies, but that would be to substitute my own poetic pragmatism for Adorno's more rhetorically scathing insight, as if I didn't get the joke. There is a range of attitudes one can have toward the truth or falsity of existing societies that allows for neither total negation nor total affirmation; this is why irony, in the narrowest sense of suggesting a binary model of assertion/rejection, is formally inadequate to allow for what a mix of comic, bathetic, and objective

7. Theodor Adorno, *Aesthetic Theory*, tr. C. Lenhardt, ed. Gretel Adorno and Rolf Tiedemann (London: Verso, 1984), p. 279. Cited by Anne Mack and Jay Rome in "Clark Coolidge's Poetry: Truth in the Body of Falsehood", *Parnassus* 15:1 (1989), 279. Mack and Rome pair this quote with another from *Aesthetic Theory* (p. 472) that suggests that art's function is "the determinate negation of the status quo".

modes might: an intercutting that undercuts the centrality of a governing narrative or prosodic strategy.

Anything that departs from the sincere or serious enters into the comic, but the comic is anything but a unitary phenomenon, and the range of comic attitudes goes from the good-humored to the vicious, from clubby endorsement of the existing social reign to total rejection of all existing human communities: poet as confidence "man", deploying hypocrisy in order to shatter the formal autonomy of the poem and its surface of detachment; the sincere and the comic as interfused figure, not either/or but *both and.* Our sincerity is always comic, always questionable, always open to mocking. We are pathetic and heroic simultaneously, one by virtue of the other, a vision of human being that is the basis of the work of the other Williams, Tennessee.

By insisting that stylistic innovations be recognized not only as alternative aesthetic conventions but also as alternative social formations, I am asking that we bring devices back from a purely structural interpretive hermeneutics. In order to fully develop the meaning of a formal rupture or extension, we need a synoptic, multilevel, interactive response that accounts, in hopefully unconventional antiauthoritative ways, for the sexual, class, local-historical, biographical, prosodic, and structural dimensions of a poem. This would mean reading all writing, but especially official or dominant forms of writing, as in part "minority" discourse in order to partialize those cultural and stylistic elements that are hegemonic and to put all writing practices on equal terms from a social point of view. At the same time, it would give a greater emphasis to the stylistic features and structural innovations of so-called marginal writings than is now the case. For every aspect of writing reflects its society's politics and aesthetics; indeed, the aesthetic and the political make an inseparable *poetics.*

Poetry can bring to awareness questions of authority and conventionality, not to overthrow them, as in a certain reading of destructive intent, but to reconfigure: a necessary defiguration as prerequisite for refiguration, for the regeneration of the ability to figure—count—think figuratively, tropically. That poetry of which I speak is multidirectional and multivectoral; while some vectors are undermining others just keep on mining.

The interpretive and compositional model I am proposing, then, can be understood as a synthesis of the three Marxes (Chico, Karl,

Groucho) and the four Williamses (Raymond, William Carlos, Tennessee, and Esther).

When convention and authority clash you can hear the noise for miles. This social noise is a sound that poetry can not only make but echo and resound. And though this convention of the permanent committees on the politics of poetic form is over, there is one last directive to pass on: Hold your own hearings.

Acknowledgments

Many of the poetry books and magazines I discuss will not be easily available from most bookstores or libraries. The best sources for information about these works are Small Press Distribution, 1814 San Pablo Avenue, Berkeley, CA 94702, and Segue Distributing, 303 East 8th Street, New York, NY 10009.

Please note that I am accountable for my several departures from conventional forms of punctuation and presentation; I appreciate the forbearance of the editors in this matter; thanks especially to Joyce Backman and Lindsay Waters.

Below I provide some information on the context of each of the works in this book, and grateful acknowledgment is made to the magazines that initially published the pieces (though often in different versions).

State of the Art. A version of this essay was presented at The Poetry Project 1990 Symposium, "Poetry for the Next Society: Assertions of Power", as part of an evening of four lectures on "Poetry 1990: The State of the Art", May 5, 1990, and subsequently published in *Conjunctions* (1991). The first two sections were originally presented at PEN American Center's panel on "The State of American Poetry" at the New School for Social Research, April 2, 1990. Stanley Cavell discusses Emerson's idea that "self-reliance is aversion of conformity" in *This New Yet Unapproachable America: Lectures after Emerson after Wittgenstein.*

Artifice of Absorption. An early draft of this work was presented at the final session of the New Poetics Colloquium of the Kootenay School of Writing, at the Emily Carr College of Art and Design, Vancouver, Canada, August 25, 1985. Thanks to Colin Browne, who organized the event. Part of my project in Vancouver was to see how much of the proceedings of the colloquium I could absorb into (or would leak out of) this work, which was completed in December 1986. Gil Ott published "Artifice of Absorption" as a special issue of *Paper Air* in 1987.

In the Middle of Modernism. Presented at a panel on "Postmodernism and After: The Culture of Late Capital" at the Socialist Scholars Conference ("Against Domination: State, Class, Race, Gender"), April 12, 1987, at Manhattan Community College. Published in *Socialist Review* (1987)—thanks to Ron Silliman for his useful comments; the Huyssen commentary originally appeared in *M/E/A/N/I/N/G* (1988).

Time Out of Motion. Presented at a panel, organized by Marjorie Perloff, entitled "Fin de Siècle: Theirs and Ours", at the annual convention of the Modern Language Association in Chicago on December 28, 1985, and published in *American Poetry* (1986).

Pounding Fascism. Presented at a panel on "Pound and Fascism" organized by Carroll F. Terrell, and including Christine Froula and Robert Casillo, at the annual convention of the Modern Language Association in Washington, D.C., December 29, 1984, and published in *Sulfur* (1985).

Play It Again, Pac-Man. Written as the catalog essay for the American Museum of Moving Image's 1989 video-game exhibition, "Hot Circuits". Thanks to Rochelle Slovin, AMMI's director. Published in *Postmodern Culture* (1991).

Professing Stein / Stein Professing. Based on a talk given for "Stein Saturday" at the Poetry Project of St. Mark's Church in New York, October 14, 1989. The essay was presented at the Stein panel (organized by Neil Schmitz and Stacy Hubbard) at the 1989 annual convention of the Modern Language Association in Washington, D.C., December 29, 1989, and published in *Poetics Journal* (1991).

Optimism and Critical Excess (Process). Based on a talk given at the "Radical Poetries/Critical Address" conference, State University of New York, Buffalo, on Tax Day, April 15, 1988. In present form, it was initially presented at the Kootenay School of Writing in Vancouver on American Flag Day, June 14, 1989, and subsequently published in their *Writing* (1989). First U.S. publication: *Critical Inquiry* (1990). My discussion of Danto first appeared in *M/E/A/N/I/N/G* (1989).

Censers of the Unknown. Written responses to Tom Beckett's questions, in 1987; published in *Temblor* (1989). Beckett is a poet and editor of *The Difficulties.* His previous interview with me was collected in *Content's Dream.*

The Second War and Postmodern Memory. Based on a talk at the New School for Social Research, February 15, 1990, and published in *Dialectical Anthropology* (1991) and *Postmodern Culture* (1991). Thanks to Stanley Diamond, who organized the event.

Comedy and the Poetics of Political Form. Presented in the fall of 1988 at the conclusion of a series of talks I curated at the Wolfson Center for National Affairs of the New School for Social Research, and published in the collection I edited, *The Politics of Poetic Form* (New York: Roof Books, 1990).

Grateful acknowledgment is also made to:

Georges Borchardt Inc., acting for the author, and Ecco Press for permission to quote from *Rivers and Mountains* by John Ashbery, copyright © 1966 by John Ashbery.

Black Sparrow Press for permission to quote from *Holocaust* by Charles Reznikoff, copyright © 1975 by Charles Reznikoff; and *The Collected Books of Jack Spicer,* copyright © 1975 by the Estate of Jack Spicer.

David Bromige for permission to quote from an unpublished poem.

University of California Press for permission to quote from *Collected Poems of Robert Creeley,* copyright © 1983 by the Regents of the University of California; and *Collected Poems of Charles Olson,* ed. George Butterick, copyright © 1987 by the Estate of Charles Olson.

The Figures for permission to quote from *Melencolia,* copyright © 1987 by Clark Coolidge; and *The First World,* copyright © 1986 by Bob Perelman.

Benjamin Friedlander for permission to quote from *Kristallnacht,* copyright © 1988 by Benjamin Friedlander.